GW00671685

HOW NOT TO BE A SUPERMODEL

'Hilarious'
CAITLIN MORAN

'Witty, gossipy, self-effacing and deeply nostalgic,
this is a joy for all of us who survived the noughties
but have forgotten quite how. Much more than the
memoir of a fashion model, this is the rarely told insider
story of the most glamorous, grotty and downright
insane industries, as written by one of the smartest
and funniest people I know.'
SALI HUGHES

'Ruth hilariously delivers all the reals!'
VAL GARLAND

'Utterly incredible and I can't even begin to express how
much I enjoyed it. A gripping and hilarious memoir.'
EMMA GUNS

'I absolutely adore Ruth Crilly's point of view. It is
wise and beautiful and funny, like she is. Strong hard
enthusiastic recommend!'
POLLY VERNON

'The perfect tonic for these endless grey days and the best
time travel experience, plus a fascinating insight into such
a glamorous and bonkers world.'
JODI CHAPMAN

HOW NOT TO BE A SUPERMODEL

A noughties memoir

Ruth Crilly

BLINK
bringing you closer

First published in the UK by Blink Publishing
An imprint of The Zaffre Publishing Group
A Bonnier Books UK company
4th Floor, Victoria House,
Bloomsbury Square,
London, WC1B 4DA

Owned by Bonnier Books
Sveavägen 56, Stockholm, Sweden

Hardback – 9781788709224
Trade Paperback – 9781785122248
Ebook – 9781788709231
Audio – 9781788709248

All rights reserved. No part of the publication may be reproduced, stored in
a retrieval system, transmitted or circulated in any form or by any means,
electronic, mechanical, photocopying, recording or otherwise, without prior
permission in writing of the publisher.

A CIP catalogue of this book is available from the British Library.

Designed by Envy Design Ltd
Printed and bound by Clays Ltd, Elcograf S.p.A

1 3 5 7 9 10 8 6 4 2

Copyright © Ruth Crilly 2024

Ruth Crilly has asserted their moral right to be identified as the author of this
Work in accordance with the Copyright, Designs and Patents Act 1988.

Every reasonable effort has been made to trace copyright holders of material
reproduced in this book, but if any have been inadvertently overlooked the
publishers would be glad to hear from them.

Blink Publishing is an imprint of Bonnier Books UK
www.bonnierbooks.co.uk

To Mum: apologies in advance.

Contents

Preface

Very little about my childhood pointed to a future in supermodelling. Yes, I was probably slightly taller than average and I was slender, but there was nothing unusual about being slender if you were a child of the eighties. It was difficult to build up much timber when you were forced to spend all of your days outside, as we were, trying not to drown in disused quarries or electrocute ourselves with kites on electricity pylons or fall prey to any one of the many and varied deaths we were warned about on public service announcements. The rest of the time we spent running away from stray dogs and throwing stones at the trenchcoat-wearing perverts who hid in the bushes – being a child of the eighties was, all in all, a high-intensity workout.

So I was tall-ish and I was slender-ish, and I had apparently inherited the natural good looks of my parents –

my dad was quite ruggedly handsome and my mum, she wouldn't mind me saying, was just utterly gorgeous – but I wasn't, by any stretch of the imagination, physically remarkable. If anything, I'd have said that I was physically sub-par, so terrible at ballet that it was suggested I cease and desist with the lessons, so inflexible of body that attending gymnastics required a special waiver to be signed so that nobody could be sued if I snapped in half whilst doing a bridge. I lacked any sort of coordination or physical grace and was pretty inept at sports and so by the age of eight or nine, I felt that the universe had – along with all the other kids who helped out in the library for fun and had to wear special glasses for their lazy eye problems – firmly placed me in the academic camp.

I was an enthusiastic reader and a keen writer, and I was good at music and had a great imagination – all fine qualities for a kid, but none of them pointed towards a glittering career on the catwalk. It wasn't as though I was practising my runway strut in the playground or brushing my hair a hundred times before bed. Even at seventeen, suddenly equipped with the worryingly lithe, full-breasted body of wet dreams and the liberal fashion sense of a Hooters waitress, the idea of actually becoming a model didn't occur to me. My room was wallpapered with torn-out magazine adverts for jeans and perfumes and Calvin Klein underwear and I certainly daydreamed about being a supermodel, but I never thought of it as a realistic option. We lived on an ordinary housing estate in Redditch, Worcestershire, and the fashion world, the catwalk shows, the models, they belonged to a galaxy far, far away.

Modelling, let alone supermodelling, was simply never on the cards. It was as unlikely and unreachable an idea as becoming an astronaut. But then, all of a sudden – *Houston, we have a problem* – the unimaginable became a distinct possibility. Modelling became a reality and (because I can never do things by halves) supermodelling became my slightly unhinged and overambitious goal.

This book, this memoir of sorts, documents my pursuit of this wildly unrealistic dream. It's a catalogue of clanging errors, it's the opposite of an instruction manual, it is – perhaps avoid if you're solely looking for inspiration and motivation – a lesson in *how not* to reach the top. Especially if you're looking to have a stab at a career in modelling in the early noughties.

Yes, we're going to time travel too. Back to the noughties, a time we frown upon for being rife with unattainable beauty standards, horrendous body image issues and deeply rooted misogynistic viewpoints. A time before smartphones and face-altering photo filters, before lip fillers for twenty-year-olds and skincare for babies. Bad old noughties, naughty noughties – aren't things better now? We're going to peer through the thick fug of fag smoke that shrouded the modelling industry and take a look at what really went on behind the glitz and the glamour. If, indeed, there was ever any glitz and glamour.

But look: this isn't an exposé. Terrible things didn't happen to me during my time as a model and I like to think I came away from my twelve-ish years in the industry relatively unscathed. Apart from a deep-seated fear of gaining weight and a hyper-critical eye for my own perceived physical imperfections, I'd say that I'm completely normal and unaffected. Everybody weighs their breakfast granola to the nearest gram, surely?

No, there have been plenty of memoirs and documentaries revealing the dark side of fashion. This book keeps things light. Because what's funnier than being told that your body looks like a turgid penis (me) or that your face is too long and shaped like a banana (sorry, Sarah)? What could be more hilarious than standing in front of a load of middle-aged Japanese men in your underwear or being measured with a tape measure in a room filled with your peers?

Why tell this story now, you might ask – why write it up over twenty years later when the world has moved on from obsessing over thinness, when people have changed their attitudes towards physical appearance, and body positivity has 100 per cent definitely taken over from the massively damaging, life-restricting culture of struggling to attain the looks of the people we see in the media? Well. Because I'm not sure the world *has* moved on all that much. I don't know whether people have entirely changed their attitudes towards their physical appearances or embraced so-called body positivity as wholeheartedly as they lead themselves to believe. To a great extent, we are still living in an appearance-obsessed, perfection-seeking, diet-trying (and failing) world.

When I first started writing up my notes and diary entries (kept meticulously alongside my Polaroid pictures and magazine tears for all these years), I thought that this book might be an interesting delve into a past that seemed so archaic and remote, it would be a fascinating contrast to the world we live in today. But as I collated my experiences and shaped them into the – let's just call it what it is – masterpiece you see before you, I began to realise that the contrast isn't all that stark. People still obsess over weight and size and the way their noses look – they just have to be more careful what they say.

Now: let us turn back the clock. No longer am I a forty-something mother of two writing bitter, thinly veiled barbs about body image in the digital era, I am twenty years old and fresh with the optimism of youth. I'm going to be a model – look at me, Mum! Perhaps I'm even going to be a *super*model. After all, I have the pillowy, plump-lipped face of an angel and the (as yet) un-split, unravaged body of a nymph. And I am brilliant and I am infectiously funny and I am kind and caring and I am – unbeknownst to the twenty-year-old me – absolutely, 100 per cent perfect.

Chapter 1

Sayonara, Suckers!

'You don't see Milla Jovovich with a fluctuating arse,' said my new model booker. She lit a Marlboro Light from the dying end of her previous Marlboro Light and sucked on it so sharply that her eyes crossed over. I had been in the agency for all of eight minutes and already it had been decided that I was on the short side, had boobs that were inconveniently fulsome and a bottom that was 'on the cusp'.

I had acquired a model booker because I was now, quite unexpectedly, a fledgling model. On Tuesday, I had been sitting in the university law library going through my Blackstone's statutes book with an orange highlighter pen and now here I was in London, on a Friday afternoon, talking to a chain-smoker I'd never met before about hip-to-waist ratio.

The model booker, whose name was Daz ('short for Darryl, nothing to do with the washing powder'), was wearing a pink boiler suit and had what looked like miniature tea-strainers dangling from her ears.

'Milla has a steady-sized, non-fluctuating arse and *that*, darling, is the result of hard work. It's dependable. You won't see her arse suddenly turning up for work one day two inches bigger.'

Daz waved her cigarette at a black and white photograph on the wall. Milla was standing front-on, no arse to be seen. Was her arse steady-sized and non-fluctuating? I couldn't tell. I would have to put my faith in Darryl.

'She works on her arse every day,' said Daz. 'Working on her arse is just a way of life for her and you just need it to be a way of life for you.'

I wasn't sure I liked this idea. It was 2001, I was twenty years old and 'working on my arse' was not a way of life I had considered for myself. I had assumed that my rise to fame and fortune would be both instant and whiplash fast, rashly leaving the second year of my law degree (*Sayonara*, suckers!) the very day I received the phone call from the model agency.

I had been skiving lectures in town when my phone had rung, which had a nice poetry to it because I'd also been skiving lectures in town when I had put in my entry for the national model search a few months before. I had scribbled my name, age, height and phone number on the back of a casual snap of myself and dropped it through the slot in the top of a cardboard box in the shopping centre on Birmingham New Street.

And then, months and months later, after I'd totally forgotten that I'd even entered, my phone had rung.

It was like in the stories I'd heard, the ones where the plain and unassuming girl gets spotted by someone connected and powerful as they're just milling about waiting at a bus stop/playing Tetris on their Gameboy/gardening, and then they're whisked away to a photoshoot and everyone gasps at the utter beauty and irresistible personality that is suddenly unearthed. Cases in point: Kate Moss, from Croydon – awkward teenager found at an airport, turned into the coolest supermodel around. Cindy Crawford, from Illinois – noticed poolside by a photographer and beamed to mega-stardom. Pamela Anderson, from Ladysmith, Canada – spotted at a football game.

Could I, Ruth Crilly from Redditch, England, discovered via a dog-eared photograph lying forgotten at the bottom of a cardboard 'search for the next top model' box, enjoy the same exhilarating trajectory to fame and fortune?

'We love you and see really great things happening,' Daz had said. 'The gap in your teeth is really cool, you've got a definite look.'

I had seen nothing prophetic about the way in which I had been discovered; the fact that nobody had actually scouted or seen me in person hadn't rung any alarm bells. Nobody had been struck mute by my beauty in the street and immediately ushered me aside to beg for my contact details, but that was OK. And it didn't feel even remotely like a bad omen that my model search entry had lain undiscovered for months in the bottom of the box because it had slipped beneath one of the flaps and hadn't fallen out when they tipped the box upside down. Nope, nothing to worry about here. The bells of realism didn't toll; I didn't see any hint of a warning shadow from the hand of fate because all I could hear was: 'We love you and see big things happening.'

What about that sentence didn't promise instant riches, limousine transfers and the next cover of *Vogue*?

'Now, I have to warn you,' said Daz, 'that you are quite old to be starting out as a model.'

She was wielding a Polaroid camera, not because she was a hipster – hipsters hadn't been invented yet – and not because she was being ironically retro, but because it was 2001 and this was the only way you could take pictures that you needed to see straight away.

Daz cupped my chin in her palm to guide my face gently from side to side, up and down, staring at me in a slightly unnerving way as she found my best angle.

'Twenty is quite late to be starting out, darling,' she said. 'In model years, you're really more like forty. Which is nowhere near *dead*, obviously, but it's fast approaching irrelevance.'

The Polaroid camera flashed and I blinked.

'Try not to blink,' said Daz. She waited whilst the camera noisily, laboriously churned out a white frame of card with an undeveloped photograph in the centre. I stood awkwardly waiting for it to fully emerge. My face appeared and my eyes were shut.

'There are other late-starters who have made it,' she said, placing the first, useless Polaroid on her desk. 'I once had a New Face who was twenty-six, which is probably the equivalent of fifty in model years. We should have called

her an Old Face, not a new one. She was virtually geriatric.
So anyway, darling, what I'm trying to say is don't let any
of this get you down.'

She picked up the camera again, cigarette in hand.

'Don't blink.'

I arranged what I now thought of as my ancient, decrepit
face atop my short, rounded body and the camera flashed.
And again, and again, and again, and again.

'Darryl,' said Daz, as we were waiting for the Polaroids
to reverse-fade into view, 'is a terrible name.'

She had taken a seat behind the desk but there was only
one chair and so I made myself uncomfortable by perching
on the glass top. Daz lit her third cigarette in fifteen minutes
and blew out the smoke slowly and ponderously.

'I sometimes wonder whether it was karma that killed
my parents.'

I wasn't quite sure what to say to this. Apart from the
time I had been flashed at in Munich by a man in a purple
velvet suit in 1995, this was by far the most disorientating
situation I'd ever found myself in. Here I was, alone in
London, with only a disgruntled, badly named lady-orphan
as my guide. And I wasn't even sure what I was being
guided through, or into. I had daydreamed about this first
meeting – my grand arrival at the agency, the moment that
would form my true discovery, when I would glide through
the doors and everyone would gasp with astonishment.

'My younger brothers are called Bernard and Clyde,'
said Daz, interrupting my thoughts, 'so I suppose I got
off easy.'

My arrival at the agency had not been the one of my

daydreams. In my daydreams, a full team of agents wearing suits and carrying clipboards would be awaiting my appearance (which would be via black Range Rover) outside a skyscraper office block with mirrored windows. One of the agents, wearing a Madonna mic, would whisk me through to a lift and then I would be shown into a vast, completely white office with white sofas (a large Dulux dog would be lying on one of them). Inexplicably, everyone would begin to clap. But only after they had all gasped with astonishment at my beauty.

In reality, things had been slightly different. To get to London, I'd driven my Rover Metro GTi down the M40 and, hitting a worrying amount of traffic just past the M25, had attempted to find somewhere to park the car that was next to a tube station. After almost choking to death on a prawn cocktail crisp, steering wheel in one sweating hand and crumpled map of the London Underground clasped in the other, I had finally found refuge in the car park of the Northolt leisure centre and clawed out enough loose change from under the passenger seat to park there for a full six hours.

My arrival at the agency had not been heralded by horn-blowers and there was nobody at the curb wearing a Madonna mic; outside the door of the building, a man wrapped in an old rug had asked me a question – 'Do you like to chop sausages?' – and the question had thrown me, so much so that by the time I'd arrived at the agency reception, via the stairs because there was no lift, I had managed to temporarily forget my own name. Which was unfortunate for the receptionist; though, when I finally remembered it after three or four seconds, she had no record of my appointment. She had stage-whispered my name to a woman in a pink boilersuit who happened to be passing the desk and she, in turn, had very obviously said, 'Who?'

Now that same woman in the pink boilersuit was telling me about her dead parents and I wasn't sure whether she was joking or not. She could have been doing Chandler Bing-style sarcasm – 'could my parents *be* any worse at picking names?' – as was the current rage, or she could have really believed that choosing the name Darryl for your child should be punishable by death.

Either way, I hadn't prepared for this part of the interview, the part where you have to work out whether the responsible adult in the room requires consoling or not, and so I just nodded and smiled more widely. My face had set into a rigor mortis grin; my cheeks started to ache as we watched the milkiness on the surface of the Polaroids begin to dissipate, shapes and shadows taking form. I wondered what my pictures would look like when my mummified old face and my rotund, short body finally plunged into view.

I had never had my picture taken by a stranger before – having my photo taken was a rare event, full stop. Because who the hell ever carried a camera around with them unless they were paparazzi? I had a mere handful of photos of myself from my teen years: one from the law school ball, in which I inexplicably chose to be a kneeler in the front row and so had foreshortened legs like two fat hams; two photos from my eighteenth birthday, my skin sallow and my eyes ringed with dark circles; and a handful of snaps that showed me on holiday with a boyfriend, leaning at a strange angle against a sea wall. It looked like the sort of joke photo that's taken at the Tower of Pisa, except I wasn't pretending to hold up the sea wall, it was my actual pose. Barely anyone in 2001 knew about posing or about best angles, because having your photo taken was simply not an activity that happened that much in normal, everyday life.

I looked at the glossy, framed photographs of super-models on the office walls. Would I look like any of them, in my Polaroids? There was a picture of one beautiful girl, naked and artfully draped over a huge rock on a beach, her thighs dusted with sand, her hair tousled. Imagine looking like that! I definitely wanted to look like that. Another had been photographed in black and white wearing latex boots that stretched up past her legs and ended in sharp points on her hip bones. She had been photographed from below and looked skyscraper tall, Amazonian, strong, her hair slicked back and her lips painted to an impossibly glossy finish. That, I decided, was also how I wanted to look.

'Wow,' said Daz as the Polaroids finally reached full technicolour. I peered over the desk to look at them. In the harsh flashed light my face looked boyish and my eyes were narrowed in protest. For the full-length photos, I stood impossibly straight-legged, with my arms like pokers beside me as though I was about to be buried at sea.

'This is unreal,' said Daz. 'Has anyone ever told you that from some angles you really look like . . .'

Daz held one of the Polaroids at arm's length and squinted at it. Who did I look like? Who? Michelle Pfeiffer? Kate Moss?

'Val Kilmer,' said Daz. 'You really do if you squint hard enough. Shorter, and with bigger boobs, obviously.'

She began to flick through a leatherbound notebook.

'I'm looking for Corrine's casting agent's number, but I know too many people and it's impossible to keep up. And they're never in alphabetical order. Look.'

She displayed a page covered in scribbles. I wondered whether she had just filled the pages with numbers and names to make it look as though she knew a lot of people. There was a number for 'Studio Toilets Simon', 254891, and one for someone called 'Dalek Dave' that started 081. 'HIRES ALL THE RABBITS' had only four digits attributed to it, 6565, and the mundane 'Cathy' was scribbled next to a fraction, 5/10.

'Cathy's is a rating, not a number,' said Daz, seeing me stare.

'This isn't just a phone book,' she said, 'it's my scouting diary. I write everything in here – if I spot someone on the street that I think has what it takes then I like to have some little memory joggers. Hair colour, height, hobbies, unusual characteristics, that sort of thing.'

'Oh,' I said, speaking for what must have been only the third or fourth time since arriving, 'do you do a little sketch of them, too?'

I had seen a little line drawing on the next page of the notebook, a girl's face in tiny, feathery biro marks. It was quite beautiful.

'Christ no, darling. That's what Polaroid cameras are for! It's not the Middle Ages! I'm not Hans Holbein!'

She picked up the telephone receiver.

'Right, here we go: Elaine. She's Corrine's casting agent and a very good friend of mine.' She pressed the buttons on her keypad and waited.

'Elaine . . . darling. It's me.' There was a pause. 'It's me, darling, me. Daz.' Pause. 'Daz from Global. We were at the David Bailey party together last week . . . yes, darling. Daz. Yes . . . yes.' She dropped her voice. 'Yes, Daz Automatic.'

Daz looked at me and rolled her eyes. 'People think it's hilarious to call me Daz Automatic,' she said to me, cupping her hand over the telephone receiver.

I crinkled my face in what I hoped was a sympathetic manner. Daz returned to her phone call.

'Listen, I have this new girl . . . yes, another one. But Corrine will *love her*. She's very quirky and cool with a definite look. And a tooth gap to die for . . .'

I felt a sudden warmth for this new booker person of mine. Quirky? Cool? A tooth gap to die for? So she did think I had something after all. Things were looking up.

Daz suddenly laughed a smoker's laugh into the telephone.

'Giraffe-like?' she said. 'Ha! Definitely not tall and willowy, darling. Think more along the lines of a panda. She's virtually an endomorph.'

Despite me being a bit short, slightly too old and virtually an endomorph, Corrine's Casting Agent Elaine agreed to look me up and down the very next week on a special type of appointment called a 'go-see'. A go-see, Daz told me, was different to a casting. A casting was like an audition for a part but without any singing or dancing, whereas a go-see was like an audition for a part, without any singing or dancing and, more importantly, without there being any actual part to audition for.

'And actually,' said Daz, 'without the person who's holding the audition really knowing whether they even want to see you or not.'

It all seemed pointless, but nevertheless my go-see was booked in for the following Monday. I felt a sense of relief that at least I had the weekend to recuperate, shrink my breasts a bit and sell enough car insurance legal protection to fund the following week's trip to London.

I realised then that with all of my daydreaming, I hadn't actually factored in the practicalities of becoming a model in London, when I lived one hundred miles away. In my fantasy version of events, the one where I straight away got picked for the next *Vogue* cover, I was collected from home in a dark-windowed Jaguar and hushed down the motorway to my hotel suite, where I awaited my turn in the swanky studio. In reality, to be able to return to London, I had to hope that there was enough money in my bank to put petrol in the car, pray that my Switch card worked in the tube station and manage to scrounge enough coins together for the parking meter at Northolt. If I worked all weekend and didn't go out, I'd have just enough to get me back for the go-see.

'Now, listen,' said Daz. 'If you can just pop back down to London tomorrow there's an induction for new models at a really cool spa space we've borrowed. I think it would be helpful for you to go.'

I tried to think of a way to convey just how little money I had but no words came out.

'Two of our very successful girls,' Daz continued, 'give a crash course on modelling and how the industry works. They're very frank, they can tell you exactly where your weak points are as a model and the pitfalls that will probably mean you'll fail.'

She wrote an address on a piece of paper.

'It's such a fun event, darling,' she said.

The next day, I arrived at the induction with minutes to spare, having driven the hundred miles home, slept for a short period of time, motored through the drizzle all the way back to Northolt leisure centre car park and then travelled almost the entire length of the London Underground's Central line.

The Cool Spa Space was actually a cordoned-off area in an upmarket hair salon – neutrally decorated, scented with mind-soothing oils but nevertheless filled with the noise of the hair dryers that roared just metres away. And the two successful models running the show? A formidable-looking girl called Conan, who was wearing a leather harness, and a self-styled model-cum-healer who called herself Cloud. I was instantly intrigued. As I took my seat with my complimentary wheatgrass shot, I began to question whether they had been hired from an acting agency, such were their improbable personas.

Conan had thick, dark eyebrows and was wearing scarlet lipstick that turned down at the corners so that she looked permanently displeased. She wore eighteen-hole Doc Marten's over camouflage leggings, but it was the interesting leather harness that really stole the show.

Fastened on top of her grey marl t-shirt, it effectively drew a frame around her breasts and invited – nay forced – you to admire their pertness. I had never before seen such a brazen show of self-confidence. Her hair was shorn almost to a crew cut and when she opened her mouth to speak, the noise that came out was low and gravelly, like something you'd expect from the multi-headed dog of Hades.

Cloud was also a top model but she made it clear in her introduction that she preferred to be known for her extensive work in mindfulness, nutrition and something called spiritual centring. I had seen her in magazine shoots and vaguely recognised her name, but she looked very different in here, on a Saturday, with no makeup on and her long, blonde hair left loose and slightly wavy. She was wearing a layered dress that was very full and luxurious in cut with lots of frills and layers, but it was made of a sort of rough, beige sacking material. She looked like a medieval can-can dancer, especially with the delicate crown of daisies in her hair, and she had placed herself cross-legged on the floor behind a tall, flickering candle.

Her being at floor level had the unfortunate effect of making everyone in the chairs, all of us fledgling models, seem very high up. The dynamic felt uncomfortable to me, like a school assembly turned on its head. Conan, on the other hand, refused to sit, preferring to pace up and down in her stomping boots, so we were all in the unpleasant situation of having to play ping pong with our lines of vision.

On the other side of the salon, through an archway, there were people having expensive things done to their hair with lengths of tin foil and I could hear low chatter, relaxing music, the rolling of chair wheels on the wooden floor. I wondered whether I'd be better off on that side. It felt more normal. Safer.

'You,' barked Conan, 'are nothing in this world.' She looked directly at me as she said this, but I assumed she referred to all eight of us. She had grabbed a long cardboard tube of something from the shelving displays that lined the Cool Spa Space and was wielding it like a truncheon.

'You are nothing,' she continued, 'until you are something.'

'I totally agree,' cooed Cloud from the floor. Her voice was so quiet that even I, sitting nearest to her, had to bend forwards in my chair to hear it. As I leaned, I saw that Conan's truncheon was actually a cardboard tube filled with a stack of pink tealight candles, their metal casings clacking together as she tapped it on her thigh impatiently.

'But also,' continued Cloud, 'you are never nothing and always something.'

'Like I said,' barked Conan, looking down on Cloud's head with thinly veiled disgust, 'you're nothing in the world of modelling until you're something, and to be something you have to go through the most gruelling assault course of humiliation and degradation you'll ever experience. It *will* completely destroy everything you thought you knew about yourself and your self-confidence *will* hit rock bottom.'

I was a bit anxious about this humiliation and degradation thing. I tended to be quite rubbery when it came to knockbacks in life and would optimistically bounce back onto the trajectory I'd decided for myself, even if it was against all good advice and common sense. I wondered whether this trait would serve me well in the modelling world or if I'd become a human version of Whac-A-Mole, popping up again and again after being hit with the wooden self-confidence mallet.

'If you still think you can hack it,' said Conan, 'know that you probably can't. Many try, most fail.'

'Fail,' cooed Cloud from behind her centring flame.

Conan stared down at her as though she was mentally willing the sack dress to set alight. I had noticed that when Conan stopped talking, she looked a bit like a sad clown. It was the downturned lipstick corners. It was funny to think about how different she must have looked in photographs.

'If you do think you've got what it takes,' said Conan, 'then listen up. You don't have a hope in hell of getting any work without pictures in your portfolio. Your portfolio, in case this is just another one of the many things you don't know, is your modelling CV. A CV but with no words. Just pictures.'

I thought about the CV I had drafted just the other week, the one I needed so that I could get a work experience placement at a law firm. How brilliant it would have looked with no words, just pictures! The mental image was cheering. Here, a sketch of me holding my A level certificates and smiling; there, a stick character playing a clarinet. A photo from 1987 of me helping the local community at the harvest festival, stuck in with small pieces of masking tape.

'To get pictures for your portfolio, you need to get jobs,'

said Conan. 'To get jobs, you need to have pictures. Even if you have jobs, you might not get pictures and having pictures won't necessarily get you jobs.'

'Well, that sounds straightforward,' I said to the girl next to me, but it was evident from her blank look that she didn't do irony. I realised that the woman to the other side of her was some sort of chaperone – her mum, maybe. The girl had a GCSE French book inside her open rucksack and a long Forever Friends ruler sticking out of her pencil case.

Conan continued on her campaign of pessimistic dreams destruction but her voice was beginning to wash over me. This all seemed very undoable and tiring, like having to fill in a UCAS form. Where was the minimal-effort instant gratification I had been seeking?

'If you think you're making money anytime soon then think again,' said Conan, her voice beginning to blend in with the whirring of the hairdryers from the next room. 'You need editorial work to get the paid commercial work and editorial work doesn't pay. If you get too much commercial work, you'll never get the editorial work and if you do too much editorial work then you run the risk of being overexposed, and that' – she hit the wall with her tube of tealights – 'is a slow and humiliating career death.'

The schoolgirl's chaperone piped up with a question. The lady had been taking notes in a Moleskine notebook using a Parker pen with her initials inscribed on it. Her initials were ARS.

'Yes, hello,' said ARS. 'I'm Annabel, Alexia's mummy, and I have to say, Conan, that your tone very much worries me.' Annabel Alexia's Mummy tried to make eye contact with Conan but could not seem to get up past the harness-framed breasts, and so instead locked gaze with Cloud, who was gently swaying back and forth, smiling benignly.

'You make it sound as though it's almost impossible to get any jobs as a model,' said Annabel. 'It all sounds rather futile. If a child has excellent prospects academically then why on earth would they ever take time out of schooling to pursue a career in modelling?'

I swivelled my head to check that Annabel wasn't actually my own mother.

Conan cracked her truncheon tube like she was activating a glow stick. A little pink tealight dropped out and rolled across the floor.

'They wouldn't,' she said.

None of this boded particularly well, but still. I was kind of wedded to the idea of becoming a supermodel now: I had waved goodbye to my degree and checked out of the law buildings, both physically and mentally. All that was left to do was learn the tricks of the trade and I'd be laughing all the way to the bank. It was just a shame that the tricks of the trade were being imparted by two people who managed to directly contradict each other at every turn. It was difficult to see how Conan and Cloud existed on the same planet, let alone in the same industry, as they briefly but intensively confused us all on such subjects as travel, exercise, working abroad and, finally, nutrition.

'Nutrition is so important,' clucked Cloud, slowly rubbing her hand in a circle over her stomach. 'Did you know that we control everything from our gut? Nourish the gut and you are nourishing your body, your soul and your mind.'

Conan grunted. 'Negative to that,' she said. 'If you over nourish your gut then good luck getting into sample size Versace. Keep control over your gut. Conquer your cravings.'

'Let your gut guide you,' said Cloud. 'When your gut needs nourishment, it will speak.'

'Become deaf to your appetite,' Conan commanded, 'or pay the price with your ass.'

'Listen to your whole being,' said Cloud. 'If you need rest then rest. If you have to go within to find peace, go within to find peace. Modelling is about being the most confident you can be, the fittest you can be, the healthiest you can be.'

Conan adjusted her leather harness and cleared her throat. Uh-oh.

'Modelling,' she snarled, 'is about being whatever the industry wants you to be. If I have to run, I run. If I need to fast? Then I fast.'

'I like to cut down on gluten to give my system the rest it needs,' said Cloud.

'I use caffeine and cigarettes to take the edge off my hunger.'

'In the warmer months, I like to eat a plant-based diet,' said Cloud.

'In Paris,' said Conan, 'I survive on smoke.'

By now, I was thoroughly confused and I wasn't the only one. Looking around, I could see the six other girls and one chaperone all thinking the same thing as me: *What in God's name is a plant-based diet?*

'Excuse me, but do you mean being a vegetarian?' asked a girl on the row behind me.

'No,' said Cloud, 'plant-based means trying not to eat any animal products whatsoever. I can point you in the direction of a few books on it if you like?'

'So not even fish, like vegetarians can eat?'

'No fish,' said Cloud, 'and no meat or cheese or eggs or even milk.'

'That's ridiculous,' said Conan. 'You're making this up. Nobody can live without milk – what would you have in coffee?'

'You can get milk that's not from a cow, if you know where to look,' said Cloud. 'And I'm not making it up. There's even something called veganism that takes things further – you can't consume honey, or silk or even leather.'

'Don't be an idiot,' said Conan, 'not even the hungriest model would eat leather. Chew it, maybe, if you were really desperate, but I've never seen it swallowed.'

I made a decision then. Partly because I was irresistibly drawn to the challenge and partly because, as I watched Conan climb into a Mercedes that was waiting outside on the street, I knew I wanted to be a part of this new, unexpected world that seemed different and a bit mad and appeared to exist at a complete parallel to normal life. Yes, at twenty years old I was a bit old; yes, at five feet and eight inches tall I was slightly on the short side, and yes, with 32D boobs some might dismiss me as matronly ('only if you wear high-necked tops, darling, so avoid, avoid, avoid!'), but I reckoned I could do it. I'd had the crash course in

How to Be a Supermodel and I knew the score. I'd overhaul my diet and eat fresh, unprocessed food, I'd take control of my smoking habit and replace it with exercise. I would cut my hair, or else I'd grow it; I'd wear a leather harness around my breasts and be photographed on a rock on the beach with sandy thighs and tousled locks. I'd have money, I'd take cabs, I'd swan about in heels and never wear flats and I'd always, always look the part. Supermodel-dom would be all mine.

Virtually an endomorph: the photo
I was scouted from.

Chapter 2

The Walk of Shame

'Jesus Christ,' said my telesales manager, 'who ordered the stripper?'

It was almost exactly six months later and I had been trying to creep into my Saturday job unnoticed. Which was admittedly slightly optimistic, considering I was wearing nothing but a skin-tight golden minidress and four-inch glitter heels. As I hobbled across the open-plan office, I was thankful that the desks were mostly empty; the last thing I needed, after the night I'd just had, was an audience. My head was pounding, I reeked of pineapple Bacardi Breezer and my feet felt like they'd been smashed with a meat mallet. I'd had three hours' sleep, my eyelashes were gluey with yesterday's mascara and there were twisted bits of party streamer stuck in my hair. And the worst thing about all of this, this wildly inappropriate spectacle, was that none of it was even my fault.

The wanton outfit, the backcombed hair, the smell of

stale fag smoke, all of this belonged in a different world – my other, crazy, modelling world. The world I went to when I drove down the M40 to London, like Alice going down the rabbit hole, never knowing what might be at the other end. Castings in Paris and studio lights flashing and famous designers in ridiculous coats. Test shoots on houseboats and go-sees in cafes and – most recently, just the night before – a TV commercial in a superclub that finished at three in the morning.

It wasn't my fault that these things didn't fit into normal life, the life that was smaller and safer and so much more secure, with its familiar faces and telesales job. The only thing I was guilty of, really, was allowing my two worlds to collide.

But honestly: what were the chances I'd end up shooting a TV commercial in Birmingham, less than fifteen miles from home? And that it would be a night shoot, on a Friday night, finishing mere hours before I needed to be at my Saturday job?

'Where's your clothes, bab?' said my manager as I plonked myself down on an office chair.

He stared at my dress, a smug expression on his face. As someone who regularly called me 'Tits McGee' even when I was fully and appropriately clothed, he surely felt that today's outfit was a gift from above. For who turned up to their office job in skyscraper heels and a dress that looked as though it had been sprayed on from a can?

'Somebody lost them,' I said, 'while I was being paid to pretend to have fun.'

It was true: somebody had lost my clothes. The night

before I had been shooting an ad for a record label in a Birmingham nightclub and all of my daytime garments – my jeans and my top and my leather jacket that I'd neatly folded into a pile with trainers placed atop – had disappeared.

The TV commercial was supposed to have been a feel-good ad for a dance music album. Creative idea in a nutshell: a group of friends were out in a club, having a good time, music was playing. It shouldn't have been a difficult brief to fulfil, seeing as though they'd got together a group of friends and put them in a club to have a good time and there was music playing, but unfortunately, the entire production crew had made the decision to get completely and utterly off their faces on a selection of pharmaceuticals, to the point where none of them really knew what was supposed to be happening, who was supposed to be manning the cameras or, as the shoot wore on, where they even were.

By 10pm, the hairstylist had stripped off his top and was dancing on one of the podiums; by one in the morning, the director of photography was slumped in a corner wearing a magician's hat and drooling onto his own chest. It was no real surprise, then, that when I attempted to find my clothes at the end of the night none of the crew had even the tiniest inkling as to where they'd safely stashed them.

It had been a disappointing end to a shoot I'd senti-mentally hoped would be something of a milestone in my modelling career – filming a TV commercial in my home city, the one I'd left just six months earlier as a law-school drop-out. I'd wanted to feel proud. *Look at me now*, I had wanted to say. *Behold my supermodel-dom.* Instead, I had spent forty minutes searching beneath tables for my lost possessions and then slipped over in a puddle of Bacardi Breezer. At any rate, nobody had been looking at me; by the time I was leaving, the hairstylist had been down to his pants on the podium, doing one-armed press-ups and mock-fellating his hair curling tongs.

And now here I was in the Redditch branch of We Insure You Too, stapling policy documents together and feeling as far from supermodel-dom as someone could ever feel. I wasn't 'swanning around' or 'looking the part', as I'd envisaged I would be by now; there was no leather harness encircling my breasts, no sand artfully dusted upon my thighs. I didn't have a driver or a personal trainer, I hadn't overhauled my diet with fresh, unprocessed food. Breakfast that morning had been a sausage and egg McMuffin and two Marlboro Lights and, despite some recent half-hearted attempts to improve my fitness levels, the effort of fast-walking from the carpark in my glittery heels had almost sent me into cardiac arrest.

'So, what you're saying to me is that you were at a club in Brum,' said my manager, who had listened to my whole story with a sardonic smile on his face, 'and everyone was off their tits?'

'Yep,' I said. 'They were all absolutely battered.'

'And then someone stole your clothes and shoes?'

'Uh huh.'

'Sounds about right for Birmingham, to be honest with you bab. Why are you even surprised?'

The telephone on my desk bleeped.

In a way, I thought, as I pressed the button to connect the call, it was quite spectacular, this sudden collision of my two separate lives. It was the big confrontation, the showdown – fight night. In the red corner we had modelling, with its big cities and traffic-stopping outfits and hair so backcombed it looked flammable and in the blue corner we had familiar domesticity, with its office job and Saturday nights out in town and everything you could possibly need contained within a ten-mile radius.

'We Insure You Too,' I said, into my headset. 'Ruth speaking, how can I help?'

There was a reason I was still doing my office job at the weekends for five pounds fifty an hour: I was completely and utterly broke. I had been broke before I began modelling but now, months down the line and with a near-daily commute from Redditch to London that had me driving more miles than a travelling carpet salesman, I had exhausted all tangible funds, all casual loans and all forms of credit. One of the biggest misconceptions I'd had about becoming a model (apart from the one where I assumed I'd become a superstar on my first day) was that I'd actually get paid. I'd naively assumed, before starting, that my pay would somehow be linked to the amount of effort I put in, that my wages would reflect the hours of effort expended. That there would be huge advertising campaigns from the off, paying thousands and thousands of pounds. But there were no wages. The advertising campaigns were few and far between. And I had quickly discovered that a lot of the things you did as a just-starting-out model, like castings and test shoots and all of the associated travelling around, were all done entirely for free.

Even magazines paid very little. Lots of them had a day rate of fifty pounds, which just about covered expenses, but some of the desirable edgy ones paid absolutely nothing. And if you did happen to hit the jackpot and get an advertising job, or one of the magazines that paid good money – one publishing house had a standard day rate of £450 – then you could then divide that fee over the previous six or so weeks you hadn't made a penny, to come up with your average starter-model daily wage. Of approximately fifteen pounds. So you could be doing very well as a fledgling model but also, at the same time, be embarrassingly, cripplingly broke. It was misleading.

Take my own situation. I'd actually had a great run in my first six months and, despite the fact that I still had a penchant for a McDonald's breakfast and had failed to establish an Olympian-level fitness regime (or any sort of fitness regime), I was really doing rather well. I'd done shoots for *iD* magazine and *Marie Claire*, and had even had a very small photo in *Vogue*. But would my Switch card work when I paid for my petrol? No, it would not. Which was why the local Texaco garage had a printout of my face behind the counter and my name on their blacklist. And also my watch. And a ring with a fake diamond in it. And my *Now That's What I Call Music: 47* CD.

So, my tattered financial situation was not a fair reflection of my modelling career thus far.

*

The aforementioned good run of fortune had started on my very first day of castings, when I'd managed to be – poetically – in exactly the right place at just the right time. Like in the films. A photographer had gone into the agency to find a girl for his test shoot that was happening the very next day and that girl had ended up being me.

'Brilliant news!' said my mum when I got home and 'Oh, really?' when I told her that test shoots were for free. And then, 'I hope it's not going to be one of those awful heroin-chic photoshoots,' she had said, when I relayed the news that it wasn't for a magazine but 'just some photos for everyone's books'. She was not at all convinced that the whole modelling thing was the greatest idea, being as she was a highly intelligent and artistic woman of the world who'd had her formative years in the sixties and seventies and knew a thing or two about things.

'Those terrible pictures where they make the girls look as though they've been chained to a radiator in someone's cellar for weeks,' she said, 'and they dress them in shredded clothes that look like rags, with horrible dark eyes and pale lips that make them look like they need to take iron tablets. I don't like it, it's glamourising something very grim.'

'Don't worry, Mum,' I had said, confidently, with my full eight hours of industry experience. 'Not every shoot is like that, just the grungey ones for the magazines nobody buys. Daz at the agency said the photographer takes really good photos and the makeup artist is brilliant.'

'Mmm,' Mum had said. 'Well, be careful. You're going to this guy's house and you've only met him once. He could be an absolute sleazebag or a wealthy pervert with a camera who's just pretending to be a professional. Do you even know his name?'

'Yes,' I had said, knowing he would be condemned before the words even left my mouth, 'he's called Filthy Rich.'

As it turned out, the idea for the shoot had been inspired by Nancy Spungen, girlfriend of the Sex Pistols' Sid Vicious, who had been addicted to heroin and had been found stabbed to death in a hotel bathroom at the tender old age of twenty.

My Mother, the Soothsayer.

'We're going to do really dark eyes,' the makeup artist had said, applying black greasepaint so thickly I could see it in my peripheral vision, 'and very pale lips.'

'Shall we go with the shredded top and the ripped jeans?' said the stylist. 'They would match nicely with the rusty radiator and the ankle chains . . .'

I had dreamed of looking like Gisele for my first shoot, with bronzed skin and a strong, chiselled body, oiled-up to gleaming perfection; instead, I spent the day looking slightly malnourished and vacant, eyes staring out from pools of black makeup, limbs looking pale and breakable. But at least nobody had actually chained me to a radiator in a basement. There had been no alarming occurrences whatsoever – I had felt immediately at home. The smell of the hairspray, the click of the camera, the way that nobody had a cigarette break because the whole thing was one big indoor cigarette break . . . it was like getting ready for a night out but periodically being forced to stand still. I had felt the same thrilling sense of transformation, of stepping out of myself and temporarily becoming someone new. Exciting. Even if the person I was supposed to have been transformed into had died a vicious, brutal and untimely death in a hotel bathroom. There were some things you just had to try and gloss over.

I had known that the pictures from the shoot would be great because I got to see the Polaroids at the start of each new shot. It was like getting a little glimpse of what the future might hold – there was something quite magical about waiting for them to develop, seeing the hair and makeup appear, seeing how different everything looked on film, with the lighting and the framing and all of the attention to detail suddenly coming into focus on this small, shiny, slightly sticky piece of card.

Nothing on set, I had discovered in my first few months as a model, was revered more than the Polaroid picture. There was no other way of knowing what the photos might eventually look like when they were developed and so, without a Polaroid, the photographer was effectively shooting blind. The Polaroid, once taken, was pulled gently from the back of the camera and then carefully waved around, or blown upon, or lovingly incubated under someone's warm armpit to speed up the developing process. And then it was placed somewhere flat and everyone would gather around as the picture came to life, like the wise men and the shepherds gazing down upon the newborn son of God.

The Sex Pistols Polaroids on the day had been brilliant. If they were a glimpse of the future, I'd thought, then the future was bright. And sure enough, a week later, the prints had arrived and my new modelling portfolio now had four outstanding pages of photos. I'd gone out on my castings carrying my new book, my makeup-less real-life face a picture of innocence as I watched the editors and art directors and photographers flick through the striking set of pictures.

'This can't be you,' they said as they stared at the grungey, black-eyed rock chick in the photos. 'It just looks nothing like you!'

But this was a blessing. For there was nothing fashion loved more than a drastic transformation and, just weeks into my newly started career, the castings rolled in and the bookings began.

So it had all been going well, despite my apparent height disadvantage and my arse being decidedly on the cusp. People liked my face, which was either interesting or beautiful, depending on who was critiquing it, and my teeth, which were either quirky or sexy or just lucky, and my body shape, which was slim but with curvy bits and a relatively impressive rack. I had a natural affinity for being comfortable and confident in front of the camera, endless amounts of chat for anyone who would listen and a self-deprecating sort of humour that seemed to put the people around me immediately at ease. I had all the right ingredients going on for this modelling thing; all I was missing was money. Money and – this was a hard thing to admit – the bravery to commit to a life in London.

'What I don't understand,' said my manager, as I finished

my call, 'is why you're even here when you've just done a telly advert. Why do you keep coming back when you could just live in London?'

I tapped a cigarette from my box of Marlboro Lights and stood up unsteadily, ready to make the arduous journey on broken feet to the smoking area at the back door. I had been working for a solid eleven minutes and was well overdue a break.

'Honestly?' I said, leaning back to put my phone on standby. 'I'm just passionate about telesales.'

His question had hit a nerve. Of course, there was the fact that I was financially destitute, but the real truth was that the idea of moving to London terrified me. That was why I had been shuttling back and forth between London and Redditch for six months, trying to establish myself as a model on weekdays and then, in the evenings and on the weekends, coming home to roost.

Was the daily four-hour commute an act of near insanity? Possibly. But I wasn't ready to let go of the anchor that my home life provided – the friends, the boyfriend, the job. Who did I know in London? What if I didn't find fame and fortune? I wasn't Dick Whittington, for crying out loud. I wasn't about to pack up my meagre belongings in a kerchief and tie it to the end of a stick. At least Dick had brought a cat along – I'd have nothing.

Anyway, I loved returning to the parental nest after a long day of castings. I enjoyed the gradual melt back to reality as I drove up the motorway in the dark, cigarette tip glowing as I held it to the window to flick out the ash. I liked that people in my home life didn't completely understand this world I had entered – it was comforting that they too thought it was a bit bizarre, that they also found it slightly unsettling. Speaking my experiences out loud and hearing how insane they sounded was a necessary sort of therapy.

'And what did you get up to today, tell me so?'

'Well, Granny, I did a hand-modelling casting for a firm who make coffins and then did a photoshoot dressed as a crow.'

'A crow! God love you. And did you get the job for the coffins?'

'I don't think so, Granny. They said my fingers were elegant but I needed to take more care of my nails.'

'Ah, away with them. You've lovely nails, so you have. And who's looking at a manicure when you're lying there dead?'

'It wasn't a casting to be a corpse, Granny. I just had to sort of run my fingers over the wood of the casket and show off the grain. Grasp the handles, that sort of thing.'

'Well, now,' said Granny, 'isn't there just a job in this life for everyone?'

No, I couldn't move to London. Not yet. London was so vast. It would be like moving to a field when you'd lived your life in a burrow. It would feel exposed. Limitless. And anyway, why reside in London, one of the world's most exciting cities, when you could live in Redditch and get the train to London, which would whizz you from Birmingham International to Euston station in around two and a bit hours? If it was actually running? Who wouldn't want to rise at 5.30am to get to a 9am casting on time; what idiot would turn down the chance to sit in standstill traffic along the A40 on a Thursday morning, exhaust fumes filling their car, Ginsters pasty breakfast sitting clammy and damp next to the gear stick?

I knew that the agency wanted me to be in London full time but I was holding off the inevitable for as long as I possibly could. Keeping my head down, selling my car insurance policies at the weekend and, on weekdays, arriving at my modelling jobs as punctually as if I lived next door. And I'd be fine living my double life, absolutely fine, so long as I turned up for castings and stayed out of trouble with the accounts department.

I just wanted to look like Gisele:
my first professional shoot.

© Richard Grassie Photography

Chapter 3

Wizards' Convention

'Beryl from the accounts department wants to see you, darling,' said Daz, as I swept into the agency in my black hooded cape-coat. 'She said to send you straight in.'

It was April 2002, almost a whole year since I'd made that very first trip to London, and I'd been planning on making a bit of an entrance. Upping my game a bit, because there was a casting at the agency for Littlewoods Catalogue and they paid really well. I'd bought the coat because I'd thought it would make me look like Whitney Houston in *The Bodyguard*, or an aristocratic Russian, or the woman out of the Scottish Widow advert. Glamorous and windswept and slightly mysterious. But in reality, the sheer size of the thing dwarfed me and the deep, oversized hood constantly shaped itself into a point on the top of my head so that I looked a bit like a Middle Earth chieftain from *The Lord of the Rings*.

'Good God, darling,' said Daz, looking up from the

papers on her desk, 'have you been at a wizards' convention?'

'I got it in the sales,' I said, hauling off the gargantuan coat and placing it carefully across the back of an empty chair. 'It was reduced from £300.'

'In the sales?' said Daz. 'I'm amazed, darling. You'd have thought people would have snapped those up.'

I went to lower myself into the chair. 'Don't sit down,' said Daz. 'Beryl awaits.'

I was mildly terrified of Beryl in accounts, mainly because each and every time I saw her, I needed to advance more money. We had the same relationship as a hopeless, terminal gambler who couldn't resist a punt on the horses and an east London loan shark. I, forever needing to borrow, was in a position of total, humiliating weakness whilst Beryl, wearing (in my imagination) multiple signet rings and a silken cravat, had to keep on doling out cash that I might never repay, always wearing the faux-reluctant expression of someone who didn't *like* chopping off arms for non-payment but would watch their henchmen do it if they really had to.

Beryl's job was clearly a job of two halves. The good half must have surely been handling the insane amounts of money that successful models made – especially the supers and near-supers – and the bad half was, almost certainly, having to dole out cash advances to the dozens of new models who made absolutely no money at all for ages. Sometimes never.

Because it was the grim truth that the majority of new models never went on to have a hugely fruitful career: in terms of people dropping dead by the wayside, modelling was the job equivalent of the Oregon Trail. A path littered with arrow-shot bodies, wide-eyed, moaning casualties and the abandoned suitcases of the deserters. (The sensible ones who saw what was truly required of them and thought *sod that*.) Even the settlers who made it to the promised land knew that their position would never be safe, that they'd probably spend their adult life on the road, living on a diet of water and a few ears of corn and wearing uncomfortable outfits.

So trips to see Beryl were never pleasant but this one held a particular sense of foreboding. Because the week previously, in a moment of vulnerability and under extreme duress, I'd agreed to give her full access to all of my financial information. Credit card statements, bank statements and, most excruciatingly, the details of the many high-interest store cards I'd been allowed to have as a student. I had quite a dirty little secret, you see: I wasn't just broke because I was a new model and because new models barely got paid for anything they did – I wasn't even broke because of how long it took to get the money through when new models *did* get paid. I was broke because, due to the slight 'love of shopping' problem I'd developed as a student, I had managed to saddle myself with a crippling amount of high-interest debt.

'Jesus Christ, you're shit with money,' said Beryl, as I stood before her in the accounts office. 'I mean you're *really* shit, to the point where I wonder whether you're on a mission to wind me up.'

She was holding a sheaf of papers in her hand and I realised, with a sudden stomach lurch, that they were my NatWest bank statements, a.k.a. The Papers That Should Never Be Looked Upon. I had certainly never looked upon them; in fact, I'd handed them to Beryl still in their unopened envelopes, feeling weirdly proud that I could deliver them so neatly, almost as though I was bestowing some sort of honour upon her. *Here are the documents, oh wise one Beryl, as yet unseen by human eye.*

'You've got some proper money problems here,' said Beryl, smacking the wodge of statements onto her desk, 'and we need to sort them out.'

Too right I had some proper money problems. One of them was that I spent money like the wife of an Upper East Side property developer, the other was that I earned the same wage as someone working a sixteen-hour week in telesales. Which wasn't surprising, seeing as though I was actually someone who was working a sixteen-hour week in telesales.

Take the cape-coat that I'd bought recently. Another ill-advised purchase that had occurred because I couldn't resist a price reduction. Ironically, it had been bought as part of my calculated effort to spend less money, my plan to curate for myself the perfect capsule wardrobe. I'd decided, two weeks before, that I was going to go late-night shopping and expertly pick out a selection of high-quality, key essentials that would all work seamlessly together, making my outfit-choosing sessions a million times quicker in the mornings and leaving me looking so striking, so showstopping, that I'd get every single modelling job I went for.

I came away from the sales that night owning: a pair of sandblasted jeans with ripped legs that were held together by hundreds and hundreds of miniscule golden safety pins; a D&G leather and denim patchwork pencil skirt with matching bolero; a pair of lime green neoprene ankle boots with stacked heels and, of course, the black woollen wizard's cape.

I liked to think that my need to buy new and shiny things was genetic, mainly so that I could pass on some – maybe all – of the responsibility for my terrible spending habit. Some of my earliest memories were of trailing my mum around the shops, legs aching with boredom as she held up item after item and carefully considered what she might or might not buy. But I also knew that it was much better all round to just face my problems head on and to be accountable for my own failings. And so, with that in mind, I fully declared that my money problems were 100 per cent the fault of the big lenders who had encouraged me, during my student years, to sign up to five different store cards and two major credit cards, and who gave me the sort of bank loan you'd normally reserve for bailing out a small country.

OK, so they didn't force me into Debenhams to buy the Gucci sunglasses (in not just one colourway, but three) and the Midland Bank didn't tie me to the reception desk and beat me over the head with an early saver's Perspex moneybox until I agreed to sign up for a loan I could never have afforded to repay. But the siren call of their easy, fast credit was too alluring for a shopper like me. I took all of it, hungrily, drinking in the funds like Augustus Gloop at the chocolate river.

The worst thing about all of this was that I had always had such a good work ethic. I knew the value of money – I'd grown up without much of it – and I understood how hard you had to work to get the things you wanted. I won't bore you with tales of my daily 6.30am clarinet practice and the after-school McDonald's shifts to pay for my driving lessons because you've no doubt come here for the glitz, the glamour and the story about the awkward time I accidentally became part of an informal sex show. But suffice to say, to spare you the growing-up-memoir montage of boring anecdotal snippets, I wasn't work shy and if I wanted something then I revelled in earning it myself, even if it was the hard way. The gratification was always worth the pain, which was why the store cards and loans were so utterly tempting: they brought the gratifaction nearer and they delayed the pain.

'You know you can't run from this forever,' said Beryl, sounding every bit the shotgun-toting East End gangster. She handed me a print-out.

'Your new diet.'

'Diet?' I felt horrified. So I *was* on the wrong side of the cusp! Was this how they were going to tell me?

'Financial diet,' said Beryl. 'You're going to cut up every one of your cards and live on an allowance. Fifty pounds,' she said, placing her book of cheques in front of her, 'a week.'

Fifty pounds a week? What year did Beryl think this was? 1986? My return train ticket from Birmingham to London was £11.55 and that was only if I went off-peak. Petrol to and from the train station was almost a fiver.

A packet of twenty Marlboro Lights cost £4.10 and I needed one of those at least every three days, depending on how much motorway driving I was doing. My Boots lunchtime meal deal, with Cajun chicken wrap, Shapers strawberry nougat bar and lemon-n-lime sparkling water cost £2.49. If I continued with my current daily commute to London then I'd be seven pounds short on train tickets alone and I'd have to siphon my petrol from the tanks of unsuspecting neighbours and/or my parents. I'd be there on my haunches, sucking on a hosepipe in the dead of night. Was I not to retain a single shred of dignity?

'She lives to see another day!' said Daz, as I returned to the New Faces desk. 'Darling, would you do a commercial for thrush cream, if the money was good?'

I sat down heavily in the chair. 'I'd do anything at the moment, if the money was good. Beryl's put me on a financial diet. I've got to live on fifty pounds a week.'

'Well, that's doable, darling,' said Daz, 'so long as you don't buy any more cloaks.'

I didn't want to remind Daz that I was still commuting to London every day. I felt guilty about it, like the hesitant boyfriend who was afraid to commit. And at present, I was still just about getting away with my double life, turning up for all the important engagements, never missing a date . . . I was there, in essence and spirit, I just didn't stay overnight. Or do weekends. Weekends were the tricky part – I needed plenty of notice if I was going to miss a day at my telesales job and now that I was on this new financial diet, I needed that weekend job more than ever.

'Darling,' said Daz, snapping me from my thoughts, 'Diane wants you to do a casting for her tomorrow, 8am on Shepherdess Walk.'

Diane head of the agency and original, brilliant boss lady. Straight-talking, frank and with an incredible, almost cyborg-like talent for seeing through bullshit, she was a beacon of relative normality in this world of fashion chaos. The human equivalent of a spirit level. If there was one person I had always been dead set on not disappointing, it was her.

'Erm,' I said. 'Does she know it's a Saturday tomorrow?'

'Yes, darling,' said Daz. 'I'm pretty sure that the boss of one of the world's biggest modelling agencies, a person who negotiates contracts with the most powerful global brands and handles tens of millions of pounds' worth of revenue each year, knows that tomorrow is a Saturday.'

Bloody hell. How could I get out of this one? Even if I didn't have my Saturday job to go to I'd have to get up at the crack of dawn to reach Shepherdess Walk for eight.

'I can't go,' I said, trying to think on my feet. 'I've got a funeral. It's for a friend of the family in . . . Hammersmith . . . and his wake starts at nine.'

'Well, you'll just have to run to it afterwards,' said Daz. 'The casting's for *Elle*, main fashion, and Diane's put it on your chart herself. Nobody will notice if you're late to the wake.' She grabbed her cigarettes from her desk and stood up. 'It's a stupid time for a wake anyway. What time are they burying him? At sunrise?'

'At eight,' I said. 'In . . . a graveyard.'

'Right,' said Daz. She stared at me for what felt like

five minutes before turning away and heading for the fire escape, tapping a cigarette from the box as she walked. 'Well, he won't notice your absence, darling, seeing as though he's dead.'

God. I was a terrible liar. I always had been a terrible liar. And I felt bad, but there was no way I could go to the casting the next day. Diane would be disappointed, yes, but I'd make it up to her in the long run.

'Did you know,' said a voice from behind me, 'that from all the New Faces that started at the same time as us, there are only six of us left?'

It was Candice, who must have turned up whilst I'd been unconvincingly fabricating a story about a sunrise burial and a nine o' clock wake. Candice was perched on the very edge of a stool wearing tight pedal pusher jeans, a white shirt knotted at the navel and white patent stiletto pumps. With her sunkissed skin, long honey-coloured hair and golden hoop earrings she looked every inch the eighties American swimsuit bombshell, so sexy and perfect that you wondered whether, if you chopped off her head with an axe, she'd have android innards. Candice had been such a hit as a New Face model that she'd immediately bagged a huge lingerie campaign and then, for the following year, proceeded to get pretty much every single job she turned up for. Such was Candice's success rate, models had begun to leave the casting queue if she happened to arrive, knowing that she'd almost definitely get the job and thinking it prudent to simply cut their losses.

Candice had the body of a Brazilian volleyball champion,

despite being from Buckinghamshire. Taut of stomach, lean of (very, very long) leg, she had large breasts that somehow defied gravity to curve up and point brazenly at the ceiling and a waist that was barely visible if she turned to the side.

Fortunately – because otherwise everyone would have hated her – she also happened to have an impediment, which was that she constantly used the wrong words for things. She had apparently wanted to study astrophysics at university before she'd been scouted as a model but nobody could ever work out whether that was true; though she was English, born and bred, it was as if she'd learned her native language from a faulty linguaphone. She'd just bought a Tempura mattresses, for example, and she got to the agency on the tube, using the Piccalilli Line. She'd told us that her cousin had recently put down his dangerous dog, a dog that had attacked a poodle in the park; the breed of his dog was a Toblerone pinscher. There were more examples but it hardly mattered – with her liquid walk, her deep brown eyes and rosebud lips, Candice was simply perfection. The early noughties fantasy woman.

'A bit boring though, darling,' Daz had said to me the week before, when I'd been droning on about how amazing I thought Candice was. 'Fashion doesn't like perfection. In fact, the weirder you are the better, in some respects. That's why I have this deep-seated belief that you'll do really well.'

'But she's getting all of the jobs!'

'Well,' Daz had said, 'money isn't everything darling. Wouldn't you rather be in *Dazed and Confused* magazine and poor than doing Freemans catalogue all the time, looking like you've been vacuum-formed out of beige-coloured plastic?'

And there was Candice now, looking outrageously gorgeous next to the chair I'd hung my cloak upon, wrinkling her nose at a magazine article about unorthodox sex positions. Golden shimmery highlights across her cheekbones, lips lightly glazed in a peachy gloss, lashes long and soft and fluttery.

'By the way, your coat's absolutely massive,' said Candice, glancing at the huge mass of black wool beside her. 'Aren't you boiling in it when you walk around?'

'Yeah,' I said. 'It was a big mistake. I have a problem with sales shopping, can't resist a discount.'

'Me neither,' said Candice. 'I always love something even more if it's been seduced.'

It took me a few seconds.

'Reduced?'

'Christ,' Stevie muttered. Stevie, another New Face model, was sitting on the floor wearing combat trousers and a black ribbed vest top, gigantic headphones on her totally shaved head, backpack hugged to her chest. With her crew cut and her fine bone structure she looked like Sinéad O'Connor, but angrier.

'How does Candice even stay alive,' said Stevie to nobody in particular, 'it's like she's been lobotomised.'

Stevie had recently been convinced, by Daz, to have what I had started to privately call the DNH, or Drastic New Haircut. The Drastic New Haircut was a hazard of the job, it seemed. It was intended to create a brand new image, a unique look, to mix things up a bit and create a point of interest to get people talking. Stevie's point of interest to get people talking was going to be 'looking more like a boy than she already did'. I knew this because I had witnessed the entire conversation the week before from behind the freestanding rack of New Faces modelling cards, where I'd been hiding in case I too got roped into having a drastic new haircut.

'I don't want to look like a boy, cheers,' Stevie had said, flicking back her mousey-brown hair.

'Look *more* like a boy,' Daz had said. 'Believe me, Steve, I—'

'Stev*ie*,' Stevie had interrupted.

'—believe me, Stevie,' Daz had continued, '*Vogue* loves the androgenous look. So does *Tank*. So does *iD* magazine. Total sexlessness is going to be your thing, mark my words, darling. It's where your success lies. You could even go so far as to trick them, really let them believe you're a boy.'

Daz waved her arm vaguely up and down in front of Stevie's body. 'Look at your clothes, darling!' she had said. 'The shapeless trousers, the shades of wheat and beige and . . . brown that you wear, and that odd army coat made from sackcloth. You could easily lull them all into thinking you're a boy. Lure them in,' said Daz, 'and then – *kapow*!'

'OK,' Stevie had said. 'Kapow. What happens at kapow?'

'They realise you're a girl. Totally fooled. Everyone will want to photograph you.'

'If they're so fooled,' Stevie had said, 'then why would they realise I'm a girl?'

'When they see you don't have a penis, darling.'

Stevie had stared darkly at Daz. 'And how would they see that I don't have a *penis*?' she said.

'Erm, when you take your clothes off?' Daz had said, oblivious to impending peril.

'It's all about vest tops and boy shorts at the moment. Black and white photos, cropped hair, no tits, wife-beater, low slung hip-hugger pants. Is it a girl, is it a boy? That is where fortune lies.' Daz paused.

'Well, not fortune obviously, but minor fame. None of those magazines actually pay anything, but you might get picked up by Steven Meisel and then you're in the money!'

She had paused again, as if working something important out for the very first time. An epiphany.

'Well, not exactly in the *money*, but you might get used for a few campaigns by big fashion houses while you're popular. For however long that is. Admittedly, some of them will pay you in clothes and some won't actually pay at all, but it's a trickledown effect, you see, darling. You do the Prada campaign and then if, I don't know, Old Navy in the US see it and book you and love you then you're quids in! Or not quids in, dollars in . . .'

I thought that Stevie was the absolute bee's knees, but there was no way she'd be friends with somebody like me. She was just so cool, with her eighties Walkman and her shaved head, but I never managed to say the right thing to her and I was sure she wanted to annihilate me with one of the grenades she probably carried about in the side utility pocket of her oversized backpack.

I tapped her on the shoulder. She had a small tattoo on the shoulder blade, I noticed. Virtually illegal for a model because clients didn't want the hassle and expense of airbrushing them out, and so we were told it was a no-go, but this was a very small round symbol, perhaps a letter from another alphabet, so intensely jet black against her skin that it almost looked like a bullet hole.

I tapped her shoulder and Stevie looked up at me.

'I love the GI Jane look,' I said, pointing to her combat trousers.

'What?' she said, pulling one headphone away from her head.

'I said, I like your GI Jane look.' I smiled and pointed to her head inanely, like a nursery teacher addressing a toddler. 'The hair really suits you.'

'Or lack of,' said Stevie. 'Cheers.' Her hand hovered next to her ear, ready to snap the headphone back into place. I had but a split second to hold her interest.

'I like your tattoo,' I said.

'Oh, thanks,' said Stevie, pressing the pause button on the side of her Walkman.

'Is it a symbol or letter from some other language?' I asked. 'Sanskrit, perhaps?'

Stevie looked at me as though I'd lost my mind.

'It's a dollar sign,' she said and pressed play on her tape.

'Diane wants to see you,' said Daz, returning from her cigarette break.

I had briefly dropped into a sort of open-eyed slumber, waiting my turn at the casting. A quiet calm had fallen over the queueing models; paperbacks were out, earphones were in and cigarette smoke curled up from the fire escape stairs. It felt peaceful. I was tired. I could easily have drifted off; I'd been on the 7.10am train that morning and hadn't even managed a nap because the man next to me had spread his newspaper so wide it had crossed over my airspace.

'She's at her desk, darling,' said Daz. 'I'd try and catch her now, if I were you.'

I stood up and made my way over to the world's greatest lie detector, like a lamb to the slaughter.

'Two quick things,' said Diane, as I hovered beside her. 'The first is that I have a casting for you tomorrow, at eight, and the second is about Japan.'

Japan?

'Don't be late for the casting tomorrow, darling, they have to make a decision on who they're shooting by nine.'

'Oh,' I said and then stopped because I wasn't quite sure how to carry on. 'Did Daz not tell you about the funeral?'

'No, darling,' said Diane. 'Tomorrow?'

'Yep,' I said. My palms began to sweat and a strange, meaty smell began to emanate from them.

'What time, darling?'

'At eight. I mean his wake is at nine, the funeral is . . . before it.'

Diane swivelled her chair around to face me.

'OK, darling, let's cut the crap here because nobody has a wake at nine. You'd have to be burying him at sunrise.'

'That's what Daz sa—'

'Why can't you do the casting, darling?'

'Because,' I said, feeling suddenly weary, 'I'm still in

loads of debt so I've been doing my insurance sales job every weekend. I'm also scared to move to London and I commute in every day.'

Diane peered at me thoughtfully for a moment. Only a moment though, because never had a person been so economical with their time.

'Yes, I knew all that already, darling.' She rapped her pen on the desk as though calling herself to attention. 'Do you want to do this?' she said. 'To model full time?'

'Definitely!' I said.

'Well, listen,' said Diane. 'The Tokyo agency has agreed to take you for a month on a guaranteed contract and I think it's a great idea. You'd be able to pay your debts off, come back and move down to London for a proper start.'

The Tokyo agency. I'd completely forgotten about them; they hadn't seemed massively enthusiastic about me when I'd met them a month or so before and I'd assumed it was a no-go. They had measured me with a measuring tape, taken some Polaroid pictures and mentioned my tooth gap at least seven or eight times. The farewell, when I'd left the room, had been lukewarm at best.

'It'll be good for you, darling,' said Diane. 'You're not their usual type, so I'm surprised they've asked for you, but your book is strong, they like your measurements and they've given you a good guarantee. You might make more than the guarantee, obviously, but at least you'll come back with your debts paid off.'

Tokyo it is then, I thought, wondering why an earth I'd ever been worried about London when there was a whole globe to be flung around. I went back to my chair, slightly shellshocked by the news that I'd be flying to Japan in three weeks' time.

'I'm going to Tokyo,' I said to Candice.

'Wow, really?' said Candice. 'Even with your tooth gap?'

'Yeah, I know,' I said. 'I didn't think they'd take me.'

I was jittery with excitement and desperate to chat but it was Candice's turn to go into the casting room and I had to watch her as she click-clacked across the agency in her white patent heels, her hips sliding sexily from side to side as though she was missing some vital ligament in her lower back. What would my parents say about Japan? What would I pack? I couldn't believe it – I was going to Tokyo. Me! I felt a burst of newfound confidence. If I could be picked for Tokyo, I could virtually do anything. It was hard to get an agency there to take you on – I thought I'd be too weird-looking, with my non-classic face and my gappy front teeth. Those things were acceptable in London, desirable even, but not in Japan.

If I could go to Tokyo then I could definitely get this casting for Littlewoods. It'd be a walk in the park. I looked at the door to the casting room that had only just clicked closed and I imagined myself strutting through it confidently in my stack-heeled boots, placing my portfolio down on the table with a winning smile. But before I'd even given my imaginary greeting, the real door opened and out came Candice.

What? She'd only just gone through! Had I entered some sort of time-warp?

Candice sauntered to Daz's desk, closely followed by the client.

'Next Tuesday?' Daz said, tapping away at her computer. 'Candice has an option for Cosmo and another for Boots but she has a free day on Wednesday?'

'In that case,' said the client, as Candice scooped up her handbag and made for the door, 'Wednesday it is. See you next week, Candice!'

I looked over at Stevie. Our wait had been pointless.

'Fight you for the thrush cream job,' she said.

Chapter 4

The Quality of the Foot

I had two main problems with castings. The first was that managing to attend them all was a logistical nightmare, due to the fact that they were never arranged in any sort of sensible geographical or chronological order, and the second was that the majority of them were a complete and utter waste of time.

'Darling,' Daz would say, when I checked in at 5.30pm every evening, pen and paper at the ready. 'Bit of a packed schedule tomorrow, I'm afraid, you might be wishing for your own death by the end of it.'

And then she would proceed to read out the eight or nine castings for the following day, all of them as geographically distant from one another as could possibly be and each with their own diverse set of instructions and requirements.

'Nine o'clock on Tottenham Court Road, darling –

you need to have wild, curly hair and be wearing casual denim and classic heels. Then the next is on Wandsworth High Street, darling – nine fifteen – and you need to be in a ball gown.'

Often the schedule was just impossible to keep.

'At ten, darling, a casting at Harvey Nichols and then you have a request in Oxford Circus at eleven and then a go-see in Holland Park.'

'What time is that one?'

'Also at eleven.'

Very occasionally, you'd even get the odd casting in Paris, which always seemed a bit of a stretch to fit into a daily schedule of appointments but, nevertheless, every now and then, there it would be: 3.30pm request casting at Studio Six-Six-Six, Rue de Chaque-a-laque, Paris. Eurostar from Waterloo at 10.05, Metro to Pigalle, Bob's your *oncle*, Fanny's your *tante*.

Fashion models of the early noughties were generally expert with an A-Z. There wasn't a location a model couldn't find in that small, spiral-bound book of London maps. Even if the street didn't exist, they had the hard-earned skills that meant they could triangulate the location to within a square metre. Mainly because they spent every day of every week, more or less, criss-crossing London on foot, tube and bus. From Islington to Battersea and then back to N1; Parson's Green to Coptic Street and then a bus across Hackney. Models could have done The Knowledge, we could have drawn the tube map in our sleep; the journey-planners and route-finders of the future couldn't have computed shortest times to destination faster than us.

We were human atlases and no discreet fourth-floor buzzer or as-yet-unmapped mews escaped our collective mind.

'You going to Denmark Street? Number 12A doesn't exist; you take the alley and it's the door with the nailed-up letterbox.'

'Hair awards casting? The entrance is by the canal.'

Getting to the castings was one thing: whether they were worth it when you got there was another. I hadn't realised that castings, those strange, unpredictable job interviews where you mostly had less than a one in a hundred chance of getting the job, would account for the vast majority of time and effort you put in as a New Face model. In my imagination (which, admittedly, had proven to be a really unreliable source of information thus far) I'd pictured there being a few castings scattered here and there – one at *Tatler*, perhaps, one for Chanel and maybe a pop-in at the Dior boutique just so they could check my sizes – but most of the time I thought I'd be rocking up to my jobs unseen, only my enviable, glamorous reputation preceding me. But no; on any day that I wasn't booked on a job, which turned out to be most days, there were seven or eight castings and the majority of them, at least at the beginning, bore very little in the way of fruit.

There were a few different types of casting and if I had to rate them, best to worst, then 'recalls' would have been right up there at the top of the chart and go-sees, the pointless, prospectless time-wasters of the casting family, would have lurked right at the bottom.

Recalls were the best and most optimistic of all the appointment types because a) they were usually for a TV commercial, which meant that there was money involved somewhere along the line, and b) if you were being recalled then you were in with a very good chance of getting the job. Just nuzzling in beneath 'recalls' you had 'request castings' and these were good because somebody, with any luck, had flicked through a load of portfolios and then given some thought as to which models they'd like to see in person. They'd begun to narrow down their selection, perhaps finding five, ten, even fifteen girls that they liked the look of for their catalogue shoot or their feature on foot creams. It showed some degree of foresight, an element of critical thinking, a vague ability to make decisions and – above all – it displayed an appreciation for the value of time. Not just the models' time, but the client's. Because who in their right mind wanted to sit in a studio all day long watching a perpetual merry-go-round of models walk in, hand their portfolio over, smile benignly and then leave?

I'll tell you who would want to do all of this – the people who held the saddest category of castings on the ratings chart: 'general castings'. General castings were the most annoying because they took up the most time. They were basically an open call and so everyone in the world tended to rock up with gay abandon, meaning, statistically, they were the least likely to end in any form of remuneration. The types of people running these general castings were many and varied. Sometimes it was the editor of a magazine, sometimes it was the owner of a hair salon, or a fashion designer, or a photographer who had been lumbered with the job of picking a girl for a shoot. But what they usually had in common was that they didn't have the faintest bloody clue what they were looking for. Even narrowing things down by something as simple as hair colour or height was beyond them.

'We know we want someone, you know, *willowy*,' the editor would say to the model bookers, 'but we're open to seeing, you know, *everyone*, basically.'

And then 240 models would egress Parson's Green tube station like some sort of massively good-looking, bannerless political protest and all sit and wait outside a studio for hours whilst some numpty inside got more and more befuddled by the sheer amount of choice.

There was never any thought as to whether it was a good idea to call dozens of people to the very same place at the very same time: the people that ran these castings were, in my opinion, utter morons.

'I'd put your name on the list if I were you, darling,' said Daz. It was the week before I left for Tokyo and I was in the agency for a catalogue casting, the holy grail of regular jobs.

'The whole agency's been asked to come in,' said Daz. 'We're expecting about ninety-five of you.'

For Christ's sake! I looked around. There were models on every surface. Sitting on desks, crouching in the corridor, lounging on the windowsill and sitting outside on the fire escape. It was as though a cloning experiment had gone horribly wrong; there were tall, thin, long-haired creatures everywhere you glanced.

I suddenly got the weird sinking feeling that I so often

got when I was in the vicinity of lots of other models – the feeling that I was being idiotic and overly optimistic by even being there. So many girls, all of them so effortless and well put-together; most of them tall and skinny enough to get away with just wearing some baggy jeans and Converse, an old band t-shirt thrown on over the top. How did they do that and still look good? Why was I wearing tall boots I couldn't walk in properly with jeans I had to stop breathing in and a tight, low-cut top that screamed 'small town mentality'?

There, by the window, a girl looking chic in a little black dress with Doc Marten boots. Sitting near reception, another in blazer and jeans. And there, near the bathrooms, a sophisticated-looking woman wear—

'Wait,' I said to Daz. 'Did you say *all* the girls in the agency have been asked to come in?'

'Yes, darling,' said Daz, 'all of them who are in town, anyway.' She was sifting through a pile of torn-out sheets from magazines and marking the good ones with little yellow Post-it notes. 'Girls from all of the boards.'

'Girls from all boards?' I said. 'Even . . . ?' I paused. Surely not. I could barely breathe with excitement. Would today be the day that I finally got to see a girl – woman – from the *Classic Board*?

'Yes,' said Daz. 'Even the Classics.'

There were three different women's divisions at the agency: New Faces Board, representing the inexperienced girls trying to build up their portfolios; Main Board, looking after all of the girls who were proper working models, earning real money that you could actually spend on things and then Classic Board, the board I'd developed a mild fixation with.

I could not get my head around this part of the agency that booked jobs for – essentially – old women. Women in their – unbelievable! – late thirties and even into their forties. Some were actually older than their forties. Older than their forties! It seemed wondrous to me, at the age of twenty-one, that this division even existed. Hadn't Daz said that I was old to be starting as a model? If I was old then what possible work was there for these ladies? When did you ever see them in adverts or magazines, unless it was for cruise ship holidays or leaflets for funeral homes? OK, so it was 2002, and magazines were getting on board with now and again featuring Helen Mirren, but no other aged women were really seen . . . anywhere. Even hair dye for grey hair was advertised using young women – surely past thirty you became invisible?

Part of the mystery surrounding the Classics was that you never really saw them around and about. You knew that these forty-somethings existed somewhere, perhaps languishing in a retirement home or being cared for by relatives in a little rose-covered cottage, bumbling around in slacks, mislaying things and forgetting what day it was, but you never saw them *out*. Not amongst the usual modelling herd.

But apparently they were here today. Right here in the agency – Daz had just said so. I looked around subtly, not wanting to draw attention by turning my head. I could see some other New Faces and lots of Main Board girls, but no Classics. I imagined them emerging from hatches in the floor in swathes of dry ice, crinkled bodies rising out from their sarcophagi.

I hurried over to the table in the meeting room and wrote my name on the waiting list, all the time checking my peripheral vision for decrepit crones. I was number eighty-six on the list, a number that would normally have sent me near-apoplectic with frustration and rage, but today it didn't bother me. The epic wait would just give me more time to observe the objects of my obsession.

Still, though, what total imbecile arranged a casting for that many people to be here all at one time? It was surely a matter of very simple logistics to stagger their arrival and make life easier. Even better, why not narrow down your criteria beforehand and invite fewer people? It was a classic example of the wrong person having significant casting control. The same thing had happened at a casting just the week before.

A casting so far to the west of London that it was virtually in Devon. It was a real hassle to get to: a tube to almost the end of the Central line, then a bus, and then a twenty-minute walk alongside a dual carriageway with lorries careering past at warp speed, spraying a constant fine mist from their tyres. Finally, safe and dry at the studio, I had waited for forty minutes in a disgruntled queue of girls who had all no doubt been on exactly the same journey.

There we all were, waiting for this casting. For a shoe campaign – an important detail. The clients had been very specific about what should be worn to the casting, too, because the clients from the German shoe company wanted to see – written verbatim – *quality of foot, turn of ankle and perfection of shin*. Translated into practical and useful language, this meant that we should turn up in a skirt or dress that showed off our legs and that it would be advisable to wear heels. This was a right pain in the arse, considering that we'd all had to hike the length of the A40 to get there. The shoes, not so much, because most of us were seasoned pros who knew to wear trainers and then just throw on the heels we always had in our bags, but the skirt/dress thing? Well. It was amazing that there had been no reports of fatal crashes in the area, the number of young, gazelle-legged girls that had apparently been striding along the side of the dual carriageway wearing bodycon dresses, Lycra wiggle skirts and cowgirl denim.

I had shunned the denim skirt and bypassed the bodycon bandage dress in favour of my current skirt *du jour*, a white broderie anglaise ra-ra skirt that was supposed to be a bit 'Sarah Jessica Parker in *Sex and the City*' but in reality was part tennis skirt, part Swiss milkmaid. It wasn't a particularly sexy skirt, this skirt, but it made my legs look more tanned and – crucially – more toned, and it was white so it went with almost everything.

But it was also ridiculously flippy. If there was even the slightest gust of wind or movement of air – say someone was drying their hair with a Babyliss Pro in the next room or a toddler in Norway was blowing out a birthday candle – the layers of skirt would begin to quiver with excitement and then they would start to flutter and, within seconds, the entire body of fabric would be flapping up and down like a flag on a cross-channel ferry. Even with a cardigan tied around my waist, my ramble to the casting had been punctuated with the beeping of car horns and the honking of trucks as my skirt repeatedly blew up in the barely there breeze and flashed my knickers. The effort level to get to the casting, had I been bothered to quantify it, would have been a solid eight out of ten.

A woman had appeared at the doorway to the casting room. 'Next girl,' she had said, 'and be quick, we have a lot to get through.'

'Next' happened to be me and so I got up from my seat and crossed the room.

'This is for a commercial,' said the woman, as she ushered me inside, 'to display the beauty of the shoe and the quality of the foot.'

'And the turn of the ankle?' I said, but she didn't respond.

There were three people behind a long table which was piled with model portfolios and scattered with cards. They all looked up as I crossed the room to give them my book, but before I could get to the table, one of them held up his hand, palm flat, to halt me. And this is where the weirdness started.

You never really knew what might happen at a casting. Sometimes, you'd be asked to do something, like demonstrate your walk, or dance, or try on an outfit. A lot of the time, you'd answer questions about yourself, or partake in a spot of small talk whilst the client or photographer or editor flicked through your portfolio in silence. Each casting had its own quirks, or lack of, and this, the *beauty of the shoe* casting, was no different. Because from the second I was stopped in my tracks, three or so metres from the table, I was hit with a barrage of weird questions.

'So, we're looking for someone who can show the beauty of the shoe,' said the man who had stopped me. 'Can you?'

'Erm, yes?'

Riddle me this, riddle me that. He looked like the dormouse from the Mad Hatter's tea party, his face almost entirely covered in a fuzzy blonde beard. Next to him, there was a woman with a high, platinum blonde ponytail.

'Can we please see your turning,' she said, 'and especially we would like to witness your ankles?' She smiled.

I turned three-sixty as slowly and elegantly as I could.

'Do you have experience with demonstrating shoes?' snuffled a man with a cold, rousing himself from his half slumber at the end of the table.

What the hell did that mean? Had I worn shoes?

'And you are free next Tuesday?' said the ponytail woman.

'I . . . think so?' I said. 'You'd have to check with my agency, though.'

'And for showing the beauty of the shoe, you can have a professional pedicure?'

'Yep, yes,' I said. This was looking promising. Professional pedicure, not a problem.

'And so finally,' said the woman, glancing down hurriedly at her watch, 'can you please tell me your UK shoe size?'

'Yes, I'm a six,' I said. 'A thirty-nine,' helpfully giving the European equivalent.

'I am sorry then, you are unsuccessful,' said the woman. 'The shoes are all a size thirty-seven.'

A size thirty-seven? A UK *four*? Sample size shoes were always a seven, or a six.

'Thirty-seven?' I said. 'That's a UK four! That's very small?'

'It is to show off—'

'The beauty of the shoe,' I said. 'Yes, got it.'

There was no point me even trying to force my ugly sister foot into the glass slipper – the pale cream court shoe they presented to me to demonstrate the beauty of the shoe looked like something you'd place atop a wedding cake as a decoration. It was miles shorter than my foot and so narrow that it would have barely fit my big toe. I left the casting room still clasping my portfolio to my chest and already contemplating the long and annoying journey back to central London.

Nearly every girl there had taken a *Planes, Trains and Automobiles* type journey to get to the casting and had worn the skirt, donned the shoes, lugged the portfolio (which hadn't even been glanced at) and paid for the TFL zones 1–6 travelcard – and how many of them would have size four feet?

But what was even more unbelievable than the clients not specifying their very particular sizing requirements was the fact that dozens of models had come out of the casting before me and not one of them had thought to say before leaving, 'Hey everyone! Just to let you know, they're only looking for someone with size four feet!' In we went, one after the other, like lemmings to the cliff-edge of despair and despondency, and then, one by one, turned around again, feeling momentarily angered but then completely forgetting about the whole thing by the time we reached the door back to the waiting room.

I saw that the waiting room was even more full than when I'd gone into the casting – at least twenty or thirty girls queuing – and there were no seats left to sit in, no sofa arms to perch on, not even a patch of free wall to lean against. I'd have to change back into my trainers outside, under the watchful gaze of the workers digging up the road outside the studio. Out I traipsed, and it was only as I was halfway down the dual carriageway, pushing down on the hem of my stupid flippy skirt and trying to remember which underpass I needed to take to get to the bus stop, that I realised I hadn't told any of the others about the size four feet.

'There's girls from Classics here,' said Candice, leaning down to speak close to my ear.

Where the hell had she come from? Had anyone else seen her? Did they know they might as well all just go home?

Candice was wearing a pink-and-white striped cotton dress, scoop-necked and short, with a large leather belt slung around her hips and knee-high white tasselled cowboy boots. Whatever she wore she looked very slightly pornographic, which I supposed was the downside of being so perfectly sexy. I didn't have that problem so much, wearing as I was my traditional uniform of bootcut jeans, brown leather platforms and vest top from Morgan de Toi.

'I've been looking for them,' I replied in a low voice. 'No Classics identified yet.'

I wondered briefly whether we might have already missed them. Perhaps they had all been paraded through early, like a sort of warm-up act. A quick outing in front of the clients and then back to the care home for bed. Or maybe they were saving them for the end, when they could dim the lights and unveil them one by one, like precious relics. . .

And then, as though I'd willed it to happen, the time came. They called her name and I knew she was one of them. I had seen her card on the wall, printed with the photo from an Oil of Ulay campaign and a cover shot from *Women's Own*.

'Number thirty-six, Irina?'

We looked around. Would I hear the squeak of the wheels first, as they pushed her across the agency in her chair? Or would there be a sudden burst of dry ice as a coffin dropped down from a hidden cavity in the wall behind the modelling cards? A slow creak as the lid opened, a moment of sweet anticipation and there Irina would be, 5'10', 34-25-34, arms crossed over her chest like an ancient vampire.

'Hey,' said Irina, standing up from a chair behind me. She had been there all along! Wearing a Breton-striped t-shirt and tight white jeans, tan suede loafers on her elegant feet and a neat watch upon her wrist. Her hair was tied at the nape of her neck with a grosgrain ribbon and she had simple gold studs in her ears and plain golden rings on her fingers. She looked expensive. She smelled expensive, like gentleman's shaving soap. As she moved, it was as though a spotlight was upon her, such was her confidence and poise and her smooth, seamless way of walking.

'Oh my God!' I mouthed to Candice, my eyes wide. 'She's amazing!'

'I know,' whispered Candice. 'And she's forty-four. She has three kids, as well. Two of them in primarily school and two in secondary.'

'Bloody hell,' I said. 'I hope I look like her when I'm old.'

Chapter 5

Tokyo Teena

There was a model in Tokyo who got all of the work and sadly that girl wasn't me. Her name was Teena and she had everything I didn't, which was – in no particular order – the body of an eleven-year-old, the giggle of a schoolgirl and the inane smile of a partially deflated sex doll. Tokyo Teena had cultivated a casting style that seemed to be irresistible to the average middle-aged Japanese man, and as most of the clients in Tokyo seemed to be middle-aged Japanese men she was doing a roaring trade. Just sixteen and on her fifth Tokyo stay, she was model casting catnip.

Now, I'm not saying that all of these middle-aged men had sexual preferences that bordered on paedophilic, because obviously – *obviously* – they were only casting what the public wanted to see. But with her Shirley Temple curls and her tiny, breast-budded body, Tokyo Teena looked as though she'd barely left primary school and the chain-smoking clients, lined up like judges behind their long narrow table, just couldn't get enough.

'Teena-*san*,' they would say, through a fug of cigarette smoke, 'please give us . . . pout.'

And Teena would pout, looking for all the world like a child who'd been denied a second scoop of ice cream.

'Teena-*san*,' they would ask, 'please give us dancing.'

And Teena would prettily bop and jig like a wind-up toy, as though someone had just put a coin in her slot.

Teena could pout, Teena could dance, Teena could also never walk in a straight line for more than two metres, which seemed to me like a terrible affliction. Instead of moving in a linear motion, like a normal human being, Teena continually twirled around and around, as though she'd been plucked from the lid of a music box and finally set free. It was like watching a demented version of *The Nutcracker*, except that Teena wore cut-off dungarees and seersucker crop tops, like an eighties Fisher-Price doll.

'Teena-*san*,' they would say to her, 'please now try on the swimsuit.'

And Teena would try on the swimsuit, pirouetting back into the room to the delighted murmurs of the clients, spectacles steaming and ashtrays full.

I had cultivated my own casting style in Tokyo but it was slightly different to Teena's. My casting style was to walk into the room, say *konichiwa* and then promptly detach myself, mentally, from the entire situation until someone thanked me and told me to leave. I found the whole thing excruciating – the queues of girls watching from the sides of the room, the nodding and the smiling, the trying on of clothing that never quite fit me. And the worst part was that there was no real way of communicating in these castings, seeing as though I hadn't used my three-week preparation period to become fluent in Japanese.

Sometimes we would bumble through together, model and client, using our joint vocabulary of a half-dozen universally known words and the power of rudimentary mime, but more often than not the clients would just examine me, point at me and – for what seemed like the length of time it took to perform a lesser-known Shakespeare play – talk about my faults. And if you want to know how on earth I found out about my faults when I understood absolutely no Japanese, then look no further than our chaperone, Takashi, who would cheerily give us a little translated summary of how our castings had gone as we all piled back into the minivan.

Yes, a minivan. Casting in Tokyo was not like casting elsewhere; unless you could read Japanese or you knew the city well then your navigational skills were virtually useless, because not only were all the building numbers written as symbols, in hiragana, the streets had no names. And so rather than have their models blundering around the city like little blind mice, the agency bundled us up together, put us in a minivan and gave us a chaperone to drive us around. It looked like some sort of kidnapping bus and once you were trapped in it for the day you had to drive to everyone else's castings as well as your own. Crawling up and down seemingly identical streets for hours and hours, waiting to be herded out when you arrived at your next cattle call.

Anyway, Takashi kept things light throughout these

long, tedious days by relaying to us his little run-down of significant things the clients had said. Which we all looked forward to when we were already at our lowest ebb, feeling defeated and totally devoid of any self-worth. After each casting, there'd be a quick cigarette break and then it would be back into the van, the side door sliding closed with an ominous thud.

'Jeanne-*san*,' Takashi might say, climbing into the driver's seat, 'clients say they like you, but not for sports shoot so maybe next time you will be lucky. Paulina-*san*,' turning his key in the ignition, 'client says eyes so nice but nose too long. Like Pinocchio.'

By this point, we all knew that Paulina's nose was too long for Tokyo because we received these little bulletins about eight times a day, after each and every appointment. It was like an exercise in positive reinforcement, but the opposite, whatever that was. Punishment.

'Ruth-*san*?'

'Yes, Takashi, hit me with it.'

'The client say only the usual, Ruth-*san*. They say: face pretty, but also face too quirky. And teeth too gappy, like crazy witch in the woods.'

Right-o.

'And hair too short,' Takashi might continue, 'cut so bad, looks chop-chopped by woodcutter.'

I mean, that was fair. I had, at that moment in time, one of the worst haircuts I would probably ever endure in my whole life, and I also had no understanding as to how I should manage it or style it. It had been a drastic enough cut at the time of chopping, looking as though it had been hacked at with a pitchfork and hoe by a medieval farmhand, but now, a month or so in, it looked as though I'd had a drunken tryst with Edward Scissorhands. Jaw-length locks with an asymmetrical tilt, different on each side, a fringe that was long but also sometimes short, and a longer back section that could only be described as a mild mullet.

I suspected, too, that these were not my only disadvantages. It wasn't a healthy path to go down, minutely examining your own physical inadequacies, but I was a realist as well as an optimist, and I knew that I didn't have the sort of classic, commercially pretty face that I saw on the Japanese billboards and magazine ads.

'Dani-*san*,' said Takashi, turning to briefly look Danish Dani in the eye. Dani was my flatmate, Denmark born but London hardened, and I couldn't have asked for a better one. Taller than me, blonder than me and with a deep, sonorous voice, she walked like a well-hung Viking, smoked like a war vet and had a deep dislike for frivolous chat.

'Dani-*san*,' said Takashi, 'the client say—'

'I don't give a fuck,' said Danish Dani, and that was the end of that.

We had two small bedrooms in our apartment, both overlooking a large graveyard, and there was a kitchen behind a folding screen and a bathroom with a tiny, sit-in bathtub. The television showed mainly chaotic Japanese gameshows, the landline phone was expensive and so our main evening hobbies, mine and Danish Dani's, were walking the streets and window-shopping for food.

The street we frequented most was the main road to Roppongi, an area that was famed at that time for its nightlife and its sordid, fetish-splattered underbelly. On the surface it was a noisy, colourful, ceaseless sensory overload, lit up as bright as day. Every shop festooned with lights, the sides of buildings covered in screens. Futuristic high-rise blocks with ramshackle lanes packed in between, impossibly narrow and cramped. It was like real-life *Blade Runner*. Singing toilets, talking doors, lifts that dropped cars to their underground spaces – walking through Roppongi was like being flicked into a giant pinball machine and left to bounce your way out.

But just below the surface, barely staying submerged, was a rank sort of sex-filth that was at once fascinating – in the same way that you might want to lift up a scab – and slightly intimidating. Vending machines selling women's used knickers, brightly lit sex shops spanning six floors and then, the weirdest thing: the men who roamed the streets with folders filled with pictures of what looked like women's spread-open genitalia.

I have wondered, now and again, whether perhaps I imagined this, or just managed to get the wrong end of the stick – after all, I'd only ever get a quick glimpse of what the men in long, shiny coats were showing in their books before the laminated pages were snapped shut. It was entirely possible that I would be, for years, operating under the misunderstanding that these men on the streets of Tokyo were flashing images of labia when in fact they were all employees of, I don't know, a shellfish wholesaler. But I was pretty certain from the shady way that they opened the pages for male passers-by but slapped the covers closed for females, as though they were trying to control an excitable clamshell, that the wares they were touting were flesh of the human kind.

And so the walk to Roppongi was potted with sex-sellers, vulva-catalogues and very drunk businessmen holding their heads in their hands, stooped in dark doorways or weaving along unsteadily. What a place. At least there were lots of pet shops along the way to soften the blow, all of them selling cute fluffy puppies, snoozing away under fluorescent lights, or fuzzy kittens having a little stretch. The same ones there, night after night, bundled together or lying alone in their Perspex display cubes with no real stimulation or life-affirming interaction with others. *Kawaii*.

If instead we went the other way from the apartment, through the rook-infested graveyard, we could walk to the big international supermarket and look at all of the food that we couldn't afford. Because the big supermarket, blessed traveller's sanctuary of Western imports, was a complete head-mash of worldwide cuisines and incomprehensible pricing. Things you'd pay a fortune for in England – sushi, raw tuna, miso sauces – were plentiful and cheap, but commonplace foodstuffs from the UK may as well have been encrusted with diamonds and plated with gold. Kellogg's corn flakes were three times the English price and a tub of Vitalite cost the same as a small car.

'Guess how much for the tortilla wraps?' Danish Dani would say.

'Old El Paso ones?' I might answer. 'I'm going with a fiver.'

'Incorrect,' Dani would announce, placing them back on the shelves. 'They're the equivalent of eight pounds fifty. Four strawberries, name the price.'

'Four? Show me.'

Danish Dani would pass me a moulded plastic container with four spherical sections, each one containing a huge, squash-ball-sized, impossibly red strawberry.

'I'm going with six pounds twenty-five,' I would say. 'Just over one pound fifty per fruit.'

'Eight pounds,' Dani might boom in her low, melodious voice. 'Eight fucking pounds.'

In this fashion, we would work our way around the supermarket, examining every single fruit and cooking ingredient before plumping for our usual pickings: some garlic, a pack of dried pasta, two lots of tinned tomatoes and a bit of raw chicken. Now and then some salad, but only if one of us had managed to get some work.

After a few weeks, it became apparent that I would not be going home from Japan draped in Gucci and driving a Lamborghini. The jobs I'd had prearranged before I'd flown out to Tokyo were done and dusted, only a few more had materialised and now I was in a tedious cycle of sitting in the minivan all day, waiting for an end to the castings, or for death, whichever came sooner. The first week in Tokyo had barely even registered, it had gone so fast, and the second had been a muddle of continued jetlag, discombobulation and a delayed reaction to the culture shock. But now, three weeks in, I was beginning to wonder whether I'd been sold a dream.

It seemed a shame that the documentary crew had gone home already because this part – where I was just sitting and waiting, the very visual representation of sad failure – would have been brilliantly poignant.

What documentary crew?

Oh, only a programme for Channel 4, directed by an award-winning documentary filmmaker – nothing very important, just a documentary about the modelling world *starring me as one of the main models.*

I had been chosen as the 'new model', the up-and-coming one, to show some of the aspects of the modelling industry people didn't usually get to see. The loneliness. The vulnerability. The strangeness of travelling alone to an entirely new part of the world. The absolute absence of any financial stability. And the crew had captured it all, following me to castings and artfully filming me at Shibuya Crossing looking tall and blonde and alien, even recording my phone call home to talk about my ever-present debt. They had captured the very essence of my trip: that it was this mad foray into the unknown but that it was also a necessary one, because I was broke.

Ironically, their presence had saved me from being quite as lonely and vulnerable and financially unstable as I would have been had they not been there. For a week, they were my family; we ate together, travelled together and talked for hours between shots. Had they not been there, I doubt I would have eaten properly. If at all. And finding my feet, in a city that was just so entirely different to anywhere else on earth, would have been far more daunting. I wished that they could have stayed on, could have witnessed the twirling of Tokyo Teena, could have documented the morning I woke up and had a minor panic attack because I thought my nipples had disappeared. (They hadn't, the client the day before had covered them with round, skin-coloured nipple covers and I'd forgotten to peel them off.) But they were gone now and I had a four-week contract, so four weeks in Tokyo it was.

I didn't want to complain – at least I had a contract. There had been a couple of girls at the agency who hadn't been so fortunate – they'd disappeared in the night and not come back, and I didn't want to go the same way. I want to make it clear that the agency didn't dispose of them, God no! They just got sent home. Still, it felt awful and shocking and slightly unsettling, like somebody unexpectedly leaving the Big Brother House when you'd become accustomed to their presence.

One of the vanished girls had been French, from Carcassonne: she had been measured and photographed and declared too fat. Not in those words, but it was made known to her mother agency that Marie-Cecile from Carcassonne had exceeded her contracted measurements, ballooned past the contingency that allowed for temporary expansion, which I imagine included things such as plane bloat or pre-menstrual water retention, and had burst her tethers and floated up into the sky, like a giant blimp. Marie-Cecile, a tiny thing, with the very slightly rounded belly of a sensuous, sexy nineteen-year-old, who looked absolutely knockout in her lacy Aubade bra. *Au revoir* Marie-Cecile, enjoy your life of eternal body hang-ups!

Next to go was Anna from Poland, who most definitely

hadn't burst her proverbial tethers, being as she was about 98 per cent sinew, but had point-blank refused to do the jobs that the agency had booked her to do. It seemed, just to a casual observer, that Anna from Poland hadn't been quite the hit that the agency had imagined she'd be, with her jet-black eyebrows that crossed her face angrily and her thin, mean slash of a mouth. She was a twist of lean, muscled aggression and had a book full of edgy magazine covers that had put us all to shame, but the only jobs she'd booked had been editorial ones. Which hardly paid. And after two weeks of solid work, total earnings approx. fifty pounds, her jobs had stopped.

'No,' we had heard her say, in the agency. 'No fittings job, I will not do.'

'Anna-*san*,' the boss lady had said, 'you have a contract to work, and this is work you must do.'

'No fittings job,' said Anna. 'I am editorial girl, I am commercial girl, but am not a fittings girl. In London am not fittings girl,' she said, 'in Paris am not fittings girl, in Tokyo – you can guess?'

The next day Anna was off home and I – well. I was fittings girl.

I didn't mean to fixate upon Tokyo Teena but she really did make an impression on me. It was the sheer determination she had to succeed, I think, which seemed at total odds with her childlike, naïve, Lolita-esque persona. She spoke basic Japanese, for example. At sixteen. Just a smattering of conversational words and phrases, but enough to set her apart from the crowd. And she was always perfectly in character – ringleted hair and freckles drawn on. But when she left after castings, her face was more cool, her smile less enigmatic, as though she'd left her act in the casting and I wondered, more than once, whether she wasn't just the cleverest model in the room.

'Teena-*san*,' said Teena's manager, 'please now hold the teddy bear.'

We were casting for a lingerie shoot and the samples line-up included pretty lace bras in unusual colours, which I loved – lime green, neon peach, electric blue – and then sporty vests in ribbed cotton and a few bits of nightwear that really did not seem to fit the ethos of the rest of the range. They were La Perla-style pure lace and silk slips that barely covered your bum cheeks, but that was OK because matching thongs had been provided. Shirley Temple, I mean Tokyo Teena, had already primped and preened her way around the room in all of the bra colours and now she was in one of the silk and lace slips.

'Ready for bed!' said one of the clients. And then they took Polaroid pictures as Tokyo Teena stood in front of them in the sort of outfit you'd wear if you wanted to be guaranteed an absolute corker of a banging, holding a small, fluffy, pale blue teddy bear. The bear had a small bell tied to the ribbon on its neck that very gently tinkled as Tokyo Teena held it close to her torso, just above the belly button, making sure that her upper arms didn't press too hard to her sides (which would squidge them and make them look fatter) and creating a lovely angle at the elbow that made all of her proportions look just right. You could just see the vague outlines of her small, button-like nipples through the lace of the slip and the dainty golden friendship bracelet on her wrist glinted under the studio lights – there a dolly charm, here a teeny heart with a little red ruby inset – and to be quite frank, there was just something a bit off about the entire thing.

'They had better not ask me to hold a fucking teddy bear,' said Danish Dani, 'because if they do then I will tell them. I will tell them no.'

'OK,' I said. I always expected more raw violence from Dani than ever really materialised.

But neither of us got the opportunity to hold the teddy in the end because the row of male clients were all smiling idiotically at Tokyo Teena and making notes on their notepads and nodding their heads stupidly up and down like the Churchill dog and so we all knew that the race was over before it had even begun. I got to try on one bra, which was so small I had to poke my breasts into the cups using the end of a coat hanger, Danish Dani just got a cursory look and a flick through her portfolio and then, gloriously, we were back outside, lighting up our exotic Marlboro Lights with their pure-white filters. Freedom.

We had to wait next to the minivan until our manager and the rest of the models finished the casting – I reckoned that 85 per cent of any one day was spent waiting for other people – but it was sunny and warm and we didn't mind being outside. And as we waited, out came Tokyo Teena, twirling her way towards her private Mercedes saloon.

'Do you think Tokyo Teena can actually walk in a straight line?' I asked Dani.

'Nope,' said Dani.

'I think she does it so that people can see her from all angles at all times,' I said, pleased with my sudden revelation.

'I think she does it so that she's constantly moving,' said Danish Dani, 'because if she stopped she would have to face the truth.'

The following week, I was back on home soil. A few days early, but it had seemed pointless to stay in Tokyo when Old El Paso tortilla wraps were only sixty-five pence in Tesco. And why spend a few days soaking up an entirely different culture to your own, with famous shrines and ancient temples and packed-together eating districts that looked straight out of a movie, when you could change your flight home for a mere twenty quid?

'You did OK, darling,' said Diane, swivelling away from her desk. 'It's a tough place, Tokyo; if you can do that then you're ready for anything.'

Had it been a tough place? Now that I was back in what felt like post-war Britain, where everyone had boring phones that didn't play videos, and the sides of buildings were covered in bricks instead of gigantic moving screens, and department stores were called things like Debenhams and House of Fraser, not DONKI!, and there was no girl in a fairy outfit with blue hair and a microphone screaming things at you that you didn't understand when you walked in through the doors of said department store: now that I was back, I wondered what the hell had even happened. I'd been on photo shoots where there had been absolutely no communication – only someone dressing me, then someone physically moving me into position, then a photographer taking photos of me without ever making eye contact. I'd been on bullet trains to towns I'd not even known the name of. I'd been to a hundred castings or more where I'd stood there lamely whilst people had said things about me that I didn't understand.

'I'm not sure I was really their thing,' I said. 'I didn't get as much work as I thought I would.'

'Listen, darling,' said Diane. 'Each market has different tastes, you'll never win them all. Paris is all about looking a bit undone and sexy and never too polished, which is why they love you. London, it's more edgy and cool. Tokyo—'

'Pre-pubescent and vacant?' I said.

'Bit harsh, darling, but OK. And then you have New York.'

'Do I?'

'Yes, darling, from next week. The agency wants you there as soon as possible.'

New York!

'What kind of look does well in New York?' I asked.

'Anything, darling, that will make them lots of money. Chic, edgy, cool . . . you can go in pretty much any direction you want, but whatever you do, make it polished and groomed.'

Polished and groomed, right. Got it.

Chapter 6

Goodbye, Moonface

I staggered into my New York agency with a sandwich under one arm and a plastic desk fan tucked beneath the other. It was the end of June 2002 and the outside temperature was nearing one hundred degrees. I had just walked thirty blocks in the searing heat to try to save money and the soles of my canvas plimsolls had begun to disintegrate, dropping little shards of rubber onto the floor with every other step.

As part of my groomed and polished maintenance plan, I had slicked my hair back from my face with the sweat from my brow and purchased a new outfit, straight from the window of a mid-level boutique in Soho. On the mannequin the cream-coloured chino shorts and lace-trimmed cami top had looked chic, but on me, the shorts were like something you'd wear to a Girl Guides powwow and the cami was distinctly Ann Summers.

'Ruth! Oh my God,' said my New York agent, 'what the hell is that underneath your arm?'

I assumed she knew what a desk fan was and so the thing underneath my arm, the thing that she was staring at with such an expression of sheer horror, must have been my sandwich. Known locally as a 'hero', due to its gargantuan size, it had been expertly crafted from an entire bloomer and filled with layer upon layer of Italian deli meats and cheeses. The size of a newborn baby and tightly swaddled in layers of wrapping, it might have comfortably fed an average-sized family at a summertime picnic.

'That,' I said, wishing I'd bypassed the agency and gone straight home, 'is my lunch.'

Obviously, I hadn't known that the sandwich would be so huge. I'd only been in New York for a week and was still acclimatising myself to the fact that America, when it came to food, spoke its very own language. Dips, chips, bowls and subs; hoagies, grinders, patties and dogs. Had I stuck to salad bars I would have been totally fine, but what kind of human could walk eight miles a day on a salad?

I had arrived at the front of the line in the deli and panicked. The sandwich menu had filled the entire space on the wall behind the counter: hundreds of fillings, dozens of types of bread, a boxed-off section with options for dressings – it was all one big jumble of numbers and letters. I felt like Alan Turing trying to decipher the Enigma code. I had just picked the first thing that jumped out of the menu. And now it was lunch.

'That's not lunch, babe,' said my New York agent, 'that's a fat man's banquet.'

Just to be clear: she wasn't calling me fat. Had she called

me fat, we might have looked at her askance because, in 2002, I was just shy of five feet eight inches tall and weighed a hundred and fifteen pounds. Eight and a quarter stone.

I had a twenty-four-inch waist – on paper at least – and my hips measured thirty-five. My bra size, because this was before the mainstream existence of small-back-large-cup lingerie, was a 34C. I could have been, with a bit of toning, a touch of tan and the addition of some skyscraper heels, not a million miles away from looking like a Victoria's Secret runway girl. Albeit the shortish one who walked like a constipated T-Rex.

But still, but still . . . I wasn't the typical waif-like character that floated down the catwalks of Milan, where the starved, heroin chic look was still at the height of its popularity. I did not have a xylophone rib cage or a jutting-out pelvis; my bones were not visible just beneath the skin like partially unearthed fossils; I was not other-worldly tall like some of the girls, who looked as though they had little stilts hidden inside their trouser legs. I was just slightly shorter, slightly rounder and had inconveniently fulsome breasts. My body had been scowled at in Paris, prodded in Berlin and one London casting agent had told me to bind my chest. And if we zoomed twenty-odd years into the future to – I don't know, let's pick a year – 2024, then perhaps the general population would be aghast at the idea that my very slender 2002 body was still not quite slender enough for certain sectors of the fashion industry. They would no doubt rant and roil over the unearthed fossil simile and the idea of a jutting-out pelvis would no doubt be abhorrent. But this was two thousand and two, not futuristic twenty-twenty-four. Magazines rarely showed anything but pictures of thin or famous people, and even thin, famous people were ridiculed publicly if they had dimples on their thighs when they ran, or overhanging bellies when they sat on the edge of a superyacht to slide into the water.

And if, in 2002, you felt slightly uncomfortable with this ridicule on a moral or political level then there was no way of finding out whether other people felt uncomfortable too, because Twitter, TikTok and Instagram didn't exist yet. Google wasn't even a thing. You could use a search engine called 'Ask Jeeves' if you liked, the butler of the worldwide web, to ask whether it was OK for magazines to be making fun of women for having perfectly normal bodies, but you'd have been asking an empty room because nobody had really written about it in any great depth. Most people were too busy enjoying themselves in the Roman colosseums that were the cheap magazines and tabloid newspapers, chuckling at celebrity mental health breakdowns and gossiping over pictures of teen stars who had been papped on a coke-bender. This was the noughties. Schoolgirls were sexualised, 'gayer' was still a widely used insult and, if you were a woman and you needed to walk past a building site, then you'd better have headphones on and the unblinking, forward-facing focus of a shire horse.

'I didn't realise it was going to be quite so big,' I said, pointing to the sandwich.

I saw, suddenly embarrassed, that grease had begun

to leak onto the agent's desk. In the space of just a few minutes, the hero seemed to have become symbolic of everything that I thought was wrong with me as a model. The fact I was always hungry, the fact I was not the sort of person who could sit and pick at a salad rather than eat a proper meal, the fact I never had any money and so I tended to choose volume and bulk over nutritional value when it came to feeding myself. I felt almost like a human version of the sandwich – a cumbersome, chaotic, meaty mess – when all I dreamed of being was a finely cut slither of cured salmon, placed carefully atop a smear of creamed horseradish. It was all so depressingly poetic. I wanted to be intense, impactful and sophisticated, maximum flavour in a neat little package. I wanted to be haute cuisine, but there I stood, feeling distinctly delicatessen. Oversized and greasy.

Oh well, I had it now, the sandwich the size of a newborn, and I very much needed to eat it. Because one thing I was not prepared to do for this job was to starve myself. In fact, I wasn't even prepared to put up with feeling hungry, not even a tiny bit – no happiness lay down that particular road. I had inherited my family's genetic quirk when it came to hunger: a quirk that presented itself as a total psychotic breakdown if any of us didn't eat for more than about three hours.

Had I gone into the agency and picked up my modelling cards *after* lunch then I'd have eaten the bloody thing by now. None of this debacle would have happened. The New York agent wouldn't have seen my gargantuan sandwich, wouldn't have made two little comments about its size, and I wouldn't ha—

Wait. Had the New York agent really only made two little comments about my sandwich? About it being a fat man's banquet? How had I made this into an issue with so many related thoughts that they would fill almost half a chapter of a book? Who had the problem here?

I made my way back to the apartment with new cards in hand, cradling the bread baby and holding the desk fan by its neck. The sun was scorching down and the traffic was stood still and there was a constant loud din from the taxi cab horns, like a bad brass orchestra tuning up. If Tokyo had been alien to me then New York was home; it was exactly the world that I'd seen a thousand times over in the movies or on TV – it was *Sesame Street* and *Taxi Driver*, it was *Godfather* and *West Side Story*. When I went to a casting in an old dance studio, with its mirrors and its peeling paint, I was an extra in *Fame*, wanting to live forever. When I hailed a cab on Broadway at night, I was suddenly in *Ghostbusters* and wouldn't have been surprised if Stay Puft the marshmallow monster had appeared from behind a skyscraper. Every man in a suit was Patrick Bateman, every 'How you doin'?' could have been Joey from *Friends*, and every brownstone I passed looked incomplete without Sarah Jessica Parker smoking a fag on the steps.

But because my New York references were mostly gleaned from watching *Friends, Sex and the City* and the cult eighties movie *Big*, I had been slightly disappointed with my living quarters. There was no shoe-filled walk-in wardrobe, I couldn't skateboard through an open plan loft space and friendly Joey and Chandler-ish people didn't live on the other side of the hall. I was not to know that the area I'd been planted in by the agency was one of the most desirable in the city – cool, arty and expensive – and that the apartment's sash windows, metal fire escapes and garbage chutes were quintessentially NYC. All I saw was the fact that the living room had no furniture, the bedroom had a bedsheet for a curtain and that there was a small terrapin living in the kitchen sink. In all fairness, the previous model inhabitant had made an effort to get things cosy – there was a cardboard box that served as a coffee table and some sparse herbs were slowly dying in their pots on the kitchen windowsill – but still, it was like an apartment that someone had started to move into and then changed their mind.

The house phone rang almost as soon as I got through the door and without picking it up, I knew that it would almost definitely be one of three people: my New York agent, Igor-boyfriend-of-Nadia or an old lady with dementia called Mrs Weinstein, who rang twice a day asking for her son, Caleb.

'Caleb?'

'Nope.'

'You again! What have you done with him?'

It would take me ages to get Mrs Weinstein off the phone, every time she called. I felt bad because something had obviously happened to Caleb, but her persistence was draining. If I hung up she would ring again; if I didn't pick up in the first place then she would ring again and again for five, ten minutes at a time until I had to leave the apartment to get away from the noise. Leaving the phone off the hook wasn't an option because this really seemed to annoy Nadia, my on-off-on-again model flatmate.

Nadia was Russian and had a psychotic, controlling boyfriend called Igor who lived in Brooklyn Heights. He liked her to answer the telephone within three rings – if it was engaged then he got suspicious and would come barrelling around to thump on the door. And then it was a whole world of trouble.

Everyone was a bit afraid of Nadia, agents and other models alike. She appeared to have supermodel-dom burned into her very destiny – it wasn't an ambition for her but a non-negotiable certainty – and I pitied those who stood in her way.

'What happen to Alberta Ferretti campaign?' she had said in the agency a few days ago.

'The option came off, honey,' the agent said, 'they went with someone else.'

'Why you no negotiate?' said Nadia.

'Huh?'

'Why you no do your job and negotiate successful campaign?'

The agent glanced across the desk at the only other agent who hadn't mysteriously vanished from the office and the other agent shrugged.

'Honey, it wasn't the money,' said unlucky agent number one, 'they went with a blonde girl.'

Nadia had huffed. 'I dye my hair,' she said. 'Always remember, I dye my hair for any job. Blonde. Back to brown-ette. Maybe I even dye it gingery-red if money is good, but only if money is very good.'

Nadia was also not above using foul play to win at her game. Because she worked in an entirely different league to me, one in which girls were tall enough to actually book a fashion show and could actually walk in the improbably tall heels they wore to do said fashion show, this foul play didn't really strike me as a clear and present danger. I was no competition. But it was still unnerving.

'This is how I win casting this afternoon,' she had explained to me. 'I win against the Austria girl with face like moon. You know her.'

'Do you . . . win at a casting?' I had asked. Surely they would cast quite a few people for a show, not just one? Why was Nadia so cutthroat about it all? I had no idea who the girl with face like moon was, but Nadia remembered every single bit of competition with near-photographic precision.

'I win at casting with new method I call glue shoe,' Nadia had continued. 'Put glue on enemy shoe. Girl walk, glue on shoe makes tack-tack-tack on floor.' She mimed sticky shoes with her hands on the table. 'Shoe makes tack-tack, out pops foot, runway casting finished.'

She slapped her hands on the table. 'Goodbye moon face.'

The landline phone continued to ring. I just wanted to eat my sandwich but the curse of the landline was that you couldn't turn it off. And if you left it ringing for too long, then the sound of it, clanging out and shattering the silence, became ominous. The longer it rang, the more the phone transformed into a present, sentient being. The pauses in between rings were the landline's listening breaks – *I know you are there* – and its buttons, if you dared stand before it, were eyes.

I picked it up.

'Caleb?' said Mrs Weinstein.

'He's not here, Mrs Weinstein,' I said.

'Well, when will he be back?' said Mrs Weinstein. There was a cat purring next to the receiver; she must have had it curled around her neck, like a scarf. In this heat!

'I think . . . try next week,' I said, in a sudden flash of inspiration. What a genius, buying myself time. 'The end of next week,' I said, 'Friday.'

'Friday?' said Mrs Weinstein. 'He'll miss his last day!'

'Last day?'

'Of junior high,' said Mrs Weinstein. 'The last day at school.'

Finally, slowly, I unwrapped the sandwich and placed a third of it onto my plate. It was magazine-worthy, stupendous. How did anyone in this city, I wondered, think about anything but food? Takeouts in cardboard cartons with little wire handles, bagels with salmon and heaps of cream cheese, pizzas and burgers and street stands with hot dogs, shops that sold salads you made up yourself.

I took a bite, hanging my face over the plate so that it would catch the falling debris. So groomed, so polished, with the shredded lettuce falling from my mouth and a trickle of dressing traversing my chin. It was heaven. Never mind your sashimi and those weird hairy bean pods you chewed with your teeth, or your nutritious Brazil nut midmorning snack (two nuts, it's as much energy as a whole apple!). Never mind your Whole Foods and your juice bar and your specialist herbs that you boiled in a brew. None of these things, all of which I had at some point heard being raved about by agents and models since arriving in the city, *none* of these things came anywhere near the sheer enjoyment of biting into a mixed meats Italian deli hero.

I'd popped into Whole Foods, actually, to see what it was all about, and noticed that they charged three dollars for a bottle of water and seven for a salad that didn't even contain lettuce. You couldn't buy Coco Pops, some of the butter was made from nuts – nuts! – and they sold sausages without any meat. It was, in my opinion, a grocery store run by maniacs.

'What in hell is that?' said Nadia, who had apparently teleported herself into the apartment without me noticing. 'Is that sandwich?'

'A third of one,' I said, food falling from my mouth. 'Do you want a bit? There's loads left.'

Nadia looked disgusted. 'I have salad,' she said, 'from Dean & DeLuca. Your sandwich is why Americans fat.'

Dean & DeLuca. A fancy deli in the heart of Soho. Now *that* was an eatery I could get behind. It looked so stylish, so clean, so reassuringly expensive . . . which was also the reason I hadn't yet worked up the courage to go in. I was worried I might get asked to leave or followed about by a shop assistant. My main obstacle to visiting, though, was that the food was priced by weight, which was one of my biggest shopping fears. I knew that deli counters had to do this, it was the only method that made any financial and practical sense, but I disliked the uncertainty of it all. Probably because I was never sure whether my Switch card would go through anyway, and so not knowing precisely how much my Davidstow extra mature was going to cost, to the penny, triggered a sense of intense anxiety. And if I couldn't cope with cheddar, which was a relatively easy foodstuff to weigh up by eye, then how would I fare if I was let loose in Dean & DeLuca? Would I be flummoxed by the size of the peppers, ordering too many and looking the fool? Were sliced eggs a salad and what would they cost? Did an ounce of spinach leaves weigh the same as an ounce of heavy pasta twirls?

I decided, as I watched Nadia stab at her tuna niçoise, that I would make a new start, eat better things and go to DeLuca the very next day.

The store was cool inside, just as I'd imagined. The styling was minimalist, with black and white bags and metal-framed shelving. Everything smelled clean and – perhaps weirdly for a food shop – also like nothing at all. Possibly due to the air conditioning being set to the same temperature you'd use for cryogenic freezing, which meant that the inside of my nose and mouth had become instantly desensitised to all tastes and smells.

On the tables, there were stacked tins of olives; on the shelves there were packets of grains and pastas and there were smart glass jars filled with pickled vegetables and gelato sauces and posh non-Heinz ketchup. No lurid labelling, no plastic lids, it was like the pantry you'd expect a serial killer to keep if he (or she!) also enjoyed good food and a fine wine. There was undoubtably a Hannibal Lecter sort of feel to the whole place.

And under the counters were trays and trays of the freshest-looking, delectable dishes. Whipped feta dips with pistachios sprinkled on top, roasted and sundried tomatoes with torn basil leaves and teeny balls of mozzarella. Things with rucola, baba ghanoush, chicken and sliced beef and all of the meats. Wedges of butternut squash, chargrilled broccoli, zucchini with a yoghurt-mint sauce – it all looked mouth-wateringly delicious.

'Could I have some of the tomato salad, please?' I asked the aproned man behind the first counter.

'Tom-ar-to,' he repeated, in my accent, 'cute. How much *to-mar-to* salad can I get you?'

'Just a spoonful,' I said. 'Oh, OK, that's a big spoonful, not quite that much!'

'I can't put it back, lady,' said the man. 'Once it's done, it's done.'

Oh my God, this was going to be worse than I thought! And now I was under pressure to choose what I wanted as well as the quantity and I couldn't even work out the prices because it was in ounces and my brain worked in grams. I looked beside me – there were three people waiting their turn. The store had been empty when I'd stepped in. I'd purposefully chosen an empty time, 3.30pm, forgoing my usual lunch break timing so that I could choose my salads in peace – and now there was virtually a crowd.

'And some salmon?' I said, moving along to the fish and seafood. 'The grilled salmon with capers and lemon? How much is that?'

The man pointed to the price card that was hooked to the front of the tray. He must have seen my look of utter confusion because he said, 'It works out to be about nine dollars apiece.'

'Wow,' I said, 'nine dollars apiece, for salmon. Cheap at half the price,' I said, laughing off my embarrassment. 'I'll take three,' I joked.

Which was how I ended up with three large pieces of salmon for my lunch that day, along with a side of tomatoes that would have easily filled a cereal bowl up to the top and one stem of chargrilled broccoli with roasted almond. Singular. Total cost of lunch: thirty-eight dollars plus tax.

'Wow, you really like salmon, huh?' said my New York agent as I sat down to eat it.

'No,' I began to explain, 'it was a joke and—'

'You know it's quite high in fat, right?' she said. 'And wow, just so much of it. It's basically a—'

'I know, I know,' I said, interrupting her. 'A fat man's banquet.'

Flatmate of Nadia: a selection of best looks.

© Taken by modelling agency's assistant

Chapter 7

Take Soda and Leave

'So,' said my New York agent, the following week. 'I think that the next step is to find you a look. Something that'll get you noticed and remembered. So that people will say, like, Oh my God, have you seen that cute English girl who wears the lacey little dresses?'

'Lacey little dresses?' I said. 'I thought that the look for New York was polished and groomed?'

'Yeah,' said the New York agent, 'in an ideal world, but what I mean is that we need to get you more of a personal style that people will associate with you. You know, an image.'

Castings had been going well enough in NYC and I'd had some interest – but not, apparently, enough interest to get an actual booking.

'An image?' I said.

'Yeah,' said my New York agent. 'So, like this is a

terrible example, but you know how yesterday you looked like a nineties sex worker who'd had her shoes stolen?'

'Yesterday?' I thought back. 'Yesterday I wore my little pink tube dress and a pair of Nike Airs?'

'Exactly,' said my New York Agent. 'I'd probably go right ahead and say that your image yesterday, if I had to name it, was a bit street, a bit cheap. A bit *Pretty Woman,* if the Pretty Woman in question wanted to be clientless.'

I'd quite liked my mini-dress and trainers look. The dress was sexy and left absolutely nothing to the imagination but the trainers had balanced it all out. Yin and yang. Of course, I hadn't actually roamed the streets in the mini-dress, I wasn't mad; I'd covered the whole thing up with a long checked shirt and removed it as soon as I'd reached the castings. To the unassuming passer-by, I was merely a chick in a lumberjack, smoking a fag.

But if the minidress look was out, then what was my image? That was the only real 'look' I'd managed to pull out of the bag in the entire time I'd been here. There was nothing styled about me and I was most definitely not polished. Everything about me seemed to be slightly chaotic and unfortunate – even my arrival to the city had been inelegant. I'd nearly had a heart attack in the taxi because I thought I was being kidnapped by the Mafia, just because the driver looked like Joe Pesci and carried a shovel in his trunk. The following day there'd been the building-scaling incident, which I will come to, and then, in a final, mortifying, 'welcome to NYC' episode, I had returned my blueberry muffin at a coffee shop because when I'd broken it open I'd thought that the blue stains all through the inside were blooms of mould.

'So, like, Nadia has an image, right?' said my New York agent. As well as speaking to me she was busy doing one of her favourite activities: rearranging my portfolio. She had an absolute fixation with my book and liked to shuffle the order of the pictures around before every important casting, curating and refining it to suit whichever brand or client I was about to see. A casting for *Cosmopolitan*? Happy, beach-babe photos were moved to the front. A go-see at *V* mag? Anything smiley taken right out.

'Nadia has a really strong image,' said my New York Agent, her voice trembling momentarily as she flicked between pages, 'which is driven and . . . and firm. You can see it in everything she does and wears. Spike heels, sharp hair, no-nonsense stare – she's, like, some kind of tough, ball-breaking businesswoman from the eighties.'

'Isn't that just her personality?' I said.

'Exactly,' said my New York agent. She slid the final two pictures into their clear plastic pockets and slammed the book shut. 'That's what we need to find you, babe. A personality.'

They rarely offended me, these throwaway comments. Not at the time, anyway. I knew she didn't mean my *actual* personality, the inner one that nobody could touch or critique and that was the foundation of all self-confidence – she was talking about the outer one. She should probably have said *persona*, really.

Lots of the good models had a persona, I had noticed. There were the boho girls with their fringed Balenciaga bags and with stacks of braided bracelets climbing their tanned arms; there were the Parisian-style babes peering out from beneath their ultra-long fringes in drainpipe jeans and nude ballet flats. Some wore Breton tops for a 'girl next door' look and some were overtly sexy, hair curling in tendrils down to shoulder-less dresses.

What was my type? I had no idea. I couldn't be like the pantherish, catsuit-wearing *femme fatale* model I'd seen slinking around who growled, softly, at any girl she fancied for tea. Neither did I want to be like the girl I'd nicknamed The Ice Maiden, a six-foot-tall Swede with the palest hair, who dressed only in white pleated Issey Miyake and never smiled. She always looked as though she'd just arrived from Narnia, miserable as sin after her journey through the wardrobe. I couldn't see that particular look working for me.

So: no femme fatale and no grumpy ice maiden, and I absolutely did not want a look that was grotty or grungey. I'd always just wanted to look nice. A bit sexy, a bit sunkissed, sculpted, toned, chiselled. Gisele, but with my own face and a body that didn't require quite so much maintenance. Preferably any maintenance. I liked the simple, healthy charm of the GAP jeans campaigns and the beachy-fresh looks shot by Steven Meisel. Denim and gingham, a bit of a curve. Hair long and tousled, if it would ever grow out from its hacked-off bob. This, I decided, would be my thing. My theme. My persona.

*

'What I see you as,' said the New York agent, 'is a proper, down and dirty rock chick.'

Oh for crying out loud, I thought. *Why does nobody ever want me to look like Gisele?*

'But, like, a really cool British rock chick,' she said. 'Create the total image. All your clothes, like, vintaged. Ripped band tees, old Converse All-Stars and denim that looks like it's come from a dumpster.'

'Marvellous,' I said, 'I'll get onto that, then.'

Needless to say, it didn't go well. I just wasn't good at styling myself: picking out clothes and putting them together was a skill that I'd neglected to learn. I could write a passable essay on *Jane Eyre*, stalactite formations or section 60 of the Criminal Justice Act 1994 but when it came to getting dressed, I tended to lack any sort of flair.

Other people seemed to be able to choose just the right things from the dressing up pile – a vintage kaftan and a brown woven belt, for instance – and make them look fancy, polished and groomed. Faced with the same pile who knew what I'd choose? A corset and a top hat? A Lycra skirt and Ugg boots?

The problem was, and I can say this with hindsight, that I was constantly trying to emulate the high fashion adverts I'd seen as a teenager. The pictures I'd had pinned to my walls. Blonde girls in Versace with their long, tanned legs and sky-high hems, brooding brunettes in Dolce & Gabbana with corseted dresses and glamorous sunglasses. And my favourite, the Polo Sport advert with Bridget Hall, her body in the white USA-emblazoned swimsuit looking like my exact idea of total perfection. No matter that these pictures were styled and tweaked and lit to a standard that could never be reproduced in a real-world setting; no matter that they were, to all intents and purposes, a fantasy – my teenage self had decided on the high fashion look as a feasible one to aspire to and that was the goal that had stuck. Which was great when I was on a shoot and a stylist was tweaking the haute couture looks, but when I was left to my own devices . . .

God, it was dismal, the rock chick look I came up with. But I couldn't be faulted for effort: masses of black eyeliner, too hard and unforgiving for my face, a ripped band t-shirt from Canal Jeans, a denim skirt and some Converse, all as suggested. Yes, in a way, it was mildly convincing and – a plus point in this situation – I did a good line in being able to clamp a cigarette between my teeth in a practised, capable kind of way, which just added to the whole *persona*. But I only needed to open my mouth for the whole smokescreen to disappear in the wind: I was no more rock and roll than your average student doing air guitar to Bon Jovi at a bowling alley.

'Oh my God,' said the New York agent, when I went in to reveal my new persona. 'Why can I smell blue cheese?'

'It's the smell of the thrift store,' I replied. I pointed at the jacket. 'Vintage item, as instructed.'

'Babe,' said the New York agent, 'you're not supposed to actually buy people's old clothing, ew!'

'That tends to be what vintage means, though,' I said.

'I said vin*taged*,' said the New York agent, 'not vin*tage*.

There's a difference. Vintaged is new, it's just made to look old. Basically, it looks cool but you won't catch someone's diseases.'

I managed to get one job in the whole time I was in New York. The shoot was outside of the city, at a music festival, where I had to pretend to be – wait for it – a rock chick. Except that the photographer obviously thought I actually *was* a rock chick and that no pretending would be necessary as she followed me around and captured my cool and crazy antics on Super 8 film. How disappointed she was.

Other than that one shoot, I generally spent my time in the City That Never Sleeps sleeping, doing castings and having quite a wild old time with the group of friends I'd managed to infiltrate. They were an unlikely bunch of people, in a way, glued together by their very active and stylish social life, filled with dinners at the sharpest new restaurants and drinks in the most exclusive clubs, but they had varying and sometimes diametrically opposite personalities. The loud, gregarious man-mountain with ambition and drive, for example, and the quiet, softly spoken thinker who couldn't stand being alone. The networking club owner who was never seen in daylight, the guy who hated flashy dinners but loved to play chess. But there was a common thread between them all, I suppose, which was that most of them were very successful, or on their way to being very successful – and if they weren't basking in the glow of self-made success, then they had instead , by way of a sort of booby prize, direct access to inconceivable amounts of inherited wealth.

Now, the cynics amongst you might be thinking that this was the reason I liked them so much. Not so. Yes, one of them was heir to the biggest car manufacturer in the United States and yes, one was the son of a famous artist, but their money was present in a quiet, understated sort of way. A full-time driver rather than a yellow Lamborghini. A penthouse overlooking Central Park rather than a mega-mansion in Dubai. It wasn't until I'd attempted to 'pay for my part of the bill' at a dinner for the third or fourth time that someone had quietly mentioned that my financial input wouldn't be necessary. Ever. Which was a good job because just the entrées at some of these restaurants cost more than my weekly grocery run.

If anything, the vast difference in wealth was probably my main sticking point when it came to being out and about with this cool, glitzy crowd of New York people. I never felt entirely comfortable being in restaurants where I wouldn't have even been able to cover the cost of the bread basket, very aware that all I was offering in return was my scintillating conversation and sparkling wit.

Oh yeah, the other cynics, I know what you're thinking too: *They definitely wanted something back for their investment and it wasn't your scintillating conversation!* But you'd be wrong because, apparently, to them at least, I was as sexually alluring as a piece of plasticine. Disappointingly sexless. Over those first weeks that I spent with them all – those humid, airless, NYC weeks – not one person made any sort of romantic or sexual advance towards me. Even the one guy I'd probably have welcomed it from. There I was, tipped as one of the *new models to watch*, dressed like a nineties streetwalker/dirty, cheese-smelling rock groupie (depending on the day) and nobody so much as laid a wandering hand upon my knee. No stereotypical 'sweaty rich billionaire taking advantage of a young and impressionable model' in *this* scenario.

Perhaps I just wasn't cool enough. Or sexy enough. And I was British, which obviously meant that I drank an uncouth amount of alcohol and said all my words wrong. I felt kind of clumsy – *lumbering* – in this expensive new life. Things frequently seemed to go wrong and the more I tried to be svelte and chic and polished and groomed, the more I failed. Take the time I wore a dress made from foil when it was 104 degrees Fahrenheit and almost cooked my own organs, for example, or fell off a bar stool in front of Chandler from *Friends*. Or the night that was to become indelibly printed upon my mind for many years to come – is, in fact, still printed upon my mind more than twenty years later. The night that I accidentally became an unwitting performer in an informal sex show.

It was a hot New York weekend, my second one there, and I was staying at a house in Long Island with a large group of people I didn't yet know very well. But that was OK because I was going to be sharing a bedroom with my agent. Not that one – another one. A man. Was there anything weird about this? I wasn't sure. I hadn't had the chance to consider it, seeing as though he'd only told me about it as we arrived at the house, which was vast and timber-clad and had a basketball hoop next to the front door.

'You two are in here,' said the agent, opening the door to a ground floor bedroom with just one bed, 'with me.'

(Oh yeah, I forgot to add: there was another model, too, so it was three in a bed. Did she think it was weird? I couldn't ask her, she spoke no English.)

I wondered, briefly, how this bedshare would look. Would the agent be in the middle, an arm around each of us as he puffed away on a cigar and made wannabe fashion models dance for him in the doorway? Or would he have the lion's share of the mattress and make us sleep at his feet like Roman slaves? He didn't elaborate and we all just threw our bags on the floor and went to lunch.

Was I worried? The other model didn't look overly concerned and I reasoned that an agent wouldn't very well risk his entire job doing dodgy things with his models on a summer weekend break. A man would never get away with that, surely. And agents were the trustworthy ones, weren't they? They were a bit like a parent, but not related to you and only there to make money.

In any case, I knew that I annoyed the hell out of this guy – it would have amazed me had he found me even remotely attractive. We were fundamentally very different. He took everything quite seriously and I didn't, for a start. I found it difficult to take anything seriously, really, especially myself, and I point-blank refused to do the sexy-sexy act that so many models were brilliant at in New York, looking as though they were auditioning for a Nelly video when all they were doing was walking out of a lift.

No, I spent my time commenting on the many differences between England and America, rather than trying to be sexy, and asking native New Yorkers (mainly the agent) to speak like Joey from *Friends*.

'Say it again!' I'd say to the agent and he'd roll his eyes, sigh and say: 'How y'doin.'

'How YOU doin!' I'd repeat, in my best accent.

'No,' he'd say, 'it's how *yu* doon. How *yu* doin.'

'How yu doon!'

And just like that, I could easily spend a good ten minutes honing my Joey impression, whilst he looked around the party, dinner table, whatever, looking for somebody – anybody – else to speak to. Were we friends? Probably not. Did I know him well enough to share a bed for the weekend? Probably not. Was I under the naïve assumption that an agent would never take advantage of one of his models? Absolutely.

And he didn't. Let's just get that out of the way right from the start. All we did, the three of us, was share a bed and sleep.

Although, it was actually too squashed for me in the bed and I couldn't stand the idea of any of our feet accidentally touching and so I bailed on the first night and went to lie on a sofa in the games room. I ranted to myself, briefly, as I tried to get to sleep. No bed, no curtain and no proper blanket, this was turning out to be a right farce. Who slept three to a bed once they reached adulthood anyway? Who did he think we all were, the grandparents in *Charlie and the Chocolate Factory*? There were just so many things I didn't know about this new, different grown-up life. *Was* it normal for people to just bunk up, randomly? Maybe it was something that the rich and famous did, maybe it was – to coin a phrase – *how the other half lived*.

Because everyone there was either rich, famous or on their way to being one or both of those things, there was a feeling of barely restrained excitement crackling in the air, the optimism of the still-young, the easy-won sense of limitless possibility that only the well-connected or those with inherited wealth ever truly get to experience. Two things struck me as strange, though, about how people like this existed. The first was that they could never seem to sit still and the second was that nothing ever seemed to impress or surprise them very much. They would bounce around, from place to place, taking their shoes off to test the soft sands here and dipping in to make a dinner reservation there, but would they sit on the beach to take in the view? Would they luxuriate over dinner and appreciate a fine wine? No, they would not. Nor would they express any particular opinion about the beauty of the harbour or the sleekness of the boat or the tastiness of the lobster – it was all a given. *That don't impress me much.* Reactions to almost everything were cool as a cucumber.

Which is probably why I didn't pick up on the fact that I'd walked into a sex scene, back at the house, until at least five long, excruciating seconds after I'd steamed on in. By which point, it was too late to retreat.

In my defence, none of the people hovering by the kitchen door had anything other than vaguely interested expressions on their faces. There was no surprise, no arousal, there was no way you'd ever have guessed that anything unusual was going on. And so I side-stepped them, desperate to get a can of Diet Coke from the fridge on the other side of the room, and for all their general lack of animation they could have been listening to a friend regale an anecdote about a parking ticket or watching a dog roll over for a treat.

But they weren't.

What they were watching, I realised, as I got to the middle of the very large kitchen, was one very well-known model lying back on the counter with nothing on her bottom half (unhygienic, for a start, right next to the chopping boards): legs akimbo, face beautifully distorted in a look of anguish, or pain, or – oh, OK, ecstasy – and there was another model standing between her legs, unidentifiable due to the fact that her head was buried in the well-known model's most private of parts.

I just didn't know how to proceed. Once I realised what was in progress I was like a rabbit in the headlights, not knowing whether to run or just try to stay as still as possible and hope that nobody noticed me. I had paused in a comedy burglar position, mid-step and on exaggerated tip toes, and the seconds seemed so unbearably long as the receiving model moaned unashamedly and the giving model growled and nuzzled.

In the end, I decided to be bold and complete my mission. I unfroze myself and forced my legs to stride to the refrigerator. It was one of those gigantic American appliances, approximately three times the size of an English fridge, and it was filled almost exclusively with what everyone else called 'sodas'. And bottles of mineral water. Anything that was convenient and disposable. Because almost everything was disposable; they didn't even eat from proper plates or drink from proper cups. Clearing up if ever a takeout was consumed (which was rare) was simply a matter of sweeping the entire meal into a bin, cutlery and all.

Anyway, because of the size of this fridge, it took the strength of about three hundred men to open the doors. The suction around the seal was so strong that you could have sent the fridge into space and back and the contents would have survived perfectly. Crisp lettuce, fresh milk and a thousand cans of assorted sodas, all still neatly stacked on their sides in pyramids. I didn't have the strength of about three hundred men and so I had to put all of my God-given energy into opening that fridge door. As the models wailed and the growing group of spectators stood there, with their strangely disinterested look, I wedged my feet against the bottom of the gargantuan appliance and heaved with all my might.

The door flew open, the pyramids of side-stacked sodas shuddered and a single can of blessed, ice-cold Diet Coke rolled – as though on cue – straight into my waiting hand. I could have cheered. It was one of those moments, like randomly throwing a screwed-up paper ball backwards at a bin and getting it straight in, that you just wanted everyone to see. But then another Diet Coke fell out, and another, and then all of them, all twenty or thirty cans rolled from the collapsing pyramid and dropped onto the floor, scattering wildly around the kitchen. One can split, the brown juices firing upwards towards the ceiling as though spurting from an out-of-control hydrant. The can spun around and around, clashing against the other rolling cans. I danced to and fro, trying at once to stem the flow of falling drinks from the fridge and prevent the already fallen from travelling too far, but my efforts were in vain. The metal cannisters and plastic bottles shot this way and that, bouncing off the kitchen units and clanging against the fridge. A particularly bold bottle of iced tea spun towards the kitchen island and hit the standing model on the back of her foot. The girl brought her head up from between the supermodel's legs, like a lioness taking a breather from devouring a zebra carcass. She turned to look at me. It was Nadia.

'Unless joining,' said Nadia, wiping her face with the back of her hand, 'take soda and leave.'

Oh, the mortification. It was only ten past one in the morning but it drove me to an early bed. The agent was already in there, alone, sleeping soundly.

'How y'doin?' I said, poking him in the chest. 'How *you* doin!'

'Oh my God,' he said, rolling over, 'go the hell to sleep.'

Chapter 8

Tell Me You'd Love to Be Me

'Hey babe,' said Texana. Texana was my new agent. I had been promoted while I was away, I'd served my time: no longer a New Face, I was now a bona fide model. A Main Board Girl.

'I need to fly you out of New York tomorrow,' said Texana.

Thank God, I thought. New York was unbearably hot and, in all, I had been away from home for over two months. I was starting to feel quite lonely, despite my lively group of friends and the colourful carousel of dinners and parties and impromptu sex performances.

'You're off to Paris,' said Texana, 'and we're putting you up at Madame Magot's.'

Oh. I wasn't sure what upset me more, the acute disappointment that I wasn't actually going home after all or the fact that Texana was making me stay at Madame Magot's. I'd never stayed there but I'd heard things; the very name of the place struck fear into my heart. Some said that this infamous boarding house for models was at the entrance to a graveyard; others uttered dark words about the food that was served. My own additional issues with the idea of staying at Madame Magot's were that a) any accommodation identified by the name of its madame was surely a place of ill-repute and b) maggots.

But I had no say in the matter; *Elle France*, the magazine I'd be flying in for, wouldn't pay for a hotel. My own coffers were bare, having paid off my debts and then failed to actually work for a month. I wasn't in a position to be choosy. And so to Madame Magot's I would reluctantly go, the mere idea of the place sending my imagination, which was prone to being over-active, into warp-speed overdrive.

But anyway, there was no way out of it: I was going to Madame Magot's boarding house, which meant, in my mind, that I was going to stay in a place that was no doubt a front for a brothel, the grubby workings overseen by a giant, writhing mother-maggot. In my mind, Madame Magot would be in her little Parisian *salon* like a smaller version of Jabba the Hut, her pale, pulsating flesh writhing about upon her antique horsehair sofa. Would she be feasting on some sort of decomposed foodstuff, served upon a silver platter? Would she be sucking up a putrid liquid through a straw as her blowfly prostitutes buzzed frenetically around her?

The whole situation made me itch. I knew a few models who had once lain their weary heads down at these particular lodgings but – mysteriously – they had disappeared from the modelling scene. Perhaps they had been ingested by Madame Maggot and her troupe of promiscuous flies.

The most frustrating aspect of the entire debacle was that my call time the following day wasn't until a very reasonable 11am; the first Eurostar out from Waterloo in the morning would have seen me safely in Paris with whole hours to spare. But instead I was to be shunted out of London the night before and placed in the care of a (potential) carrion-eating bawd.

And I did arrive at night, too. Not in the evening, as would have been civilised, but at around ten-thirty, when the only restaurant still serving dinner was a McDonald's and the Place du Clichy was alive with people up to no good. Still, it set the tone. I bought some cigarettes from a *tabac* owner with one eye and then stopped in the doorway of the shop to surreptitiously read my Paris equivalent of the A–Z, the *Paris Poche*. It was never advisable to let anyone see you with a map at any time of day, but at night, near Place du Clichy, making it obvious that you didn't quite know where you were going was an invitation to get press-ganged into the sex trade. And so, being able to read your map in secret, whilst pretending to do something else completely different, was a vital skill for an international fashion model.

I, *par example*, did a very good line in sticking my head into my bag to look at my street map, which would already be open to the correct arrondissement, whilst all the time pretending to rummage for a lighter. I'd take a long hard look at the pages whilst jangling my keys and noisily stirring around in the bag, memorising each and every street name and Metro station for the next part of my route as though I was playing an intense, high-stakes version of Kim's game: having a quick peek of the goods, covering them up and trying to remember as many *rues* and *boulevards* and *avenues* as I possibly could, just to get me to the next place of safety. *Place du safety.*

There was no other option though. How else would you have found your way around, in 2002? Telepathy?

As it turned out, Madame Magot's wasn't a brothel at all. Though, to be quite honest, that would have been preferable because at least there would have been some sort of life in the place. As it stood (creaky, dark, a concreted-over front garden filled with dying plants), I appeared to be the only resident.

Madame Magot, who was wearing a skin-tight t-shirt and leggings, both in a disconcertingly maggoty shade of peach, had taken a full three minutes to come to the door and hadn't seemed to be expecting me. Still, she had gruffly let me in and then led me down a dimly lit corridor to my room, passing as we went lots of other rooms off to the right and left, each containing just a simple single bed and small bedside cupboard. And each of them empty. Where were all of the models?

At the end of the corridor, she threw open a door and flicked a switch.

'*Et voilà!*' she said, as the strip lights on the asbestos-tiled ceiling flickered to life. The room expanded before me like something from a nightmare: beds, beds and more beds –

eight of them altogether – all of them neatly made up but very obviously unoccupied. It was like a scene from a horror movie, possibly about orphanages, and the hairs on the back of my neck instantly prickled. Giant maggots I had mentally prepared for, and I had even practised the French for 'I'm not for sale!', but there was no way I was going to sleep in a room with that many empty beds. It would be asking for trouble, especially from the spirit world. Which I didn't really believe in, by the way, but I was always wary of giving too much easy encouragement – you had to be careful not to set the scene with these things. There were situations that almost demanded paranormal activity: for example, walking through a graveyard, alone, at night. Why would you ever do that unless you want a hand to suddenly appear from the side of a tomb? Going into a dark basement for no reason when there was a storm outside. Again: complete no-no. Sleeping in a room with seven empty beds in a creaky house in a backstreet of Paris? You'd have to be insane!

'Uh,' I said, gesticulating wildly at the cavernous room with its primrose yellow walls that looked so sickly in the striplight, '*Il y a une autre chambre, Madame?*'

'*Non,*' said Madame Magot, '*c'est le seul.*'

And that was that. Me, the beds, my frantic mind – suddenly all alone together.

There was also the room's *piéce de résistance*: a huge, self-contained shower cubicle made from brown and cream plastic that stood to one side like a portal into another world. Or just a portal to the 1970s. It was singularly one of the most disturbing things I had seen in my life, perhaps because of my moderate claustrophobia but also because it could have been a centrepiece to pretty much any frightening movie I had ever seen. The door was made from smoked brown plastic, so that if someone had been crazy enough to ever take a shower in it then they would have been just about visible from the outside. Now, I appreciated that nobody in their right mind would want to shower inside a completely sealed, windowless plastic box, but equally, why would anyone want to wash in full view of seven other people? What a decision to have to make: shower in the dark within France's scariest bedroom (*Tourisme de France* awards 2001) or put on a sort of disturbing body-washing peepshow performance for numerous spectators who may or may not be ghosts.

It was late but I couldn't sleep until I had inspected the unit. I was at once repulsed and fascinated. What secrets did this shower stall hold? The inside of it was so spattered with various stains that it looked as though someone had been cooking their dinners on the tray. On the back wall, a long brown hair; on the shower attachment, a smear of soap. The curious thing was that there were still a few water droplets here and there, suggesting that the horror shower had been used fairly recently – who the hell had been in the shower?

By this point, it was almost midnight. I smoked a cigarette at the window looking over the front garden with its grave-like stone planters. In my heightened state of paranoia I couldn't bring myself to actually lean out of the window, lest one or more ghouls crept up behind me and pushed me out – or worse! – and so I stood side-on, the eight beds kept permanently in my peripheral vision. This meant that

I almost set fire to the nylon net curtain, but the numerous scorch marks told me I hadn't been the first to assume that particular smoking position. I envisioned all of the models before me, sidling up to the window and gingerly lifting the sash. What had become of them? How I longed for one of them – just one would be fine – to be here.

This was my eternal conundrum as a travelling model. To share or not to share. On the one hand, sharing my personal space with a virtual stranger wasn't the most enticing of ideas, but on the other, I had never been good at sleeping alone in an empty house – every creak was the psychopath edging nearer, every glint in a tree outside was the man who'd been watching me through binoculars for the past week, tracing my every step from room to room.

Unsurprisingly, it was a fitful sleep that I had in the *chambre of forgotten souls*, with all the striplights kept on and a long sock tied around my eyes as a makeshift sleep mask. I descended the stairs in the morning, very obviously unwashed and in a state of mild shock.

'You didn't want to use the brown shower, no?' said Madame Magot. She appeared to be drinking wine, which seemed unusual for such an early hour, but perhaps, I thought, one person's getting up was another's winding down time. Maybe it had been a busy night for the blowflies.

'Many girls hate the *douche brun*,' she said.

Now, look. I don't want to be sued so I'll make it really clear that Madame Magot was absolutely not a brothel owner. Had I been of normal mind and not cursed with the imaginative faculty of a horror film director then I'm sure that my stay in the room of eight beds would have been an entirely different experience. I would have slept soundly and without a sock tied around my head.

But it just so happened that I had been cursed with an imagination that was both overactive and morbid, which posed a real problem for me seeing as though half of my job description could have been summarised as "attractive lone female traveller". And my incessant fantasy-factory of a brain had once more been on a self-sabotaging rampage, scaring me half out of my wits and leaving me bone-tired, ever so slightly jumpy and with a head of unwashed hair.

My travels so far had been pockmarked with harrowing incidents that had only occurred within the confines of my own mind. There was that suspected Mafia incident that marked my arrival to New York, when I was certain that the taxi driver was going to use the shovel in his boot to bury me alive. Or the time in Norway when I'd taken a ghost bus to the airport. There was the driver in Holland who'd stopped for a sleep, the taxi in Turkey with banging in the boot, and a whole load of other plane, train and automobile rides that had given me enough material to write a series of thriller novels. And yes, *fine*, the coach trip in Norway had been alright in the end, it was only empty of passengers and creepy as all hell because most of the flights at the airport had been cancelled. And yes, OK, the banging in the boot of the Turkish minivan had actually been a small goat, not the first kidnapped person in what was obviously going to be a busy night of kidnaps, but try explaining any of that to a highly-strung brain that loves to predict the worst.

People would ask me whether I loved the travelling part of my job.

'Oh, it must be absolutely brilliant,' someone, probably called Brian, would say. 'Your mum said you've just been in Italy! What an adventure!'

'Goodness, to go to Paris,' Jean would chime in. 'I'd love to be you, so young and free and just travelling around. Croissants, little bookshops, the Eiffel tower.'

Oh yes, Jean, that's all I do when I'm in Paris, eat croissants that'll make me fat, visit bookshops in all my spare time and stand in front of the bloody *tour Eiffel* waiting to be mugged. Not on your nelly – I'm too busy avoiding sex traffickers and dodging ghosts in graveyards, all thanks to my wildly out-of-control imagination. My life is like a high-adrenaline video game, Jean. Every blind corner hides an axe murderer, every lodging could be the place of my demise. Try living with that inside your cranium and then tell me you'd love to be me.

Chapter 9

Kill You Stone Dead

I mostly blamed my dad for this highly morbid and pessimistic way of viewing everyday life. Thanks to my dad, I had developed what seemed to be a near-pathological preoccupation with health and safety. Throughout my childhood and continuing well into my adult years, he had provided me (and my siblings) with an almost constant stream of death-related anecdotal material: ways you could accidentally die, things that could – in a very rare but entirely possible fluke of nature – kill you, and an ever-growing list of activities and events that should be avoided at all costs if you wanted to live a full and healthy life.

The fact that my dad was possibly one of the most unhealthy people in England, who collected vices like fridge magnets and who 'managed' his type 2 diabetes by seesawing between insulin overdoses and Mars bar-induced comas, was an irony not lost on me. He once lectured me on the present-day dangers of the bubonic plague whilst testing his blood sugar, and then excused himself halfway through his summary to eat a Cadbury's Creme Egg and then smoke a cigarette in the garden.

The first death warning I can remember was when I was about four and we were feeding the ducks.

'Aye,' he had said, staring darkly at the lake. 'You don't want to be getting too close to those geese. The size of their wings! They'd break a grown man's leg.'

'Daddy?' I must have backed away from the water at this point because the lake was chockablock full of geese.

'A swan, too,' my dad had continued. 'There's probably enough power in a swan to break a man's neck. It'd kill you stone dead.'

'Kill you stone dead' was one of his favourite phrases. Many things could kill you stone dead: those huge hay bales tumbling off the back of a lorry (I never drove behind one, would even pull over at the side of the road to put some distance between), touching a plug socket without rubber gloves on, most of the plants in the garden and absolutely, most definitely lightning, if you were in the wrong place at the wrong time.

'Never drive with one hand,' he said. 'If you have a tyre blow out then the force of it would rip your bloody arm off. If you flipped the car into a ditch and hit your head on the steering wheel, it'd kill you stone dead.'

'Never eat from a can of tinned salmon that has a dint on the outside,' was the opener to his favourite tale of caution, 'you only need the most microscopic hole to break the vacuum and any bacteria on the outside will be sucked in.' He usually paused here to make a dramatic sucking motion. 'And if it's botulism that gets inside and you eat that salmon . . . it'll kill you stone dead.'

Dad's accident scenarios weren't limited to the mundane; we ticked off food poisonings, electrical hazards and inappropriate work/leisurewear (never don a necktie whilst operating a woodchipper; don't wear hoop earrings whilst horseriding through a forest), but he also had a plethora of possible death-causes that were so unlikely, so niche, that it was impossible not to find them fascinating. My favourite (if that is the right term) was 'death by banking'.

'Some of those massive vaults,' said my dad, settling in for another comfy and enjoyable chat about loss of life, 'weigh about twenty tonnes. Twenty tonnes! Imagine that coming at you!'

I tried to imagine. I had no idea what he was talking about, really, but I knew that something was about to kill someone stone dead.

'Those big Swiss banks,' he said, 'you'd want to be well out of the way when the vault doors open. Because if you think about it,' he said, 'that door swinging into you would be like getting hit with a twenty-tonne truck. It'd kill you . . . kill you stone dead.'

'I'll make sure I stand well back next time I break into one,' I said.

To which he replied, 'Don't get fucking cheeky.'

As a result of this intense, decades-long neurolinguistic programming, I now catastrophised almost every situation I found myself in and, thanks to my overly active, morbid imagination, it was possible to work out exactly how and why one could – probably would! – die from the most unassuming and vanilla actions. Bearing in mind my dad drilled it into us that a mere *lightbulb* could kill you if you tried to replace it with the light switch turned to 'on' (he would make one of us stand right next to the switch if he was performing this particular act of DIY, and if the new bulb flickered as he touched it to the holder he would shout OFF! OFF! and jig around at the top of the ladder as though he was being swarmed by bees), you can only begin to imagine how my brain whirred when faced with more perilous activities. Standing on a tube platform, crossing a road, boarding a ferry when there was a storm a-brewing – all of these rather pedestrian, non-daring feats came with a continuous internal monologue. The narrator of doom.

Then again, what might have befallen us, my siblings and I, had we not endured years of this traumatising life advice? I would probably have stood next to an open window during a lightning storm and been burned to death by an errant thunderball; my brother maybe would have been imprisoned and sentenced to death in a far-flung country for taking an old lady's heavy suitcase through customs that then turned out to be packed full of drugs ('NEVER TAKE ANYONE'S CASE FOR THEM, EVEN A FAMILY MEMBER'S! . . . WHAT? ESPECIALLY NOT MINE!'), my sister could have been felled by any number of things. Quicksand ('you'd never see it until it was too late'), a hippo ('they look lovely and cute but my *God* those things can run and they'd kill you stone dead, not a second thought boyo, not a second thought') or perhaps a biro. Biros were dangerous as anything, especially if you walked with them in your mouth ('straight through the soft palate, and that isn't easy to mend, I can tell you') or poked them up your nose.

I'd no idea why my dad had so much death and injury-related anecdotal material. I only remembered him having two accidents ever and they weren't even that bad: once he walked through some patio doors thinking they were open (he cut his arm) and another time, his eyeball got scratched by a rose thorn.

It was almost inconceivable, then, that he would finally meet his demise in such a pedestrian way. Not by getting hit in the head by a professionally spun cricket ball ('the speed of those things, they'd knock you stone dead!') or drinking too much water ('hyponatremia, you basically drown inside your own head') but by boring old garden variety heart failure. What would lead to the heart failure, all those years in the future, would possibly be a much more colourful story, but the death itself would surely have been a bit of a disappointment to him. After he had described such dramatic ways to go, after he'd set all of those stages, he never actually got to play on them.

But for me, for someone who was, as a result of these colourful stories, unable to use an escalator in a relaxed fashion or indeed touch the handrail of an escalator ('If you got your fingers caught under that moving belt they'd probably be sliced clean off!'), the smoky, Polaroid-filled world of fashion seemed like an anxiety-inducing hotbed of health and safety nightmares.

One of my best friends, on one of her first shoots, had

been submerged in a water-filled glass tank inside a studio crisscrossed by electric cables and the water-filled tank had collapsed. Had 'the floor is lava!' been a thing, I'm pretty sure it would have been uttered by the half a dozen or so crew members who were trying to jump out of the way in an attempt to not be electrocuted horribly to death. My first modelling shoots had been tame in comparison, but that summer I was to collect a few near-death experiences of my own. I was a Main Board girl now, traversing the globe – crossing paths with people who had absolutely no respect for human safety was going to be par for the course.

The first photographer, a Romanian man called Satin (warning bells!), had me balancing perilously over jellyfish-infested waters and the second, let's call him Monsieur de Rigeur in case he sues me, had me risking life and limb in the middle of the Caribbean sea. I couldn't tell whether these people were devoid of all common sense or simply didn't care, but in both cases I saw my life flash before my eyes and also, in those crucial last seconds, imagined the little news story that would accompany the announcement of my death. No doubt written in an incredulous tone, surprised that anyone would be balancing on a narrow sea wall in heels or hanging from the end of a boom above shark-infested waters. She obviously had it coming.

Satin (no relation, or perhaps he was) was a stern man with a dark beard who smoked small, narrow cigars incessantly and had very little facial expression.

'Posing with the arms high,' was one of his set phrases, as was 'Now we are waiting,' which he used whenever the sun came out (this was in Turkey, so it happened a lot) because the more muted, indirect light was better. And then there was his favourite: 'Now we have the shot.'

The 'now we have the shot' phrase was actually quite confusing because each time he said it, I took it to mean that we had finished that particular shot and that he was done with it. What he meant – inside his own head – was that it was all looking good and he was happy (if he was capable of happiness) to continue in that setting with that pose and with whatever light the sun was casting from its hiding place behind the clouds. ('Don't come out, sun, for the love of God!')

'OK,' he said, as I stood wide-legged in a power pose, with my arms stretched out towards a raised flag. (No idea, even now. It could have been political, I would never have known.) It had taken forty minutes to get me into this perfect position, with both art directors, the makeup artist and the stylist hopping in like crows to arrange my limbs. An array of golden jewellery had been carefully draped over my shoulders and arms and it was heavier than carrying a whole other person; I could barely keep my hands from shaking – which were, incidentally, adorned with about three dozen diamond rings.

'OK,' he said, clicking away with the camera, 'now we have the shot.'

'Great,' I said, dropping my arms and therefore about ten million pounds worth of jewellery onto the concrete floor. There was a collective gasp of horror.

'Back in position!' he shouted. 'You have ruined the arrangement!'

I'm sure that Satin tried to punish me, then, with the

final shot. I was to balance on a harbour wall that had a drop of at least fifty feet down to the water below. A quick glance told me that the water was swarming with what appeared to be either stingrays or jellyfish – the wonders of the natural world have never been my forte. Either way, I wasn't keen on the wall-walking set-up. Especially not in 150mm high Christian Louboutin Pigalle pumps.

Anyway, there was a bit of a standoff. There was no way I was balancing on a thinnish wall with jellyfish below me – this wasn't a seventies Bond film. I could hear my dad's voice delivering my eulogy (this was many years before his death):

'If only I had covered off maritime accidents, Ruth would be here now. The perils were threefold and I failed to prepare her. First, the sudden drop from a great height, the shock of the fall, the bone-shattering impact. Then the drowning, which – if I can digress momentarily – is actually a very peaceful way to go, and then the stings from what was established by the coroners to be over one hundred and thirty individual large jellyfish, which we all know will kill you stone dead.'

I'd like for there to be an exciting twist here but I just refused to get on the wall. Dad 1: Fashion 0.

Monsieur de Rigeur was equally ambivalent when it came to seafaring safety.

'Climb out to the end of the stick,' he said, 'using the netting.'

Sounded pretty tame until you clocked that by netting he meant rigging and by stick he meant boom – a boom that was jutting out into the open sea, upon which we were bobbing about on a sailing ship around fifteen miles from shore.

I spent a week with this man and can only give you only three facts: he was small, he was angry and he shaved his chest. Everything I did sent him apoplectic with rage. He pointed the camera with all the violence of someone taking aim with a bazooka, he changed lenses frequently and noisily, as though trying to find an angle, any angle, that wouldn't make him want to die of hatred.

'Climb out to the end of the stick,' he said again, 'and then try to pose but not like your usual.'

There was no way I was going to climb up any rigging, let alone slide along a boom. I was greased up with factor fifty and the seven pina coladas I'd drunk the night before were already threatening to make a reappearance. I looked to the rest of the crew for support but one was pretending to throw up over the side and the others had disappeared 'down below' to 'get some water'. Bastards!

'*S'il vous plaît*,' said Monsieur De Rigeur, 'help her up the netting.' One of the young boat hands came forward, shrugging. Even he was reluctant to get involved, despite the fact he'd get to cradle an oiled-up model in his strong arms, thus fulfilling one of the most classic teenage fantasies.

We were (possibly) in shark-infested waters. The huge wooden boom creaked as it swung gently from side to side; a light breeze lifted the napkins on the table that had been set for lunch – a lunch we could only enjoy, apparently, if I risked life and limb for a photo I'm not even sure would have worked. I mean what was he expecting? Me to stand Amazonian-like at the end of the boom, bronzed and strong like a carved figurehead? More likely I'd be clinging onto the pole looking like a terrified sloth. It was a standoff; the boat was silent. Anger seethed from Monsieur de Rigeur – it was almost visible, like a dark, dense steam. That could also have been, though, thinking about it, the sweat rising from him because he insisted on wearing black all the time, despite the fact that the average daily temperature was about thirty-seven degrees Celsius. Whatever: he seethed. And then, just as I was running through the list of possible – fatal – accidents that could occur if I gave in and climbed the boom; just as I was running through my list of demises, I was saved by the bell.

The art director popped her head up from below deck waving a pair of crochet bikini bottoms like a white flag.

'I think I'm going to change her,' she said. 'The clothing and the shot. I'm not sure I like the Missoni one-piece and her legs are too short to look good on the boom.'

There were many other incidents. If I'd had a mental filing cabinet then there could have been a whole drawer labelled 'Some of the Times I Could Have Been Killed But Thankfully Wasn't'. And it would have been stuffed to the gills already. And I was only a year-and-a-bit in. Going all over the world with people I barely knew, flying alone to far-flung places, turning up to castings in creepy unfinished warehouse conversions, killing time at the weekend in foreign cities where not a single familiar soul in the world knew where I was or what I was doing – all perfect opportunities for something drastic to happen. It was amazing I was still alive with all four limbs attached.

One of the most dramatic 'Times I Could Have Been Killed' incidents on file was the one where I had scaled the roof of my eight-storey New York apartment block, Spiderman-style, because I'd locked myself out. My first proper day in New York, I popped out for fags and a Mountain Dew and returned keyless to the cold, hard stare of a locked entryway. It was so inescapably hot that day and I had no phone, no memorised numbers and no friend to call. In the end, a woman huffed up to the doorway carrying grocery bags and she kindly let me into the lobby.

Which was nice, but listen to this for a psycho alert: the woman was carrying a handbag that was woven from hair. Human hair? OK, so it couldn't be confirmed with any real confidence without lab testing, but still. That is what it looked like. Who had a handbag made from hair? What was the zip fashioned from? Children's milk teeth? Perhaps it wasn't hair but some form of straw or wicker, I don't know, whatever; when the lady with the hairy bag invited me up to her top floor apartment for a glass of water – no doubt drugged – I was hesitant to say yes.

'Aw, come on,' said the lady, who was also wearing an evil eye pendant with an incredibly realistic eye. (What the hell was this? Wear your trophies day?)

'I'll call the super,' she said, 'and get you a spare key. Just come on in hang out for a while.'

Which is what they all say, surely. But it was impossible to refuse without seeming rude and with rude not being an option for this newly arrived Brit, we went on in to her apartment. It had roughly the same layout as the one I was sharing with Nadia (oh, for Nadia to be here!):

an open-plan kitchen-living area, a bathroom and two doors going off to the bedrooms. The only big difference was that one whole wall in the living area had floor-to-ceiling shelving which held – *abort! abort!* – dozens of wooden body parts. Jointed wooden hands, intricate wooden feet and row upon row of perfectly smooth wooden milliner's dummies. Brown and gleaming, like rows of decapitated bald men's heads. I don't know, it all just gave me a bad feeling about things. I didn't touch the glass of water, despite it clinking seductively with ice, I just perched myself right on the edge of the sofa, trying to avoid looking at the carved wooden craniums, whilst the lady tried to reach the superintendent on her phone.

After an excruciating ten-minute wait I could bear it no more; my overactive imagination had already seen me drugged, skinned and then fashioned into a practical rucksack, my fingernails used decoratively along the shoulder straps like shards of mother-of-pearl. I went over to the window to look out at the fire escape, mainly to see how quickly I'd be able to throw myself onto it if I needed to.

'If you're apartment 10A then you're off the other fire escape, honey,' said the lady, watching me closely with the phone clamped between ear and shoulder. 'I thought about the fire escape right away when you said you'd left your bedroom window open. I thought, *why doesn't she just go down the fire escape?* But it's the wrong side.'

She paused.

'You know, you could try the roof?'

The roof? What would I do from the roof? Abseil?

'I don't know for sure,' said the lady, 'but maybe you can get onto your fire escape from there.'

It was worth a try. At least it would get me out of her flat – anything was better than sitting about with body parts.

So I found myself on the bare, scorching rooftop of the SoHo apartment block, dazed in the midday heat and totally disorientated. I felt like a criminal who had escaped capture and who was now waiting for helicopter rescue – I was up in the sky! On a proper New York roof! The only problem was that the fire escape I needed didn't directly drop down from the roof; first, there was a waist-high wall at the edge of the roof to be negotiated and *then*, if you were daring enough to lean over far enough to see, there was a four- or five-foot drop down to the first platform of the metal fire escape. Not only that, the waist-high wall was not a normal waist-high wall, the sort of wall you'd get in a garden; it was curved, smooth, perfectly possible to traverse if you were an action hero who could vault over burning cars, roll beneath moving trains and then ride an alligator over a waterfall whilst firing a semi-automatic. But if you were a normal person, untrained in scaling oversized humps and who couldn't even jump a primary school hurdle – well, then it was a little more dangerous. Not only did you have to get yourself over the rounded top of the wall, you had to hope that you were going to land on the fire escape when you dropped down on the other side, or else you were going to be dropping a very, very long way.

'Oh, be careful,' said top-flat lady, clutching her scalp bag, 'it's so high.'

No shit, I thought, as I pressed myself to the hump and felt all of my skin instantly sear off from the heat. Was this how I would die? Falling from the top of an apartment block, my seared-off skin carefully swept up by the resident psycho and kept in a labelled jar, later to be made into a patchwork hanky?

I didn't die, obviously, but had anyone been flying overhead that summer's day in 2002 then they would have most definitely alerted the emergency services. A young woman, dressed only in terry towelling shorts and vest top, dangling over the side of a building with her sandalled feet pedalling frantically in mid-air. And when I had finally climbed down the fire escape and in through my bedroom window, which had indeed been left ajar, I was met by a chair-wielding Nadia who very nearly took me out.

'Why you use window?' said Nadia, putting the chair down. 'Was thinking you were my boyfriend, Ivan. Was about to kill him but pretend was accident, that I thought he was burglar.'

'I forgot my key,' I said. I was absolutely buzzing with adrenaline, my legs trembling and hands shaking violently. 'I've just climbed over the roof of the building, can you believe it? Oh my God, I can't believe I just did that!'

'Next time ring buzzer,' said Nadia, coolly, 'and I let you in through front door.'

Chapter 10

A Thousand Unsafe Pins

It's funny that the one time I *was* sort of kidnapped, in a roundabout kind of way, my hyperactive imagination just completely switched itself off. Nowhere to be seen. Hiding, probably – thinking *Shit! This is not a drill, I'm outta here!*

But I wasn't properly kidnapped, my imagination had nothing to worry about: I just accidentally ended up, in the summer of 2002, on a five-day holiday with a man that I hardly knew. At no point was I physically held against my own wishes; it was more 'holidaying under false pretences'. With a bit of horse-riding and jet-skiing thrown in.

I'd met the man in question once or twice, which wasn't a lot, I'll admit, but he was loosely linked with my friends in New York and so I felt relatively safe in the knowledge that he wasn't a psychopath. I suppose I had also lulled myself into a false sense of security with my safe, mutual friendships and sexless existence over the summer. I'd not had one single indecent proposal and therefore, when Tarek, who I'd met twice before but never on my own, phoned me and said, 'Ruth, come to Morocco,' it didn't even occur to me to question the premise of the trip.

'Who's going?' I said. I was back at home with my parents for the very end of the summer because Paris was closed and London was slow. Boredom was setting in and the offer piqued my interest.

'Ruth,' he said, 'everyone is going. I am booking your tickets, tell me which airport.'

'Everyone?'

'Ruth, everyone,' he replied.

'Fabienne? Billy? Patrick and Sarah? Jean-Bernard?'

'Ruth, don't worry,' said Tarek. 'It's going to be cool. We can all hang out. My uncle's hotel has this club on the beach, the food is great. Ruth, let's party.'

I didn't need to be asked twice.

Here is what I knew about Tarek before the accidental holiday for two: 1) he had a girlfriend who was potentially a mute, and 2) he waxed his entire upper body. I'd seen it on the beach in Ibiza, it was the sort of thing I noticed. Mainly because I wasn't into waxed chests.

In retrospect, there were a couple of incidents that may have raised red flags. The fact that he never asked a question, for example, only made statements that were basically well-disguised commands. Or – and this was far more pertinent – the fact that when I'd seen him with his girlfriend, he'd always ordered her food for her. Without any sort of discussion. Or consideration of the fact that she was very obviously vegetarian and left the meat and fish on her plate every single time.

Danger! Danger!

The tickets to Morocco were there waiting for me at the airport when I arrived. I text Patrick to see if he was on his way, I text Sarah to say I was about to board the plane, I text Jean-Bernard as we were taxiing along the runway to tell him my arrival time in Morocco and then I switched off my phone to enjoy the ride.

More sun. More fun. This was turning out to be quite the year. As I drifted in and out of my high-altitude snooze, I thought about how bizarre it was to have these friends from a totally different world, who travelled at every opportune moment and were completely au fait with jetting off to meet up with friends at the drop of a hat. Who didn't dread paying the bill, like normal people. Who hardly glanced at it. Lobster starters at forty euros a go. Club tables with a thousand-dollar minimum spend. A two hundred euro cod! Here was a group of people who just seemed to go from one amazing place to the next, having a constant good time and never having to do any washing up. Eating out for every single meal. People who could get taxis whenever they wanted to if they wanted to, but they didn't, because someone would always drive them. People who never queued, shopped where they liked and always had a light tan.

There was a sun-soaked optimism to spending time with them. I was twenty-one and I was living the dream: I couldn't wait to see them all again.

'On my way where?' said Patrick's text, which scrolled

across my screen as the plane reached the gate and the overhead lights came on.

'Where are you off to on a plane?' asked Sarah, in a text that arrived as I sped through border control and headed to the luggage carousel.

'Ruth, why are you going to Morocco and why do I need to know what time?' Jean-Bernard messaged, as I wheeled my trolley through the sliding doors and into arrivals.

Uh-oh, I thought, as I glanced around the arrivals hall. There were no familiar faces. There was no happy, tastefully neutral jumble of the usual crowd with their leather luggage and their sunglasses perched on expensive highlighted heads, the girls talking loudly, sounding like a parody of some sort of Californian teen soap opera, and the guys with their understated watches and their shirts rolled up to reveal tanned American, French, Italian forearms with just the hint of exclusive, musky cologne.

None of them were there.

'The hell, Ruth?' text Jean-Bernard. 'Have you gone on vacation with Tarek?'

But it was too late to reply because there he was, standing in the arrivals hall with his babyish handsome face and his cared-for twenty-something physique and a crisp white shirt against his dark skin – and he was completely, one hundred per cent, on his own.

Well this is odd, I thought, as we left the airport arrivals and headed for his car. But if there was one thing I was used to – and you know this already – it was arriving in a strange country in the small hours to be greeted by an unknown man who would drive me along dark, empty roads to an unfamiliar destination. These drivers nearly always had a disturbing quirk: one in Tunisia coughed up phlegm balls and then inserted them into an open can of Fanta using the rolled-up tip of his tongue. Another driver, in Rome, would close his eyes every time he needed to navigate the taxi through a particularly narrow gap. He wouldn't open them again until we were through it, three or four seconds later. One British taxi driver taking me from London to Oxfordshire kept up a lengthy text conversation for the duration of the journey, tap tap tapping on his phone buttons even whilst doing ninety up the M40; another had unscrewed his false leg and placed it on the passenger seat because it was 'chafing in the heat'.

Tarek was a relative dream. I'd met him before! I knew where he lived (Morocco) and that his girlfriend was a mute. No wonder my imagination was quiet and inactive: in terms of warning bells, there was only one, tinkling far in the distant hills: the fact that I'd been expecting a fun group holiday but nobody else was here.

'Ruth,' said Tarek as we reached his car, 'your sandals are too small for your feet.' He had parked right in front of the entrance, his car gleaming, whilst a whole car park of lesser vehicles festered in the dust beyond the trunk road. There had been no ticket on his windscreen, the airport staff who patrolled the front of the terminal did not glance twice at Tarek as he sauntered to the driver side door and blipped the car into action. Not just central locking on this thing but wing mirrors that went in and out – on their own! Blip blip!

'Your sandals do not fit,' he said.

'They're *Havaianas*,' I replied, as though this would explain everything. Which it should have done because everyone knew that it was impossible to get your sizing right in Havaianas. They were from Brazil! They used different – foreign – sizing! The rubber flip-flops causing a storm in the fashion world could only be bought from certain sellers on eBay and nobody ever knew whether they would come up small, whether you should size up or size down, whether you should trust the size stamped onto the rubber itself or written on the eBay description . . . I had four pairs of Havaianas and only one pair fit. And even then, apparently not.

'Ruth,' Tarek said. 'I know that they are Havaianas. Of course. When anyone goes to Brasil, they are the disposable sandals you buy for the beach. This doesn't mean they shouldn't fit you correctly.' He steered out of the airport and onto the open road. 'I find it strange that you would wear a disposable shoe for travel.'

Disposable shoes? Bloody hell. They were as coveted as Cinderella's glass slipper back in the UK, despite them arriving in poorly sealed Jiffy bags held together with elastic bands. The little Brazilian flag stamped on the rubber! The bright colours they came in! The superior comfort sole!

'It's hard to get the sizing right,' I said to Tarek, but he was concentrating on the road, driving determinedly to our destination at a smooth and constant speed of circa 115mph.

You'll be pleased to know that he wasn't a psychopath. Yes, he went on to criticise the way I used a fish knife, boarded a jet-ski and held a champagne coupe (all skills

I had been apparently too poor in life to learn), but at no point did I wake to find him staring at me in my bed, entirely devoid of emotion, holding a pair of pliers and a Polaroid camera.

Praise the lord.

Not a psychopath, then, but still, the whole situation was most definitely irregular. By the time we reached his uncle's hotel on the beach – architectural inspiration taken directly from the Disney castle – I had established that 1) no other guests were coming, 2) his girlfriend was no longer on the scene (I assumed dumped but perhaps should have had him clarify) and 3) I was about to embark on a five-day luxury mega-trip with a full, action-packed itinerary of wealthy-person pursuits, including riding Arabian race horses, lunch aboard a yacht and a two-night vacation-within-a-vacation on a private island. Additional flights included.

Crikey. It beat sitting around in England waiting for a casting to come in, I supposed.

I know, I know. *Get the hell out of Dodge!* you're thinking. *This is like in the movies when the woman goes down to the basement, in a lightning storm, armed with only a flickering torch. Because she's heard a thump and Granny has gone missing. Never mind Granny! Run, run like the wind!*

But there was simply no real sense of impending danger. Apart from the fact I hated to be given an itinerary and felt slightly anxious about the horse-riding part, I was A-OK.

By day four, I was enjoying his company in the same sort of way that you'd enjoy the company of a work colleague. Perhaps if you'd become stranded together at a pharmaceutical sales conference in Florida, due to cancelled flights. We'd had separate rooms the entire time; he'd not tried to kiss me – he'd not given any indication of wanting to do anything remotely sexual to me, niche or other-wise – and I'd dined out in lovely places and topped up my tan. Oh, and much to my own amusement, I'd also made a deeply disappointing companion to Tarek in nearly every single one of the activities he'd organised. Clinging to his back inelegantly, like a beige-coloured seal, as he'd crashed his jet ski through the waves. Managing to misinterpret the expected dress code at almost every mealtime. Screaming 'We're all going to die' when his yacht had hit what I thought was definitely a tidal wave but was, in fact, just the wake of another boat.

Yes, I thought, as I lay there on my sunlounger, reading my paperback novel, *life could be a lot worse*. I'd had a free holiday, despite it not being with someone I'd have picked to go on holiday with. The waves were lapping at the shore of the private, sandy beach, the sun was beating down on my lotioned skin and everything was right with the world. I wondered, fleetingly, what my problem was with Tarek, anyway. Aside from the fact he'd 'surprised' me with a romantic vacation on our third ever meeting. Apart from that bit. He was obviously very eligible – rich, handsome, polite, educated – and so what was it about him that I found so wrong? I just couldn't put my finger on it.

'Ruth,' he said, 'this is disgusting.'

Tarek's head suddenly appeared in my line of vision at the end of my sunlounger, popping up between my raised knees like an unexpected gynaecologist. A near-naked, waxed-chested gynaecologist.

'Ruth, you should take better care with it,' he said, as though referring to a pet, 'and make sure that it is all neat. All trimmed.'

I lowered my book. Was this man really passing comment on the neatness of my bikini line?

'Ruth,' he continued, ducking his head down again, 'you have hairs spreading all around down here.'

I was fairly sure that I didn't; I was not a hairy person and there was no way that I had suddenly sprouted a full, meandering muff overnight. But how long had Tarek been down at the business end, silently appraising my nether regions? Quite honestly, it's not something I'd have been comfortable with a lover doing, not in the full glare of the sun, and this was a man who'd not even touched my hand.

Had Tarek been harbouring painful, secret urges for the entire trip? Perhaps this was his opening gambit, in terms of taking things to a more sexual level. Perhaps he had been lying on his lounger, toasting away, trying to think of good lines to seduce me with and 'this is disgusting' had been the best he could think of. Maybe he thought that discussing intimate, private things was the same thing as . . . actual intimacy? What were his usual openers, I wondered, when he wanted to advance a relationship to the next stage.

'Jenine,' I could imagine him saying. 'From the smell of your bowel movement this morning I think you could benefit from more fibre.'

'Cecile,' he might venture. 'I have noticed through your kaftan that your nipples are very slightly different to one another in both circumference and depth of tone.'

Sexy.

'I don't trim it at all down there,' I said and snapped my knees shut, almost decapitating him in the process. 'I am very unhairy. I have the sparse pubic hair pattern of a ninety-year-old woman.'

If that didn't put him off . . .

Reader, it didn't. It was simply added, apparently, to my growing list of perceived faults. He hated my smoking, he disliked me drinking – even if we were at a bar, which is quite literally designed for drinking – and my lack of important life skills irked him. My inability to jet ski, already alluded to; not knowing the difference between a caprese and a carpaccio; the fact that I liked to drink a glass of champagne to the bottom, because it was champagne, when I should have waited for it to be refilled when it was halfway down.

'Ruth,' he had said, 'it is not attractive to see your big, wide, open mouth through the glass as you tip it upside down.'

He frowned upon my disposable shoes, looked slightly despairingly at my non-Eres bikini and couldn't understand my obsession with ordering burgers, everywhere I went.

'I like the fact you get lots of flavours in one,' I said. 'When I worked in McDon—'

'Ruth,' Tarek had said, cutting me off before he heard something he could never come back from, 'they will make you fat and then you will die from it.'

So many dislikes, it was borderline rude. Especially

as he was the one who'd kidnapped me! He should have checked out my credentials before committing to the airfare. If he'd wanted a little blonde bombshell who'd know what to wear for black tie and who would cling to him like a limpet on his various speedy seafaring vessels then he should have looked for one with some pedigree, or at least an ambition to marry rich. Instead, he'd gone for a little blonde bombshell with half a law degree whose total previous boat experience involved a blow-up dinghy on Bournemouth beach. *Tant pis,* Tarek. You win some you lose some.

But none of this deterred him. Perhaps he was just determined to see his investment through, now that we only had one night left of the trip. There was just one more Tarek Test to complete: the horse-riding session.

I'd always had an off-kilter relationship with horse riding – the reality of it never met my expectations. I loved the idea of horse riding. Throughout my childhood and teen years, I had romantically imagined myself cantering over the moors on Black Beauty or clip-clopping down muddy lanes in the Lake District à la Beatrix Potter – but in reality, I was mildly scared of horses and had detested nearly every minute spent in the saddle.

When Tarek suggested bareback riding on the private beach, I got my all-familiar sense of thrill and expectation. I briefly did wonder whether he meant sex rather than horses, but he quite quickly elaborated on his plans.

'Ruth. This evening you will wear something more suitable for riding horses into the sunset.'

'I have just the thing for riding horses!' I said, and it

was true. For once, in the entire trip, I had just the right thing for the right activity. I'd worn battered denim shorts to a swanky members' club, a sequin evening gown to a beach BBQ and a bikini on a boat trip where everyone else had been covered up from head to toe, but finally, I had the correct attire. Jeans. Granted they were my special jeans, the Jeans of a Thousand Safety Pins, slit up to the thigh on both sides and re-fastened with hundreds and hundreds of tiny golden pins, *but* they were pre-distressed jeans, they were rugged jeans and they were pliable enough to allow me to straddle a horse. Canter a horse. Perhaps even jump on a horse, if the opportunity arose. That would show him, bloody Tarek, thinking I was useless at all of the important things in life.

'Just hold on,' shouted Tarek, galloping up beside me. I could barely hear him over the rush of wind. The beach was a blur, I had horse mane inside my mouth and the was being pummelled in the pelvis, over and over again. I was hurtling towards the sunset rather than riding, the horse angrily careering over the sand as though he had been given just one task, which was to destroy me. I was like an out-of-control missile heading straight for disaster; death was surely imminent. I could barely open my eyes for the amount of sandy air that was blowing into my face and I was having to grip the horse's neck with every ounce of my strength so that I didn't fall off.

Through my eye slits I saw Tarek lean over and grab the reins, having failed to tell me he was apparently an accomplished trainer of Arabian stallions in his other life, as well as an Olympic-level jet skier and an experienced sea captain. Was there any leisure activity he didn't excel in? Bloody Tarek. We slowed to a faltering, exhausted sort of trot and then my horse finally began to walk again, round and round in still-agitated circles, snorting and puffing.

'Ruth,' said Tarek, 'you can open your eyes.'

I opened them. We were about two hundred yards down the beach – I could still see the little colourful tent where the man organising the horse riding stood.

'I thought I'd gone miles!' I said in disbelief. 'Wow.'

'No, Ruth,' said Tarek. 'We had only just set off.' He glanced at my feet, pointedly. 'Disposable shoes are not suitable for riding a horse. You have cut your feet,' he said.

I knew that I had cut my feet. Didn't I just! The flip-flop toe-posts had sliced through my flesh like cheese wire. But that wasn't the worst of my injuries, oh no. For as we had been riding, all thousand of the safety pins on my ridiculous jeans had popped open and then stabbed themselves into my inner thighs and calves. Obviously the pressure of my grip had frenzied the pins into some sort of mass pin protest and they had all pinged at once and then lanced into me like I was Gulliver and they were the tiny spears of Lilliputians, with—

'Ruth,' said Tarek. 'You said you could ride.'

It was just one disappointment too many, I think, and he indicated with a nod of his head that the adventure was over. He helped me down into the sand where I pulled my flip-flops from my bloody, cloven feet and he slowly walked us all back to the tent, me hobbling behind the horses in the Jeans of a Thousand Unsafe Pins.

Chapter 11

Amazing Furrycollared Steamcoat

In a way, that episode neatly drew a line under what had been the most intense, crazy summer of my life. It had been a sort of coming of age: over the space of a few months, I'd gone from being a girl who never left home to a jet-setting model who thought nothing of jumping on a plane to do a few castings on the other side of the Atlantic. OK, so I had accidentally gone on holiday with someone I didn't particularly know or like, but apart from that I was so much wiser. So much more worldly. The world of modelling was no longer some strange unknown that I had no clue how to navigate; this was a new era.

I was back in London after my disjointed summer of non-love, the autumn leaves were falling and big things were afoot. Not only was the modelling documentary about to air – *This Model Life* – I had just been optioned for a huge ad campaign. Putting an option on a model was just a client's way of making sure they'd be free on the shoot day, it didn't commit them to anything whatsoever. But still. If it confirmed, it just might turn out to be the biggest job of my entire career.

'Babe,' Texana said, 'this casting in Paris could be for the biggest job of your entire career. You always look great, my babe, but for this casting you have to look the very best you've ever looked. Like, groomed, polished and an extra layer of shine.'

With that in mind and knowing that the job I was casting for was worth the same amount of money as a small house in Bethnal Green at the time, I decided that I would indeed turn up to my casting – on the outskirts of Paris – looking the best I had ever looked. With an extra layer of shine. I would wear my newest and most prized possession: my red shearling coat.

It was a quirk of the job that some of the time, instead of being paid for work in money, you'd get given clothes. The designer – often massively wealthy and with huge investment backers behind them – would note your inability to afford even the smallest amount of rent, see that you'd spent your last five pounds on a tube ticket to get to their studios and then find it appropriate to pay you in fabric.

It was absolutely bloody fantastic. Who needed money when you had stacks of posh clothes? Although not always posh, actually, because there was a rub to all of this: the clothes you got given were more often than not samples. And samples, unlike the finished garments you'd see in the shops, were a mishmash of designs that hadn't quite made it: zips that wouldn't work and hems that someone had got bored of sewing three quarters of the way through.

That summer, in between Tokyo and New York, I'd walked for a very successful and popular London fashion label. The show would end up being one of the very few of my career – I had been so very bad and slow at walking on the catwalk that I'd caused a catastrophic bottleneck. But still, despite my failings, I had been told to go to the label's sample storage lockup and pick seven or eight pieces to keep for myself.

'The walk was shit,' said the owner of the label, in her cracked, raspy old voice, 'but you looked great. Fabulous tits.'

The samples were stored in a gigantic warehouse in west London and the man who showed me in, who looked like Lurch and had a huge ring of jangling keys, seemed annoyed that I was there. Not wanting to inconvenience him for any longer than was necessary, I picked items from the first two rows near the door. Six dresses, one little skirt and the biggest, furriest shearling coat ever seen outside of Siberia. Dark, blood red in colour and with the most dramatic, glamorous collar that rose up behind my head so that I looked like a medieval baroness.

'Never made it to production,' said Lurch, pointing at the coat. 'It was too expensive to make. Five grand.'

It was also possible, I thought, that the coat had never been signed off for production because it was so large it could have been used as a caravan awning. Or because wearing it was like voluntarily sitting inside a furnace in a glassworks. It would have been too hot in the midst of an arctic winter.

And so my version of the coat was a mock-up. This huge, red, glamorous monster hadn't been made to the same high standard as it would have been for the shops, but I didn't care. It was a masterpiece. And it was this coat that I decided to wear for The Most Important Casting of My Life.

I should have seen the warning signs before we'd even left England.

'Your ticket is red,' said the man at the check-in desk, but I was already too hot and too bothered to take it in. I'd left home at 4.30am to drive to the train, coat on the passenger seat beside me like a huge, maroon St Bernard, and then I'd had to wear it through to the Eurostar at Waterloo because it was too bulky to carry. It was so large that people were pointing at me as though I was a circus attraction. And so, when the man had told me that my ticket was red, I hadn't had the capacity to be massively worried.

'It's because it has been in the pocket,' I said, slightly dismissively, 'of my new coat.'

'Is that what it's called?' said the check-in man. He nodded to his colleague. 'Coat,' he said.

'I know,' said the second man. 'Saw it.'

At security, the passengers stared too, as they watched me try to feed the coat, which even balled up was the same size as a grown man in the foetal position, through the scanner.

'What is this, madam?' said the woman at the scanner. 'It needs to be in a tray.'

'It won't fit in a tray,' I said. 'It's just a really, really big coat.'

'Are you going on an arctic expedition?' said the lady.

'Paris,' I replied. 'I have an important casting. Like an audition.'

'Oh,' said the woman. 'Cabaret or circus?'

On the Eurostar, things took a turn for the worse. There wasn't enough space in the overhead shelves or on the luggage racks for half of the passenger's cases, and so my coat, which I'd taken off to light applause, was filling the entire space in front of me. I'd also become vaguely aware, when I'd stood up, that people had been staring at my face and neck. It was worrying. I was sweating, yes, but surely that wouldn't attract that much attention?

I tried not to fret. I had planned the morning meticulously. Arrive in Paris at 11.30am, go to a department store (Lafayette most likely) to use their loos and do my makeup; get a taxi to the casting and then bingo. Lunch, wine, get the plane home. I'd be back just before pub closing, probably, to celebrate my jet-setting day in my jet-setter's coat with a lovely cold glass of terrible Chardonnay.

Except that the train turfed us off before Paris and we transferred to a coach, which also had no space to stow the amazing technicolour dreamcoat, or, as it should have been called, the amazing furrycollared steamcoat. I had to sit, stewing inside it, as the coach made its way through sleeping villages and nondescript towns before finally passing through the outer suburbs of Paris.

Il fait chaud.

Beneath the coat, I was wearing a brand new Pringle

cashmere jumper in palest cream, faded blue jeans and leather boots that came up to the knee. My shins were sweating, my breasts were sweating, my entire person was beaded with clammy perspiration but still I could not remove my coat. I couldn't remove my jumper either because all I had on underneath was a bra. The saving grace was that after the sort of grey, depressing journey you'd see in a war film set in the 1940s, when I finally stepped down from the transfer bus it *was* quite unseasonably cool outside. A little rainy, which was unfortunate because I had no umbrella, but at the same time, something of a gift from God because I was so hot that every tiny rain drop that hit my scorching, feverish skin instantly sizzled, steamed and promptly evaporated. *Trés bien.*

I sauntered into the *Galeries Lafayette* to looks of abject horror. I didn't care though: I just couldn't wait to take the coat off. I would stuff the bloody coat in the bin I was so sick of it. Bloody coat, bloody bloody . . . BLOODY HELL!

I looked in the mirror in the loos and couldn't believe my eyes. My entire neck and the bottom of my face – jawline, mouth, chin – were dyed a dark, bloodlike red. And not only that, when I opened the coat, my brand new cashmere jumper had tie-dyed itself into something unrecognisable. Pinkish blotches, all over, with bright red centres. It looked as though I had gunshot wounds all over my torso. And my legs! My jeans! Mottled red, worse down the seams and on the knees. I stared at the coat, which was hanging on the corner of a toilet door, sparkling with raindrops and dripping bright red water onto the tiles.

This was not good for the The Most Important Casting of My Life. I had a face that looked as though I'd been tearing into the open carcass of a recently killed antelope. My entire body was a tie-dye nightmare. Sweat was still coursing down my shins and pooling in my boots.

I used the complimentary liquid soap to try to wash my face, but the dye wouldn't shift. I needed flannels – I needed towels! My hands were red, thanks to keeping them dry in my pockets, my neck and chest were red, even the ends of my hair had a fetching pink tinge. What I really needed was to check into a hotel, just for an hour, and do a complete wash. But what hotel would have me? I decided to phone a friend. The only friend I had in Paris and a tenuous one at that, because he didn't sound too keen to help.

'Hey Jean-Bernard, it's me, Ruth.'

Jean-Bernard was one of the friends I had made in New York. Born to wealthy parents, he lived between New York and Paris and sometimes Italy, and just about wherever he wanted to live, really. 'I have an emergency, Jean-Bernard. You *have* to let me wash in your flat!'

'My flat?' he said. 'What is it, my flat?'

'You know, your apartment! In Paris! Jean-Bernard, this is a life and death situation. I'm completely red!'

'OK,' he said, 'but . . . it's not my apartment, you know? It's my mother's.'

'No, I didn't know, but please, I just need to use your bath. I've dyed myself red.'

'My mother,' said Jean-Bernard, 'she, you know, I can't just bring back girls.'

'Jean-Bernard I'm not a *girl*! I just need to wash in her bath! I've dyed myself red! Red, Jean-Bernard!'

There was a lengthy pause.

'Please, Jean-Bernard,' I said, feeling as though I'd landed myself in some kind of desperate movie, 'you're my only hope.'

Jean-Bernard's mother was in whatever the French version of the living room was – the *salon*? She was facing away from the doorway reading a book and so he snuck me past her and hurried me into the bathroom. It was all terribly posh.

'Listen to me,' he said. 'Don't use the towels, OK? Please, don't touch anything apart from the water, *d'accord*? It has to be like you were never here.'

'Gotcha,' I said.

Twenty minutes later and it was like a dreadful scene from an educational film about abattoirs. A veritable bloodbath. The tub was red. The taps were red. The floor around the bath was red and so was the smudge on the tiles where I'd levered myself down into it. The more water I added, the redder everything went. Some of the red water splashed down onto the white bath mat so I began to wash it under the tap, but the more I washed it, the redder that became too.

'Hurry,' said Jean-Bernard from outside the door. 'She won't stay in there forever, OK?'

The thought of Mrs Bernard coming into her bathroom now was horrifying. It was a murder scene, a cult ritual involving exsanguination. I was naked and mottled with stains, my hair was wet but not washed and my face was raw from scrubbing. I had managed to not use any of the white fluffy towels, which remained neatly folded over a rail, but the bathmat was ruined. I would have to take it with me to the casting, get it laundered and return it.

'A big bin bag, Jean-Bernard!' I hissed through the closed door. '*Un sac de poubelle!*'

Into the bin bag I forced my rolled-up coat, the soaking wet bath mat and my leather boots and socks. Fortunately, I had brought heels with me to change into at the casting, but I had also – oh, praise the absolute lord – slipped a pair of cheap old flip-flops into my bag. In case the weather turned hot and sunny.

I redressed in my sweaty clothes, still damp from the bathwater because I had dab-dried my body with a sopping bathmat, and I looked in the mirror. My hair was scrappy, my face was now pink all over, I had patches of irritation where I'd used hand soap to try to wash my skin. I was going to have to do my makeup on the Metro or else I'd be really late.

'You cannot get a taxi?' asked Jean-Bernard. The idea of taking the Metro wasn't something that appeared on his radar.

'It would take too long!' I said. 'I'm so, so late.'

I tried not to cry. The coat had cursed it all. Stupid non-budget mega-coat, stupid outfit planning. Obviously I was aware of precisely how fortunate I was to even be in Paris, with a potential life-changing job on the horizon that would earn me big bucks for standing about in a studio for a day or two, but at that particular moment, as I made way down the street in the rain, carrying a bin bag with my coat in and a wet bath mat that I had effectively stolen from my friend's mother, I didn't feel fortunate.

And I didn't feel at *all* fortunate as the heavens suddenly opened and the rain began to really hammer down. I had no umbrella and so I held the bin bag above my head, which was no mean feat considering it was about the same size and weight as one of those plastic-wrapped bales of hay. I pushed along the pavement in my cheap flip-flops, trying to keep my bag on my shoulder and my binbag shelter over my head, and then something bad happened. As if everything that had happened so far hadn't been quite bad enough. The sudden, extreme downpour had formed a small river that was racing down the middle of the pavement. It was twisting and furious, the little river, gathering up all of the mini streams that were pouring from the gutters, carrying bits of debris, empty plastic bottles and cigarette ends down onto the road. I momentarily stumbled, as well you might when trying to carry Hulk Hogan in a bag above your head in a monsoon, and in the split second I unclenched my toes, my left flip-flop slid off my foot. I watched, dumbfounded, as it sped away from me, carried by the rapids, reaching speeds of approximately ninety-five miles an hour before it even passed the pedestrian crossing. There was no point chasing it and so I just stood and silently observed. Watched as it hit the curb, flipped over to enter an even faster tributary of the new river, flew along the road between the tyres of a car, emerged the other side and disappeared abruptly through the gap in a drain.

*

The incident, which became widely known as 'Bloody Coat Day', left me feeling war-torn and slightly humiliated. The fact that I had appeared in the lobby of the headquarters of the biggest beauty brand in the world wearing only one flip-flop and carrying a bin bag of fabric over my head had not gone unreported. Ditto the information that the entire lower portion of my face had been dyed red, as though I had been the victim of a terrible stag-do prank. I had managed to sabotage what would have been biggest job of my career. It felt so final. Like another opportunity this big would never come along again.

'Babe,' said Texana the following week. 'You'll never guess what. I've just confirmed you for a job that is probably going to be the biggest job of your *whole career*.'

'The Paris beauty job?'

'No, babe,' said Texana, 'that particular superyacht has definitely sailed. I think that the fact you trailed sewage into their lobby on your bare feet—'

'Foot.'

'—bare foot,' said Texana. 'Whatever, babe, I wouldn't expect a call. Anyway, this is so much more amazing! It's shooting with David LaChapelle for the new Patrick Cox campaign!'

'Oh . . . wow. But I haven't done a casting for it.'

'No need,' said Texana. 'They want you and only you.'

I couldn't believe the turn of fate. One minute, a modelling pariah, banished from one of the world's biggest beauty brands. The next, confirmed to shoot a high fashion campaign with one of the most famous photographers in the world. Surely – because my life just did not work this smoothly – there had to be a catch.

'Now listen, my babe,' said Texana, 'you'll be totally naked for this shoot. But don't worry, they're only going to photograph you from the side. Nobody will see a thing.'

It was a definite negative, the nakedness element of the job, but this was a shoot with David LaChapelle. For a Patrick Cox campaign. What if this was my big chance? How naïve I'd been before now, to think that you could just become a supermodel overnight. *No, I thought, this is how things happen*. It was all coming together. The TV documentary would get me noticed – there'd be interviews and features and maybe even opportunities to get other TV work – and shooting with David LaChapelle would make me a cool new thing in the fashion world, suddenly desirable to all of those editors who had dismissively flicked through my portfolio, maybe even to the casting agent who'd told me to come back to him once I'd bound my breasts flat to my chest.

If I played my cards right, I could probably be supermodelling by the following spring! It was satisfying to know that all of my efforts had finally paid off: the long-haul travel, the hundreds of castings that had felt so pointless at the time, the dozens of test shoots where I'd been dressed up as a doll, or had been spray-painted green, or had spent three hours sitting inside the rim of a giant button pretending to be a Borrower. And I had jogged – twice – which must have made a difference, and had been balancing out the heavy partying of the summer season with eating at least one salad a week. And, possibly most impressively, I had finally made the biggest commitment to modelling that I could possibly have made, considering how attached to my family home I was: I had moved to London.

Only on weekdays, but still. I could do castings at 9am without having to leave home in the middle of my sleep cycle and I could turn up for early shoots – 7am, sometimes 6.30 – without looking as though I'd just been disturbed by a graverobber after a three-year stint in the soil. Pale-faced, wild-haired and with jet-black circles beneath my eyes, like a slightly shorter, less snazzily dressed version of *Beetlejuice*.

My quasi-move to London had been both prompted and facilitated by the unexpected offer from some close family friends: use of the cosy spare room at the back of their house on a lovely, leafy west London street in exchange for . . . absolutely nothing. You read that right: a room, in a nice part of London, with the safety and security that comes with living as part of a family, all completely for free. Why anyone, especially with a school-age kid already in situ, would offer to take in someone else's 'just out of the troubled teen years' daughter I have no idea, but my quiet gratitude would have no end.

Imagine suddenly sharing your bathroom with another adult, one who never remembers to squeegee the shower screen after using the shower and who has an annoying habit of hanging wet towels over the corners of doors to dry them off. Imagine being woken up by that same person when they try to tiptoe in at half past eleven, setting off the burglar alarm and noisily falling over the stack of *National*

*Geographic*s in the hallway. Pretending not to smell cigarette smoke when that person routinely cantilevers their entire upper body out of the spare bedroom sash window to smoke Marlboro Lights above the glass-roofed kitchen extension. Imagine all of this and then imagine also offering lifts into the city in the morning, warm conversation in the evening, enquiries into how castings went and where they were and which exact route you had to use to get there. The generosity they showed was simply off the scale.

And had I not had this kind offer, which I'm sure I thoroughly abused as any self-respecting young adult would – forgetting to say when I was going to rock up or depart, forgetting to feed the dog on time on more than one occasion and also nearly setting fire to some dry leaves in the gutter when a lit fag rolled down the roof during a drought – had I not had this place to stay, this refuge, I am absolutely certain that the rest of my life would have looked completely different.

Maybe the modelling career would have fizzled out, or I'd have ended up in – God forbid! – the model flat, or I'd have given up on the whole London idea and decided to go back to my law degree. I don't know. But what I'm sure of is this: had I not had this always-welcoming house to retire to at the end of a long day of castings, I'm not sure I'd have ever properly moved to London. Having this home-from-home eased the transition. I had my warm, feathered, familial nest at the weekends and I had my warm, feathered nest during the week too. In this way, I managed to maintain the soft embrace of a comfortable home life seamlessly, seven days a week – the gentle chatter, the kind laughter, the banal enquiries into each other's day. I threw myself into my new, weekday family as much as I relished in my original family at the weekends.

So yes, I had moved to London and my career had taken this sudden turn. I'd had a spate of bookings for high street campaigns that had been nice earners and my editorial work (still nearly always unpaid and with long hours, still nearly always in a freezing studio or 'super cool abandoned printing factory') was going from strength to strength. But this was different: this was the biggest job of my entire career. Yes, I'd be naked and I wasn't one hundred per cent sure about how I felt about that, but they were only shooting me from the side. Nobody, Texana had said, would be able to see a thing.

My mum had only been properly, properly annoyed at me a handful of times in my life. I'd no doubt irritated her repeatedly over the years but mums are good at hiding their irritation, it's just one of their superpowers. It goes without saying that one of those rare times when she didn't hide her irritation was when she phoned me to say that she'd happened to glance at a newspaper, only to see her daughter right there on the front page.

'Totally naked,' she said.

Which wasn't entirely true. OK, so I didn't have any actual clothes on as I straddled the lap of an innocent-looking Sophie Dahl for the Patrick Cox campaign, but I was wearing some rather fetching retro sweatbands as well as a delightful pair of spike-heeled sandals.

'I'm only naked from the side,' I replied desperately.

But even as I said it, I knew it was a lie. I'd been there in real life: being naked 'from the side' had felt exactly the same as being, well, naked. It had been a baptism by fire, the nakedness thing. Being unclothed on a photoshoot had turned out to be entirely different to being unclothed in the comfort of your own home. For a start, people wanted to do things with you, like add shine to your legs and strap shoes to your feet, and very soon, you found that you ended up in completely shameless positions – one foot on the stylist's knee and the other leg stretched into the hair and makeup area, for example, ready to be basted with MAC Strobe Cream.

And anyway, there was no 'only from the side' about it when it came to nakedness, and when I saw the photos in the newspapers – plural – there they were, the instantly recognisable curves of the peachy bottom, the slope of the pert breasts, all looking quite admirable, if I was going to be objective about it. It was a tennis-themed campaign, if anyone bothered to notice, and Sophie and I were perched on a bench in a cleverly constructed fake locker room. Sophie Dahl entirely clad in a towel looking slightly bashful and confused, me on top of her wearing just shoes and sweatbands, like a sport-obsessed nymphomaniac. *I love sex but I'll never forget about tennis!*

Was I proud or ashamed? I couldn't work it out. Nakedness was everywhere, editorially, so it wasn't as though I'd done something particularly groundbreaking or unusual. When it came to high fashion, nudity seemed to be exempt from the usual scorn and judgement poured upon, say, page three girls. Appearing nearly nude in

Vogue whilst adorned with three million quid's worth of diamonds was *not* the same as having your hooters out on page three. Apparently. The reason being, as far as I could fathom, that fashion models didn't tend to have large tits and so were therefore not really getting them out for the male gaze. In fact, the majority of editorial shoots where there was any breast showing used girls who were teetering on the edge of androgenous and had chests as flat as ironing boards. When you removed the sexy element, it seemed to make it OK.

But what if you did have sexy knockers? Was it bad to get them out if it was for fashion? If it was edgy, if it was skilled, if a photograph had been taken by a world-famous photographer, then wasn't it just . . . art? Nobody got their knickers in a twist about all the nudes in, say, the National Portrait Gallery. What had the parents of those Renaissance girls said when they'd casually dropped into the conversation that they'd just sat naked for a team of assistant painters for the entire day?

Had the parents shouted, 'You bloody what?' and taken up their swords, marched around to the painter's studio and brutally run the assistants through?

I just don't know. Maybe their mums would have been OK about it.

'Darling, that's wonderful! We love Botticelli's work. Did you make sure that your nipples were nice and perky and looking their best?'

'Mum! God! Ugh!'

'And what about your muff, darling? Was it waxed or au naturel?'

'I held a shell in front of it.'

'You held a shell in front it! That's wonderful darling, what fun.'

You had to wonder. What made one thing art and the other thing filth? Intended audience? Was I proud to be in a major fashion campaign or ashamed that my mum had been subjected to the shock of seeing her middle child naked (only from the side!) on the front of the newspaper?

Luckily, it was 2003 and yesterday's news really was the next day's chip paper and so we never needed to discuss it again. By the end of the week, there were no more stories about our cheeky little tennis tableau on the newsstands – the mini-scandal, once it had served its intended PR purpose, sank into the quicksand of unimportant histories along with all of the other trivial happenings. So quickly did the story disappear, in fact, that it made me realise just how hard non-famous people had to work to become and to stay famous. Not the ones who were famous because they had talent or were hugely successful – Julia Roberts, for example, or Brad Pitt, Kate Moss, Liam and Noel Gallagher – but the ones who wanted to be famous for not very much of a reason at all. They must have been exhausted. It was quite difficult to get in the paper, I thought. If shooting a big campaign with one of the biggest photographers in the world – virtually naked from the side – only earned you a couple of one-off mentions then imagine what you'd have to do to stay in the public eye long term.

My next small brush with fame came the following month when *This Model Life* finally aired in a three-part series and I started to be recognised in the street. It happened at least ten times, which was enough to give me a good taste of what life would be like if I was Mariah Carey. At the height of my fame, in week two, I was papped trying to go into a nightclub, by not just one photographer but four, all of them running backwards alongside me as I attempted to cross the pavement. It was a real Whitney Houston in *The Bodyguard* moment.

'Oi, love,' the first one said to me. 'Over here, love!' And then he said, 'What's her name?' to the second photographer, who was circumnavigating a bin in reverse whilst flashing his camera at me repeatedly.

'Don't know,' the second photographer said. 'What's she from, Jim? Did she get voted out early on *Big Brother*?'

'Something on the telly, I think,' photographer number three said. 'Something about models.'

'*My Modelling Strife*,' the fourth photographer shouted as he strode purposefully backwards, narrowly missing a Vespa that was propped up at the side of the road. 'It's a programme on Channel 4.'

Ah, the sweet smell of success.

In truth, though, I didn't feel as though the Channel 4 documentary had served me massively well. It was a gorgeously produced piece of film and gave a brilliant insight into the weird world of modelling, but I felt that it hadn't quite captured the person I knew that I really was, the person I'd constructed purely using my very own imagination. When the opening scenes appeared on the television screen, I had expected to see myself reflected back as the lithe-bodied, utterly glamorous goddess I knew I was, gliding elegantly through Tokyo airport before saying something pertinent and/or witty in a fine, sonorous voice. But instead, there was this sallow little shrimp who spoke in near-squeaks and wore outfits that looked as though they'd been put together by somebody who'd recently suffered serious head trauma. A denim pencil skirt with a corset – a corset! – that was so bedecked with ribbons it wouldn't have been out of place in the window of a fancy dress shop. Rubber clogs. A beige zip-up hoodie the exact shade of a World War Two-era prosthetic limb.

More than my physical appearance, though, I had been quite shocked by the way that the documentary had portrayed me as a very naïve, very poor, massively struggling model. Yes, it was true that I had created a debtometer to track my earnings in Tokyo because I owed so much money and, OK, so I couldn't put a full tank of petrol in my car, but I wasn't *struggling*. How very dare they! I had been booking campaigns and editorial shoots left, right and centre – Vivienne Westwood! Jigsaw! *Elle* magazine! *VOGUE*!

To make things even worse for my ego they'd counter-pointed this (entirely fictitious, if you asked me) young pauper character against the very rich, very successful, very statuesque supermodel Erin O'Connor. It was like having a mirror held up to my own inadequacies. New inadequacies that I wasn't previously aware of. Not only was I not quite tall enough, not quite thin enough and with a gap in my teeth that divided opinion, I now had an irritating voice, a strange forward-leaning walk that looked as though I was trying to battle against a gale-force wind and a dress sense that was even more terrible than I'd realised.

How was this television version of myself so completely different to the person I thought I was? Someone who was cool enough to be shot by a world famous photographer, naked from the side?

I was no stranger to having my perception of myself constantly messed with. In any one day, I could be told that I was too chunky by one editor but then a bit too thin by a catalogue client, two hours later. I had been on a close-up beauty shoot where the makeup artist had commented on my nose, saying that it was as cute as a button, but less than ten minutes after that I had heard the photographer complaining that it was unrefined and blobby. I was used to the rapid chopping and changing of opinion when it came to my physical appearance and keeping the resulting – inevitable – dysmorphia more or less under control, but this was different. Seeing how others saw you, watching yourself being observed through someone else's lens and then not truly recognising the person you were presented with in a neat little television package – that was potentially a whole new level of insecurity.

Fortunately, my little tennis player naked-from-the-side show had garnered quite a bit of interest from the fashion world and, in a fortuitous turn of events, my self-confidence was saved. I'd done a whole load of magazine shoots looking really quite sizzling and I rather liked this new me. I wasn't a grungey rock chick or a freshfaced innocent, I was a minxy little bombshell and it suited me just fine. For the first time in my career, nearly two years in, I suddenly felt that I had a little bit of control over my own destiny, the power to make people want to book me –

I had something that people wanted and that set me apart. That didn't require me to be poker-thin or ultra tall. I was edgy but I was also just a little bit sexy.

And it was no coincidence, I'm sure, that it was during this brave new era of spirited self-assurance and sexually charged studio shoots that I fell completely and utterly head over heels in love.

Chapter 12

Filthy Rich

For a fashion model with big ambitions, falling in love was a terrible idea. It had been Nadia, the merciless Russian cut-throat of New York, who had floated the idea of this particular pitfall to me. Though I'd only shared the SoHo apartment with her for a few weeks, she had nonetheless managed to find the time to gift me with a few pearls of her mercenary wisdom.

'Falling in love,' Nadia had said, one humid summer's afternoon, 'is terrible idea for model. First,' Nadia had continued, 'falling in love will make model fat.' She puffed out her impossibly sculpted face. 'Woman in love,' she continued, 'is woman who thinks mission is complete. And so this is what she does,' she said. 'She eats, eats, eats and then has big ass, and then woman wonders why her lover makes switch-over to Nadia.'

This particular lecture had started in response to me saying I had a boyfriend at home. I had only been half-listening to her, occupied as I was with trying to work out how to get my tri-band mobile to work. The man at the phone shop in London had promised that this new-fangled business phone would work outside of the continent, but it hadn't, and so I had found myself on the other side of the world with no practical way of calling home – or my boyfriend – unless I wanted to pay the eye-popping charges to use the apartment phone or stand in a public booth stuffing the machine with coins, quarter after quarter, like some demented slot machine addict.

'But why you call boyfriend back home?' she had pressed, when I'd said that I needed to be able to stay in touch. 'What is his use? He sends money?'

I'd shaken my head, concentrating on the tiny writing in the instruction booklet I'd received with my new, useless piece of technology.

'This boyfriend,' Nadia had continued, sensing an opportunity to expand on her lecture, 'he provides security, like Igor boyfriend-of-Nadia?'

'No,' I'd said. 'Nothing like that. I just like seeing him.'

'You see him?' Nadia said. 'You see him when Susan is in New York and he is in – where you say?'

'The Midlands.'

Who the hell is Susan? I thought.

'There is opportunity for loving?' said Nadia, 'When Susan is in New York, or Paris, or Susan is in Hong Kong? And this boyfriend is in Midlands?'

'Who's Susan?'

'Your name, it's not Susan?' Nadia had said.

'It's Ruth.'

'Huh,' she had shrugged, 'just as bad. But anyway, you tell me there is opportunity for love,' Nadia said, with no hint of apology or embarrassment, 'when Ruth is in New York and boyfriend is in Midlands?'

'No, of course not,' I had said. 'That would be impossible.'

The opening strains of Nelly's 'Hot in Herre', the big hit of the summer, had floated up from the street far below.

'Then is completely pointless,' Nadia had said. 'Is prison sentence without guard benefits. Is best find boyfriend with uses – Igor is bad lover but has good motorcycle. Is very good when lots of castings, lots of shows. Is very fast.'

She had paused for a moment to watch me struggle with my opened-out page of instructions, its bible-thin paper and miniscule font.

'And I will tell to you one more thing,' she had said, obviously on a bit of a roll. 'Fall in love and you will soon hate travel. Oh!' she had exclaimed, throwing her head back like a fainting damsel and fanning her forehead with a flappity hand. 'Oh, no, Mr Armani, sorry but I do not want your nice job on runway – love, *love* is most important thing for me.'

She had then ceased with the hand flapping to pick up an imaginary telephone. 'Oh, hello my booker at agency,' she'd acted out, 'no, I do not want amazing opportunity to stay in Paris and get rich, is too far distance from my love.'

I had fundamentally disagreed with her at the time, though I hadn't said this out loud. I didn't have a death wish. Why the hell, I had thought, would you even think about your modelling career trajectory if you were currently experiencing the exquisite sensation of freewheeling into the abyss of total lust and infatuation? It would have taken a very driven, laser-focused sort of person to behave that way. Nadia, basically. Because you couldn't help falling in love once it started to happen, could you? You might try to delay it, to deny it – you could even try to dodge it by completely dismissing your own feelings – but if love had its sights set on you, then surely there was very little that could be done about it.

A whole year later and Nadia's words still vaguely floated around in my memory. I had left my old life, my old friends and my old boyfriend and I was starting completely anew. I was shooting brilliant things and starting to make just a little bit of money, I was jetting off here and there and everywhere, and I was really starting to be good at my job. *Maybe Nadia was right*, I thought, *maybe falling in love is bad for business*. If your job description largely consists of 'staying thin and living out of a suitcase' then was it such a marvellous idea to do the very thing that would make you want to drink copious amounts of red wine, eat shepherd's pie and cosy up on the sofa each and every night?

I wasn't sure, but I was about to find out.

When I saw him at the party, he looked as though he had just jumped off the back of a military truck: he was dressed in full army fatigues with big black boots and a combat jacket – he even had a set of silver dog tags around his neck.

'Have you signed up,' I asked him, 'or did you come in fancy dress?'

He did look quite hot as a soldier, actually, but then again

I had always thought he was pretty hot as a photographer too. Hot full stop. Tall, dark, handsome – a well-worn cliché but he ticked all of those boxes and it would be remiss of me not to mention it – and with the most amazingly white and even teeth that I'd ever seen on a non-American. Had I been choosing by looks, breeding and vitality alone, like a farmer at market, then I'd have hitched him to my wagon without a second thought. As it stood, there were some things about him that I couldn't quite come to terms with. The fact that he rode a tiny Vespa instead of driving a car, for example, or that he wore enormous vintage Pucci sunglasses that made him look like a seventies porn baron. It was all so confident and individual and so . . . London. I had grown up in a place where often it felt as though the ultimate goal was to have a nice motor and to try to fit in with the crowd, and here was this guy riding about the place looking like a Hollywood extra on a clown bike. And what was with all the camo print?

'How can you not like camo print?' he said, looking down at his outfit and trying not to laugh.

Ah, Filthy Rich, I thought, *you are so very, very lovely.*

For yes, it was he. The photographer who had booked me for that very first shoot, almost two whole years before. The one inspired by the down and dirty punk era and wild-eyed antics of Sid Vicious's girlfriend. This was to be the man I fell head over heels in love with.

We hadn't got together on that very first shoot (amazingly, for nothing says romance like a tragically murdered drug addict) and we hadn't got together on the second shoot either. Or the third, or the fourth.

179

By the time we saw each other at the party, which had been thrown by David LaChapelle to celebrate the Patrick Cox campaign – the gift that just kept on giving! – it was almost two whole years after that fateful shoot. We were at least finally on the same relationship page – both single – and his outré Pucci sunglasses and lack of grown-up car no longer seemed weird to me. The stars were aligned and his opinion of me was still entirely positive and unblemished. He was not to know that I was about to give him the runaround for a number of months, letting him repeatedly take me out (for a quick drink, a bite to eat) but never committing. It was a time of blissful innocence and naivety because he had also not yet witnessed how ridiculously messy I could get when I'd had too much to drink; this party, as it turned out, was to be a sort of initiation ceremony.

Maybe this all puts me in a bad light, admitting that I gave him the runaround, but in truth I was just a bit of a hot mess. It was 2003, I was twenty-two and I was still trying to extricate myself from the web of my old life and all of the things and people in it – all of the elements that had been my comfort blanket of deep familiarity. I was trying to build a new life in a new city whilst doing one of the most batshit crazy jobs on the planet. It was really quite scary. In a relatively short amount of time, I had gone straight from school into university and from the second year at university into this mad, incredibly adult world of fashion and modelling.

I was careering about in this new life arena almost entirely unsupervised; my agency was looking out for me, and out of all the agencies in the world they were the most nurturing and compassionate and truly committed to making sure that their models were looked after and safe… But ultimately, I was at liberty to be a total loose cannon if I wanted to be. Which was probably why, at the tail end of the David LaChapelle party, I found myself in the toilets at a West End club with my knickers around my ankles and a sanitary bin on my lap, trying to decide which end (if not both) the night's indulgences might come flying out of. On the scale of things, it was a pretty tame scenario; some people would have come off a lot worse had they been let loose in London at the age of twenty-two with a growing disposable income, a modest taste of minor fame and an absolutely cracking pair of tits.

I was content with merely consuming excess booze, which was the trademark vice of girls who had come of age in the 1990s. Growing up in the ladette era, with Sara Cox and Denise Van Outen downing pints, and with its boisterous, rowdy female presenters who were easily as funny and confident as their male counterparts: it gave us balls. For most of us, drinking to excess was a perfectly acceptable way of life and no one was telling us otherwise. Throw in visible thongs, low-slung jeans and the excessive use of the middle finger and you had yourself a whole generation of women who believed that they'd finally achieved sexual equality. Until they went on to have children a couple of decades later and realised that being able to hold your drink didn't necessarily equate to *having it all*. Girl Power!

'Hello,' said Filthy Rich, his head popping up over the top of the toilet door. 'Are you OK down there?'

It's testament to just how drunk I was that I was hardly even bothered that Filthy Rich was bearing witness to my vulnerable, partially undressed state.

'You can't stay in here all night,' he said, dangling his arms over the door.

I wondered, briefly, how it was that he was even managing to look over the top of the toilet door. He was tall, but he wasn't a giant, for crying out loud. Tops of toilet doors were high up for a reason. Did the man have no boundaries? And what was he standing on? Stilts? Maybe his army outfit gave him special tactical skills. Perhaps he was attached to the other side of the door with suckers.

'I can't move,' I said. 'I don't want to see anyone.'

'Elton John's gone, now,' said Filthy Rich. 'So you're safe to come out.'

Oh God. Elton John. I had spent at least two or three minutes, immediately before my exit to the toilets, leaning quite heavily against a man on a leather banquette who'd been wearing a very jazzy hat. He'd not responded massively well to my enthusiastic attempts at conversation and had even tried to remove himself from my clingy person as I regaled him with some anecdotal material about Philip Treacy the hatmaker and a shoot I'd just done for *iD* magazine.

'They used me for the hat shoot,' I'd slurred at the man in the hat, 'me specially, because recently I was on the telly and so now I'm just a little tiny bit famous.'

Bloody hell. My stomach lurched, my head span; I could hear the toilet attendant charging someone fifty pence for a spritz of deodorant.

'I'm going to take you home,' said Filthy Rich. 'You can sleep on my bed and I'll sleep on the sofa.'

That seemed like a sensible idea. I couldn't even contemplate going back to the little spare room in west London at . . . what time was it anyway? I tried to focus on my watch face . . .

The horrors began before I even opened my eyes the following morning. There was a stiff, plasticky covering around my face that was rebounding my sour breath back at me and causing drops of condensation to run down my cheeks. Was I in a body bag? Had someone kidnapped me? Was a serial killer storing me in his cellar for later use? I searched for a zip to pull down but was relieved to find that the covering simply moved away when I pushed at it, for it was just a bedsheet. A bedsheet made of scratchy, unyielding canvas with a print of green, splodgy camo . . .

'Morning,' said Filthy Rich.

He was perched at the top of the stairs to the bedroom with a glass of water in one hand and a can of Coke in the other. I was on his futon, fully dressed beneath a camouflage-print sheet, a camouflage-print duvet cover and some sort of throw made from what looked like the remains of an army-issue parachute. For God's sake.

'Muh,' I said. 'What time is it?'

My entire body had steamed itself inside the man-made fibres and I felt drenched in sweat. The mascara on my eyelashes had melted and then redried, effectively gluing my lids together, and on the floor beside the futon lay a half-full packet of Marlboro Lights, my bra and a lighter, sitting inside the bowl of the right-hand cup.

'Half ten,' said Filthy.

'Shit!' I said. 'I was supposed to be at a really important casting at nine! I feel so sick. Have I been sick? How did I even get here?'

I shakily slid a cigarette from the packet and lit it up, not even stopping to consider whether or not the bedsheets might spontaneously catch fire due to the fact that they were evidently made from 99 per cent petrochemical waste.

'You would have stayed all night in the toilets if I hadn't torn you away,' he said, passing me the water. I gulped it down and then flicked my cigarette ash into the empty glass. 'You were very, very drunk.'

'Bloody hell,' I said. 'Well, at least there was a soldier on duty to return me to base camp.'

How was Filthy Rich so together and mature, I wondered? Granted, he was over ten years older than me but still. Even if I lived to a hundred I couldn't imagine ever being so . . . grown-up. He had his trendy industrial live-work studio, for a start, right at the top of a warehouse conversion in Shoreditch. So what if 2003 Shoreditch was a bit grimy with no proper shops and questionable transport links? A pad was a pad. And he kept it all so immaculately organised, with no dirty dishes lying about in the kitchen and all of his clothes hung neatly on rails behind floor-length curtains. Why? Why on earth did he do this, voluntarily, when there was nobody to force him do it? The mind boggled.

I was no stranger to his studio because I'd done photoshoots there quite a few times, but I had to admit that it was a novelty to be lying on the futon staring upwards at the exposed beams of the mezzanine ceiling, listening to him clattering around in a cupboard and muttering something about people who didn't use ashtrays. As I did a quick damage assessment check on my mind and body (results: searing headache, mild sore throat, reasonably intact pride and one blister due to my new high-heeled boots) I realised that I felt really very at home on that futon. Safe.

'Babe,' said Texana, 'where are you? You had a request casting at 9am!'

It had taken me until the fourteenth ring to even find my phone, buried as it was between the many layers of Desert Storm tent canvas.

'I'm so hungover,' I said. 'Sorry.'

'Me too, babe,' said Texana. 'I didn't leave until three and that was only because security asked me to stop leaning against Elton John.'

'You were leaning on him?' I said. 'I was leaning on him too! I wonder whether it was you who was leaning on him from the other side?'

'Was it you telling him about hats?' said Texana.

'Yeah,' I said.

'Babe, can you get to this casting for eleven? The client is waiting.'

'Eleven?' I scrabbled in my bag for my A–Z. 'In Battersea Park? I don't think I can. I'm in Shoreditch. I stayed at Filthy Rich's. The photographer.'

'Don't tell them that!' shouted Filthy from downstairs, his head still in a cupboard. 'Make sure you tell her that I spent the whole night on the sofa.' There was a clatter as he evidently found what he had been looking for. 'Or they'll think I took advantage of you.'

I wouldn't mind you taking advantage of me, I suddenly thought. *That doesn't sound too bad at all.*

You might be wondering why he was called Filthy Rich and I have to admit that at this point in time I wasn't absolutely sure. In reality, there were two obvious explanations and neither were the sort of thing I wanted to casually drop into conversation. The first school of thought was that he was dripping in wealth. The second was that he was just pure filth – as in dirty – and seeing as though he was one of the cleanest and tidiest people I'd had the fortune to meet, it was wildly apparent that if he *was* nicknamed filthy due to some sort of personal habit, then it was highly likely that it would be of a sexual nature and not because he was somehow unsanitary.

But how to ask? Plunging on in with 'Are you massively wealthy?' seemed embarrassingly crass and 'Do you do terribly naughty stuff to women in bed?' just felt far too much like encouragement, or an invitation. There was no way of finding out. Even the bookers at the agency had been divided over the origins of Filthy Rich's name.

'Apparently he's from old money, darling,' Daz had said when I'd first asked, the day before the Nancy Spungen shoot. 'His father is some kind of landowner on the south coast.'

'Not true,' said Lewis, who was another booker on the New Faces team. 'It's because he does devilish things in bed. I've heard it on the grapevine.'

Lewis had paused his typing to look up at me with a

smirk. I had smiled back, unsteadily. Bloody hell, I'd only been modelling for a day and I'd just agreed to do a shoot with a man who may or may not have had sexual proclivities so renowned he'd been named for them.

'Ignore Lewis, darling,' Daz had said, handing me a piece of paper with Filthy Rich's studio address written on it. 'Lewis is just obsessed with sex.'

'Stinking rich or filthy dirty,' Lewis had said, 'either way, he's cute.'

So we'd all been none the wiser back then and we were all none the wiser now, as I hobbled down his stairs made from scaffolding to see what delights my toilet trip would unveil.

'Do you need a lift to Battersea?' he said, as I crossed the floor of the studio, back hunched against the full weight of my hangover.

'Only if it's by helicopter,' I answered. I shut the bathroom door behind me.

You'd never catch me on that stupid Vespa scooter. Ridiculous contraption. How anyone could think that it was a good idea to ride around a busy city on something that looked as though it had been stolen from a travelling circus was beyond me. It was noisy, it was absurdly tiny and it was almost definitely a death trap. A lift on the Vespa? Over my dead body.

We did Old Street to Battersea in twenty-four minutes flat. *What wizardry is this?* I marvelled, as the little scooter weaved its way through traffic and sped over bridges. No having to scurry into the underground, no descent into the stinking belly of London, with its floors carpeted in discarded *Metro* papers and the stale wind blowing out of its dark tunnels. No standing beneath someone else's armpit in a lurching carriage, no trying to avoid the unwavering, aggressive stare of the man sitting opposite with his arms folded tight and his shaven head prickling with stubble. Just the rush of fresh air as we noisily charged along, my arms clamped tightly around the waist of my knight in shining armour (son of a major landowner, saver of the day), engine thrumming wildly beneath my—

This was how it all started. More or less. The Grand Rich and Ruth Runaround Tour of 2003, a highly tense sporting event in which both contestants had to simultaneously be on the same team and also play against one another. An event famed for its unfair advantages, unlevel playing field and cruel twists of fate, in which one contestant (Rich) had to try to decode mixed signals coming from the other contestant (Ruth) whilst walking the perilous tightrope of playing it cool but not too cool.

This sporting event continued for many months, seeing us through the spring and almost into the summer, until one fateful night when the games reached an important climax, a climax that almost finished off the Rich and Ruth match for good.

We had been out for a bite to eat and he had, for the first time, invited himself back to my place. My place, it should be noted, was now a small bedroom in a flat in a not very desirable part of Hackney that I'd just moved in to with my new best friend (who was always away – that model life!) and her friend (who was also always away – that stylist life!), and that had contained a futon, a set of white metal IKEA lockers and a wardrobe that wasn't big enough to handle more than my coat. Granted, it was the infamous dark red fur coat of Paris nightmares, which would have filled a small shipping container, let alone a wardrobe, but still. Space was tight.

So tight, apparently, that the only place for Filthy Rich to put himself was under the covers of my futon.

'I'm getting in,' he said.

'You're already in,' I answered.

This situation was far from ideal. He had very obviously decided that enough was enough and that if anything was ever going to happen with us then this was the night. He was clearly at the very end of his tether and could bear it no more – if I didn't want him now then, at least he'd know and then that was that.

But here was the thing: it wasn't that I was *never* going to sleep with him, I just couldn't sleep with him that night. Not only did I have raging cystitis, I had a dodgy-feeling stomach from the coconut milk in the Thai soup I'd eaten an hour or so before and I knew that I was just about to get my period. Because I was about to get my period, I had a couple of massively painful cyst-like spots coming up under my skin, one under my chin and one in the crease just below my nose, and as well as an ulcer inside my lower lip, I'd developed a weird case of crackly skin in the corners of my mouth.

There was something wrong with pretty much every orifice and so, unless he had some weird earhole penetration fetish (*Oh my God, imagine if that was the devilish thing he liked to do in bed!*) there was no way that sex was ever going to be on the agenda. Or kissing. I felt like a diseased toad and so I did what any normal girl would do in this situation: rather than communicate discreetly and kindly that perhaps it wasn't the perfect time for intimacy, especially the first go at it together, I dressed for bed in a way that could only suggest an absolute and vehement rejection of sexual intercourse of any kind. I put on layers of clothing that not only discouraged the idea of reaching out with a loving touch but created an actual physical barrier against it.

'Why are you wearing a cagoul to bed?' he asked, as I slipped beneath the duvet in the dark.

'I'm cold,' I answered and assumed the plank position, facing away from him towards the curtainless window with my buttocks clenched tightly and my arms clamped straight down at my sides. Across the street, I could see the windows of another block of flats, some of them lit warmly, some of them dark. Was anyone else lying rigidly on their futon wearing seven layers of clothing because they hadn't yet developed their communication skills adequately, I wondered?

'It's May,' said Filthy Rich. 'What's . . . is this . . . are you wearing a fleece underneath it? For God's sake!'

He turned on the bedside light and got out of bed. I was at once surprised and – I'll admit it – slightly aroused to see that he was stripped down to his underwear, but before I could think of an appropriate comment to make, he had dressed and pulled his shoes on and his hand was on the handle of the bedroom door.

'Look,' he said, 'I'm just going to go.'

Don't go, I thought, but I didn't say it out loud, and after a few long moments of silence he went.

If this was a romcom, I thought, turning to face the window again, *then I'd probably go after him now and kiss him in the street*. But it wasn't a romcom and I couldn't go after him because about ten seconds after he'd shut the front door, the full force of the coconut milk came into effect. I legged it to the bathroom, shedding layers of Regatta outerwear as I went, realising as I Klinsmann'd myself towards the toilet bowl that I'd really and truly cocked things up.

Chapter 13

The Epiphany

Three things happened the next day. The first was that I had a bit of an epiphany. It wasn't quite an angels singing, shaft of heavenly light bursting through the ceiling sort of epiphany, but then again, it wasn't really the right time or place for that. Seeing as though I was working for a department store at their autumn/winter press event, showcasing fashion and homewear launches for the upcoming seasons. It wasn't the most demanding of jobs, wearing an unoutrageous outfit and hanging about near the bath towels, but still. I don't think the clients would have been massively impressed had I experienced some sort of orgasmic biblical meltdown right in the middle of the new season handbags display.

I hadn't ever done a press event before and it seemed slightly off-key to be doing one now, just when things with my modelling career were really starting to take off. I currently had a six-page (very naughty, semi-naked) spread in *Arena* magazine, yet here I was about to spend the day being an actual human mannequin, shifting my weight from foot to foot and smiling benignly at anyone who happened to look my way.

The client was busy organising people, pointing at cardboard backdrops that needed straightening and clothes rails that were as yet unfilled. The three-storey event space had been magically transformed into a leaf-strewn wintery wonderland with bare-branched trees in huge terracotta pots, garlands of pinecones strewn from the ceilings and enormous vases filled with decorative twig arrangements. I couldn't help thinking that the cost of the twig arrangements alone was probably multiple times my fee, but I supposed that we were about to perform similar duties and so it was only fair. Stand straight, look wooden, try not to snag anyone as they brush past.

'If you could just pop on this dress from the autumn/winter collection,' said the client, who had a bleating voice and short, curly, off-white hair. Like a sheep. 'Just the dress, and then the brown leather boots and the beige cashmere coatigan . . .'

Coa-oa-oa-tigan.

It was the middle of May but unseasonably hot – too hot to be wearing a dress, boots and a coatigan. But then again, the night before, I'd gone to bed wearing a fleece and a cagoul, so who was I to complain? It was obviously karma.

'Then just hang about by the homewares, if you please could,' baa'd the client. 'There are some cushions on the three-seater velvet sofa that contrast really nicely with your dress, so if you wanted to you could always . . .' She paused, as though what she was about to suggest was somehow deviant or illegal.

'Sit on the sofa?' I ventured.

'Would you mind?' said the client. 'I know it's a bit boring.'

Would I mind? Like hell I would. I was undergoing period cramps so violent my eyebrows kept shooting upwards and I had barely slept six hours thanks to the previous night's Thai Soup Coconut Explosion. Sitting on a sofa and nicely contrasting with some cushions was, at that moment, my dream job.

'I don't mind,' I said, trying to look as martyr-like as I possibly could.

And it was as I reclined there on my sofa, pretending to be a dummy so that none of the editors would come over and speak to me, that I had the aforementioned epiphany: I had been dithering when it came to Filthy Rich because he was just too good to be true. I wasn't used to it. I simply couldn't believe that a man could be that pleased to see you, could be that genuinely interested in everything about you – your thoughts, your plans, your past – and I hadn't been aware that someone else could make you feel so excellent and so valued and so completely worthwhile. It was all totally beyond my realm of experience. After my recent relationship history, I'd have been happy just to be with a guy who could see me in daylight hours and who wouldn't throw a coat over my head if a member of his extended family walked past, but this was a completely different level of happiness. I was so delighted by this epiphany, this realisation that I could potentially exist at this whole new level of happiness, that I ate three Pret half-baguettes with tuna mayonnaise and an entire bag of Percy Pigs on my lunch break.

The second thing that happened that day, whilst I was lounging amongst the contrast cushions, was that someone unexpected appeared at the event and, like a Ghost of Christmas Past, forced me to reflect on my own behaviour. And when I say forced, I mean . . . forced. In she walked, the straight-talking editor who was also one of Filthy's best friends, her hair a shock of platinum and her skin so heavily fake-tanned she was the same colour as the pinecones. She was wearing leopard print trousers, leopard print sandals and a leopard print top and proceeded to help herself to a glass of prosecco from a tray near the door.

'Don't mind if I do,' she said, before turning to examine a rail of hot pink faux-fur bomber jackets and turquoise sequinned dresses.

If I stay incredibly still, I thought, *she will just glide on past me and be none the wiser*. She was the last person I wanted to see today, of all days; she'd grilled me only the week before about my intentions towards her friend and now here we were again, after I'd worn a cagoul to bed, brushed him off and then uncaringly let him leave.

What if he's told her? I thought. I watched her take a second glass of prosecco as she placed down the first. *It will all be fine. She's heading for the owl-shaped toiletry bags and russet-toned flannels.*

'Oi!' she shouted as she spotted me on the sofa. She padded towards me like a radioactive wildcat. 'What's with you putting all of the fucking clothes on then?'

'Oh,' I said. 'He told you then?'

'What are you on about?' she said, narrowing her eyes. 'He told me what?'

'Rich told you about all the clothes I put on.'

'No, he didn't,' she said. 'I was just wondering why you had on so many clothes when it's about forty-five fucking degrees outside, but pray tell.'

I had to relay absolutely everything.

'A cagoul?' she said, draining her prosecco. 'Didn't it rustle under the duvet?'

'A bit.'

'Fuck's sake,' she said. 'Listen to me, right? You need to make up your mind about him. This has gone on too fucking long.' She put her empty glass into my hand and pulled up on the waistband of her leopard print trousers, shifting her weight from foot to foot, like a boxer getting ready for a new round. Ding-ding!

'Be with him,' she said, 'or let him go.'

And with that, she was gone herself, off to stalk through another part of the fashion jungle.

And the third thing – well, let's just say that the combination of 'epiphany' and 'stern talking-to from a leopard-clad East End pocket rocket' was an effective one and most certainly paved the way for the finale.

That evening, at around eleven thirty, I asked Filthy Rich to come and collect me from outside the Hackney flat I'd slept in for a total of three nights (and would never sleep in again, making it more expensive per night than a two-bedroom suite at the Ritz) and the rest was history.

I say I asked him to come and collect me – it was more

of a rescue mission. It had started with a dried-up dog poo next to my bed (left there by the resident puppy, who had evidently been strolling about the place finding interesting new places to shit) and it had ended with two very drunk girls coming home and playing Justin Timberlake at full volume, right through my bedroom wall. I was so very tired that night. Already wracked with various period-related pains and still suffering the dull ache of the mild cystitis case I'd not quite managed to get rid of, I now had to deal with the emotional exhaustion of my epiphany and all of the thoughts that had followed it. And on top of all of that, I had to get up at 7am to do a lingerie shoot.

I'd heard them coming from the bus stop, singing a line from 'Cry Me a River' over and over again, their voices filling the dark street.

'Oh – oh!' they sang. 'The damage is done so I guess I'll be leaving!'

A dog barked, a car alarm bleeped momentarily and then stopped; there was the distant, oppressive roar of an aeroplane tearing its way through the sky.

'Oh, oh!' sang the girls, taking turn with the 'ohs'. 'The damage is done so I guess I'll be leaving!'

'Shut the fuck up!' shouted a man from the flats across the way.

I put my pillow over my head.

'OH, OH, the damage is done so I guess I'll be leaving!' The voices were close now, right outside of the flats.

'If you don't shut it,' screeched a woman's voice from somewhere down at the end of the road, 'I'm going to come down there and beat the shit out of you, you stupid bitches.'

THE EPIPHANY

This was one of the more desirable streets in Hackney, the estate agent had said. Hackney was on its way up.

'Oh, OH, the damage is done so I guess I'll be leaving!' the girls sang cheerfully, woozily. There was a laugh and a clatter as a bin full of cans crashed over onto the road. *At least they are moving along*, I thought. *All will be quiet again soon.*

'Oh, OH, the damage is done so I guess I'll be leaving!' they sang, getting closer.

'That's it, you fucking bitches,' screamed the woman from down the road. 'I'm coming for you.'

I peered out onto the street. There was potentially about to be a double murder and I can't say that I was too upset about it. At least I'd get some peace. But to my annoyance, I realised that one of the girls was my flatmate, the stylist, and the other was her friend. I couldn't allow them to be murdered.

They were absolutely rip-roaring drunk, standing outside the flats smoking cigarettes and emptying the contents of a leather bag onto the pavement.

'Keys!' shouted one of them. 'I've found them!'

'Thank fuck for that,' said the neighbour across the way, angrily sliding his balcony door closed.

The party continued when they finally got inside the flat, having spent at least four minutes ricocheting along the walls of the corridor outside. When I realised that there was no sign of it stopping, I called for emergency help. Now, you might think that this was all very convenient, me having my 'oh I do actually really like him' epiphany on the very day I needed someone to SAS extricate me from my own flat, but that is simply the way it had panned out.

The phrase 'panned out' doesn't scream romance but oh God, it was. So romantic.

Because once I'd realised, that day, that I wanted to be with him, the fact that he cruised around to pick me up in the dead of night and took me off to blissful silence and a clean bed that an animal hadn't defecated next to . . . well. He could have given me a fireman's lift from a burning building and I'd not have been any more grateful. Or delighted. Because I was there, with him, and I would never be without him again. Twenty-two years later, after sixteen years of marriage, two children and seven house moves, I would still remember the feeling that I had that night and it would be crystal clear – the feeling that I was exactly where I was supposed to be, that I was home.

At least, it would be home once I'd moved in my stuff and infiltrated his organised, masculine space with some of my most pointless-yet-necessary possessions. A Georgian-style four-storey wooden dolls' house, my television from 1995 (that still handily had Teletext), the red furry coat that I hadn't worn since that terrible day in Paris, my midi hi-fi system that played both CDs and cassette tapes that I'd had since starting my first job at McDonald's in 1996. I didn't own much, because I had only just left home, but what I did own: priceless. There was Rich, thinking he'd been happy in his industrial-style warehouse conversion studio, with his wall of vintage metal swimming pool lockers and his bedroom made from scaffolding, but I like to think that my home décor contributions gave the place a bit of an eclectic lean. For who didn't want a five-foot-tall dolls' house next to their telly when they were a grown man of thirty-three years of age?

My old life was very seamlessly melded into my new life and things were, without getting all vomit-inducing about it, quite marvellous. Everyone was young, we were always out – at The Cantaloupe, or The Bricklayers, or Charlie Wright's (which everyone called Charlie Wrong's, for a variety of reasons) – and then, when we'd had enough, we'd rent a DVD from the twenty-four-hour petrol station up the road and hide inside, ignoring the buzzer when friends tried to call up.

Ah, blissful union. Falling in love. It was nothing like Nadia had predicted; it had not been a terrible idea. Work was booming, my weight was steady and my boyfriend, thankfully, had not made the switch to a woman with a smaller ass. Yes, parting for the many jobs abroad was sweet sorrow, but no opportunity had been turned down in the name of love. Yet.

But there was one – potentially catastrophic – side-effect to being in love that Nadia had overlooked. Perhaps because she hadn't been the type to consider non-practical matters of the heart – i.e. other people's feelings – it hadn't occurred to her, but there was another aspect of a model's job that potentially presented big problems in a relationship. This was the fact that models spend a fair whack of their time in varying degrees of undress, making love with their eyes to camera-wielding men (and women) whose job it is to capture this person on film looking their most tantalising best. Men and women who literally transform their subject and produce imagery that ultimately seduces the end user into wanting something. Whether it is a fourteen-year-old sneaking looks at his mum's lingerie catalogue or a woman staring at a welly boot advertisement in the London Underground as she waits for the tube, a model is there to spark people's desires. Desire for the new shoes, the better convection oven, the bigger car or a smaller arse; desire for clearer skin, thinner legs or simply for the grass that seems altogether greener on the other side.

And to create that seduction, that desire for people to want something, there needs to be some sort of rapport between photographer and model. I don't mean sexual tension, though that is sometimes the case (always brilliant for relationships, a bit of extra-curricular sexual tension!) but an understanding. A sense of professional respect, or a genuine history of friendship, or a shared motivation to produce some brilliant images. Or, at the very least, just a mutual inclination to get the job done and dusted and get the hell out of there.

For the most part, these shoots would present no problem for a loving couple who had no reason to be plagued by trust issues. A model wearing red dungarees and yellow waders, holding aloft a plastic carp and smiling inanely didn't tend to be anything that anyone would get massively het-up about. But take off the dungarees, fling away the plastic carp and lay that same model down on a sheepskin rug, *Playboy* 1967 style? Now, you might have had a problem getting your head around things. Especially if she kept the yellow waders on.

I hadn't been lying on sheepskin rugs wearing yellow waders but I had been folding myself languorously into chairs and onto beds and over the tops of stools wearing little else apart from $2,000 boots and necklaces so priceless they came with their own security details. I had also been shooting a lingerie campaign in which I wore nothing but an oversized velvet bow. (Seemed counterintuitive from a marketing point of view, but hey, who was I to argue?) I'd been dressed as a sexy batgirl, worn a full latex bodysuit for a TV casting and done more shoots than I could count wearing lacy bra sets, glamorous swimsuits and little silk nighties with matching shorts. I went on with my work, developing quite the little sex-kitten character (put that persona in your pipe and smoke it, New York agent) and Rich carried on with his work, taking portraits and shooting fashion features with other girls, no doubt being just as charming with them as he'd been with me on the shoots we had done together. It felt pretty even and balanced, the relationship, and our jobs held no surprises for one another – he'd been there on my very first shoot, for crying out loud! There were no secrets, no mysteries and we were both chilled, content and free from insecurities. It was all under control.

Or so I thought.

Reader: I married him. (Later.)

Chapter 14

I'm Drunk and I'm Not Wearing Knickers

'I'm filming with Jude Law today,' I said to Rich, before he'd even managed to have a wake-up coffee. It was 9am and I'd just put the phone down to my agency. The sky was stormy and dark outside and a hard, autumnal rain was hammering down at the studio windows. '*With Jude Law*!'

So great was my excitement that I'd been booked to shoot photos that might appear in an actual film, with an actual film star, I didn't even stop to see Rich's reaction. Perhaps if I had, I might have been able to do some early damage control, but I didn't. I woke him up screaming, told him that I was about to go and film with one of the most famous, most sexy actors of the moment and then I said: 'And it's shooting in lingerie! Agent Provocateur!'

At this point, all of the blood had most likely drained

from his face, but he managed to strangle out a few words.

'Who's shooting it?'

It could have been anyone shooting the pictures. Some vanilla catalogue guy who just clicked and got the job done; maybe one of those film-set photographers who roam about behind the scenes and shoot candid snaps in black and white. It could even have been one of Rich's friends, which may have helped with what was about to unfold. But no. The photographer shooting the pictures was Rankin, current *enfant terrible* of the photography world, famed for his brilliant, twisted imagination.

I had worked with Rankin before and he had always been the perfect gentleman (more considerate and respectful than most, in fact) but at that time, if you were shooting with Rankin then you could almost guarantee that the resulting photos would sit in one of the following categories: sexy, outrageous or raw. Probably all three.

'Rankin?' said Rich. 'Right.'

He went out for his coffee that morning and took an umbrella. It didn't really compute that he'd left, so busy was I doing an emergency leg shave and Immac-ing the hair from my entire pubic region, just in case the underwear was sheer, but when I went to get in the car that the studio had sent it occurred to me that Rich never took an umbrella anywhere. That there was only one reason he would take an umbrella and that was if he was planning to take a long, long walk in the never-ending rain.

In fairness, I wasn't totally oblivious to his pain. Once in the back of the car, shoes kicked off and legs stretched out, I thought about how he hadn't seemed massively ecstatic when I'd woken him up with my triple whammy newsflash. Jude Law! Lingerie! Rankin! I considered that maybe my bedside manner had been quite abrupt, what with all the excitement, and that my delivery of the news had been something akin to an optician bursting out with 'YOU HAVE CANCER OF THE EYES!' during a routine contact lens fitting. Just minding your own business, thinking you're going to have a good day and then *BAM*.

I made up my mind, there and then, that what I would do to make Rich feel better – all throughout the day, as often as I could – was update him on how sexy I was feeling and how ravishing I was looking so that by the time I got home, he'd be so hot under the collar he would barely be able to restrain himself. He, on the receiving end of all of this, would in turn know that I was thinking only of him and that there was absolutely nothing at all to worry about.

I should give you a bit of backstory here that might help you to understand how utterly naïve I was when it came to jealousy, its workings and the correct way to handle it. I was (still am) an absolutely atrocious liar. I simply couldn't do it properly. I *tried* to lie – I'd have loved to be *able* to lie – I was just really bad at it. It was inconvenient. I thought that because of this, people could see straight through me and I assumed that I was something of an open book. In my formative relationship years, my late teens and early twenties, I naively thought that any guy I went out with (we didn't 'date' in the nineties, that was just for Americans) would automatically sense that I was this relatively readable, non-shady character and therefore they did not need to ever be jealous because if I did do something that perhaps wasn't within the expected boundaries of a mutually respectful relationship (I said I was bad at lying, not that I was a modern-day saint) then they'd know about it fairly soon.

Writing that down just clarifies that I had totally the wrong end of the stick with all of this, thinking that my inability to be effectively deceitful should have equated to a sense of trustworthiness and loyalty. Why would anyone be jealous when the person they were with had nothing to hide?

'But why would you be worried that I'm about to go to a pool party in Long Island armed with a string bikini and a magnum of Veuve Cliquot? You know I can't lie, right? If anything happens out there then you'll be the first to know about it. You just need to ask.'

This was the sort of thinking that lay behind my decision to stay in full radio contact with Rich for the whole day, giving regular updates and providing some exciting titillation. Cheer him right up. Never mind the fact that his reaction had been totally out of the ordinary for him and he barely knew what to do with himself, what he needed was a constant reminder of what I was up to so that he could feed his imagination with vivid mental images.

So sure, I might be wearing knickers that had criss-crossing ribbons instead of a gusset, spending the day draped over a film star, but so long as I kept Rich regularly updated, I thought, he'd be absolutely fine. I mean, it wasn't as though I was going to be drinking.

'Champagne?' said Rankin. 'Or are we doing more of this rosé?'

It was early evening and by God had it been a fun day. There had been another girl on the shoot (I made sure I relayed this by text: 'It's a Jude Law threesome') and we'd both had the sort of hair and makeup treatment that models dreamed of. The kind of Bond Girl Pure Sex look that made you do a double take at yourself in the mirror, with feline flicked eyes, big tousled hair and body skin sheened with golden-flecked lotion. We had waited for Jude Law to arrive, which had taken quite some time, and then we'd done some lighting tests with Jude Law, which had also taken a while, and now, with the sky having darkened outside and most of the country settling down to dinner, we were about to get cracking. Main instruction for the models on this particular shoot went something like, *He's Alfie, an irresistible womanizer; you're both good time girls, out for a bit of fun.* It was quite literally our job description for the day to paw over Jude Law, who, at one point, was wearing only trousers.

'He's playing Alfie,' I text, 'and I am a good time girl, out for a bit of fun.'

Send.

There was no reply when I returned to my phone twenty minutes later, as we took a break whilst the lighting was being changed. There hadn't been any reply to my last few texts either.

'The bra I am wearing has stars over the nipples!' I had text at around 3pm.

'I feel really sexy!' I had text at a quarter past five.

And now here we were, at just after seven in the evening, and he'd still not replied. Had I known it was because he was sitting in the mental equivalent of a dark, damp cave, slowly cheese-gratering his own skin off, then I'd probably have stopped with the updates. Had I known that he had unexpectedly lost the power of rational thought then I absolutely, one hundred per cent, would not have been sending him updates about the fact I looked like a golden-hued goddess and was throwing myself over another man in underwear that was definitely not meant to stay on. But I didn't know that he had spent hours pacing around the flat in a state of utter fury and devastation, like a recently caught panther, his wild imagination fuelled by the texts I was sending. (In fairness, he didn't even need a wild imagination: I really was wearing virtually nothing and wrapping myself around another guy.)

It would have been better had I said nothing for the entire day – each text I'd sent had been like a taunt, when all I'd been trying to do was to keep him in the loop. Every moment of contact had fanned the flames of jealousy when all I'd wanted was to show I had nothing to hide. *See? An open book. If anything happens, you'll be the first to know!* And so my final text was the nail in the proverbial coffin, sent as I got into the car home.

'I'm drunk,' I text, 'and I'm not wearing any knickers.'

Well. By the time I got back home, mouth feeling sour and dry from the champagne and undercarriage feeling really rather chafed from sudden lack of protective hair *and* having no knickers on, Rich really had driven himself to the brink of insanity.

I was shocked. There I was thinking I'd done a decent job of providing a day-long foreplay session and that I'd be arriving home to a hero's welcome; instead I walked in to the man I loved slumped on the sofa, deflated, inexplicably holding a whole raw cauliflower on his lap. He looked devastated and shellshocked, as though he'd just survived a natural disaster and had witnessed terrible things, as though he'd escaped an earthquake on the back of a Jeep (probably an army one) and seen women and children fall to their deaths as a deep crevasse split the ground in two.

I felt kind of sorry for him, because anyone cradling a raw cauliflower has to be in a bad way, but I also felt quite cross. All I'd done that day was my job, after all. (I mean, draping myself on and around Jude Law wasn't specifically my job, obviously, but now and again the Lord provided.) OK, so perhaps the text updates and the tipsy voicemail messages (five) hadn't been the best plan, but my intentions had been solid.

I tried to offer him a bit of sympathy, which was good of me, I thought, considering that he'd had nothing to actually worry about all day, but after about fifteen seconds it became clear that my efforts were futile. He had been completely overtaken by the force of his feelings.

Oh for God's sake, get a grip, I thought, as I went into the tiny kitchen to look for food. I needed something to soak up the booze and there was only so much coddling a working girl could do after a long, hard day at the office. *Just get a bloody grip.*

What I couldn't get my head around with the whole thing was that Rich should have been the last man on earth to be jealous or worried about a famous man and a photographer. After all, he'd worked with loads of famous people and – more to the point – he was, himself, an actual photographer. He knew what went on at a photoshoot, that it wasn't some filthy cesspit of uncontrollable urges. He knew that what was represented in the final versions of photographs wasn't the reality of the job: a gleamed-up, half-naked supermodel making eyes at the camera would probably have had two assistants beside her, fanning her head with bits of cardboard to give her hair movement, and that there would have been a makeup artist just off camera eating a croissant from the breakfast table and telling the stylist about her weekend in Barcelona. He knew all of this, that any sexual tension between model and photographer is usually purely artistic, that photographers see beautiful women constantly and so look upon them differently, almost as art subjects rather than objects of desire.

'What I don't get,' I said, popping my head out of the kitchen, unable to stop picking at the scab, 'is that you know exactly what goes on in a photographer's mind. So why would you be worried?'

'It's *because* I know what goes on in a photographer's mind that I was worried,' he said.

Oh.

We got over it, of course we did, but at the time I was so cross that he'd had this momentary lapse in strength and judgement. I'd fallen for his calm, practical ways and the fact that he always felt so solid and in command; I couldn't be dealing with irrational episodes that seemingly had no solution. I was a twenty-two-year-old model with a chaotic attitude to finances and a fear of rejection, for crying out loud – I was the very definition of an irrational episode with no solution. He was supposed to be the rock that I could anchor myself to, like I was one of those frondy, wavering sea anemones, but briefly, for a very short flash in time, he'd turned to sand.

I did what any unsympathetic, self-centred twenty-something would do and ran home to my parents for a couple of nights, and that straightened things out. The jealousy, that strange and sudden emotion that had never been there before, left the building and never returned again. In some ways, it would have been nice for it to have popped its head up every now and then, but it didn't. I'll just repeat this for emphasis: Rich never got jealous again. I don't know what part of his brain – or heart – he had to permanently shut down to achieve this, but even in the most outrageous of scenarios he was as cool as a cucumber.

'I'm just off to rural France for this *GQ* job,' I'd say.

'Oh yeah, I'd forgotten you were going to France. Do you know what the shoot's about?'

'It's me and two male models, apparently. They're both in love with my character and we're like this weird threesome going about looking as though we're shagging everywhere.'

'Brilliant! Well, have fun.'

'I'm sure I won't. We're out in the middle of nowhere

and it's going to be freezing and I'll barely be wearing any clothes. Also, it's shooting with that French model who's just been voted the sexiest man in fashion, and apparently he's been really big-headed and unbearable since it happened.'

'I'm sure he'll be fine.'

'Maybe. Well, don't worry if you can't get hold of me, it'll be terrible reception out there.'

'OK, see you in a few days. Make sure you wear your knickers, you don't want to go getting cold.'

Minor drama over, we settled into a blissful existence of lively evenings, lazy mornings and me running late for just about everything. The Vespa became my personal, chauffeured time machine, it being the only mode of transport that could conceivably get me to my various job and casting destinations fast enough within the tiny windows of opportunity I left myself with. Work at ten? I'd wake at nine, even if the location was an hour away and I still had to wash my hair.

'Where do you have to be?' Rich would say, muffled inside his motorcycle helmet.

'Notting Hill. At nine.'

'But it's twenty-five to nine now! For God's sake . . .'

And we would do it, Old Street to Notting Hill, twenty-four minutes including a brief meander about at the end of the journey for me to consult my A–Z; faster than a taxi, faster than a helicopter, faster than anything, other than perhaps teleportation. Sure, I arrived with flattened hair and a ringing in my ears that wouldn't disappear until lunchtime, but if it meant that I could hit snooze on my Samsung phone until the very last possible minute, I was in.

I snoozed, I worked and I started to make – for the very first time – very real money. Money that landed with Beryl in accounts and then, via a convoluted, lengthy process that involved taking off lots of expenses and producing statements I couldn't understand, appeared in my bank account.

'You might fancy contributing to the bills, at some point,' said Filthy Rich, after a few consecutive months of cohabitation. 'Now that you've left your flat.'

I was shocked and outraged. I'd thought I was exempt from bills, seeing that they'd never been discussed. And yes, I'd left my Hackney flat for good, which meant that I was paying no rent at all, anywhere, but really. Did that warrant such an abrupt discussion – demands for money, right out of the blue?

'I thought you were the son of a lord or something,' I said. 'Surely you don't need my meagre amounts.'

'What?'

Of course, Filthy Rich hadn't been party to our in-agency discussion about the origins of his name. I hadn't ever given it much thought but subconsciously I must have ruled out the sexual option, seeing as though no shocking oddity had arisen in that department, and settled, quietly, without ever asking, on him being the son of some sort of property developer or well-to-do businessman. The owner of the local car boot.

'Doesn't your dad have loads of land?' I tried to remember what Daz had said.

'He lives in a semi-detached house off the M27,' said Rich.

Bloody Daz. It was a good job I wasn't with Filthy for the money, I'd have been well disappointed. As it was, though, the thought that I could seduce my way to a fortune, that marrying into money was a realistic option, hadn't really crossed my mind. Had it, then perhaps I'd have tried a bit harder with Tarek, commander of seafaring vessels and heir to a generous fortune. Or one of the other millionaires. I had always assumed, from a pretty young age, that I'd be making my fortune for myself. Lawyer? Model? Over-zealous health and safety inspector? The means hardly mattered, all I knew was that I'd need money in life (especially with my irresponsible spending tendencies) and so I'd better get on with earning it.

And that's what I did. In fact, when it came to modelling, I realised that I was actually getting quite good at it. I still wasn't sure what the magic formula was, in terms of making that leap from a model to a super one, but whatever I was doing was OK for now. I had a whole arsenal of facial expressions I could call upon and knew how to work systematically through the sequence of 'I'm a little teapot' poses required on a catalogue shoot. (One hand on hip, both hands on hips, no hands on hips, wide-apart legs in a strong lady stance, repeat to fade.) OK, so I still couldn't walk in very high heels but I was amazing at standing still in them, and the fact that I wasn't the beaniest beanpole in town could easily be overlooked when I did such a good number in fake-striding and fake-jumping.

Of course, there were things I still hated about the job –

notably the castings, many of which seemed pointless, the sometimes dire working conditions on shoots and the fact that quite often people would talk about you as though you weren't there – but mostly, overall, it was alright. So long as you had reasonably thick skin, were immune to the cold, didn't mind occasionally being so bored that you wished for a quick, sudden death, perhaps by natural disaster or alien invasion, and had the stamina of an Olympic long-distance runner.

The most important thing was that you were unique, it seemed. This is what the industry craved. So long as there was nobody else like you, that you had something novel and new, you were in with a chance. And that was the easy bit – because what were the odds that anyone in the world would look exactly the same – totally identical – to you?

Chapter 15

Congrats on Australian Vogue

'Congrats on Australian *Vogue* darling,' said Daz, 'the pictures look fab.'

Australian *Vogue*? Was Daz daytime drinking again? Daz had recently moved across to be a Main Board agent, which was nice because it meant I'd once again benefit from her passive-aggressive insults. Good for keeping self-confidence in check and an essential part of growing a thick skin.

'They're over on my desk, darling,' said Daz. She was over at her wall of model cards, taking out the old ones and slotting in the new. I made my way over to her desk to take a look at whatever magazine she had mistaken for Australian *Vogue*. I had recently shot for French *Elle*, so she probably meant that. Or Austrian *Vogue*, if there was one – I'd done a smaller Austrian magazine so perhaps, by some amazing stroke of luck, the pictures had been picked up and run by Condé Naste.

'Australian *Vogue*?' said Lewis as I passed his desk, 'let's have a look. I didn't even know you'd shot for them!'

'Neither did I,' I said.

We reached Daz's desk together, having gathered a following of another two bookers, all keen for a little break and a bit of a nose.

'Oh my God, darling,' said Lewis as he took hold of the magazine and slowly flicked through the pages. 'You look absolutely sublime!'

It was true. I did look sublime. I looked so utterly sublime, so unlike my usual self that I momentarily welled up. *This* was what I had been waiting for: me, the human equivalent of a thoroughbred racehorse, reclining on a picturesque beach. There was the bronzed skin, there was the stomach, toned and taut, a testimony to my many minutes of half-hearted sit-up practice. My hair! It was tousled and honeyed, and my thighs were artfully dusted with sand. Finally, after all these years, I looked every inch – every single inch – the supermodel.

'It's almost as though it's not you, darling,' said Daz, barging through the growing crowd to get to her chair. 'I mean, look at those eyes! Sparkling with vivacity and joy, darling. And the legs, so long and graceful and lean. Do you think they retouched them?'

Had the people at the magazine retouched them? Now that I examined them, they were inconceivably long. I glanced down at my own real-life legs, starting under their denim skirt pelmet and ending in some clompy suede clogs.

'I didn't know you'd been to Bali, darling,' said Lewis. 'When did you go to Bali?'

I hadn't been to Bali.

I leaned in and looked at the credits on the last page of the spread: 'Shot at the newly opened Bulgari Resort, Bali.' Well, this was odd. Had I, in fact, been to Bali but not realised it? Had I thought at the time that I was somewhere else? But wait, now that I looked at the photos, I couldn't even remember shooting them. The swimwear was unfamiliar – I'd have definitely remembered the Missoni one-piece with the criss-crossing laces up the side – and what was with the furry Mukluk boots when it was so obviously scorching hot? I'd certainly have had something to say about that – at the very least I would have recorded my disgruntlement in my secret diary of complaints. There was only one feasible explanation.

'They've used my head and stuck it onto someone else's body!' I exclaimed, not entirely unhappily. And I say 'not entirely unhappily' because even though my brain had only had a few seconds to process this new bit of completely bizarre information, it was already managing to put a positive spin on things. *Surely*, it was saying, *this is the best of both worlds? Someone else's taller and slightly thinner body, someone else's slightly more excellent hair but with your face. Everyone will think that the goddess is you.* And my brain was right. Everyone would think that the goddess was me!

'Darling, I think you may be right about them using your face,' said Lewis. He took a magnifying loop and ran it over the open pages, looking for some sort of tell-tale retouching flaw. 'Let me get on the phone to them now.'

'Don't be ridiculous,' said Daz, returning to her desk. 'It looks exactly like Ruth, it *is* Ruth, we just need to try to remember when we sent her to Bali.' She tapped at the keys on her computer. 'Could it have been after we did the Christmas drinks and none of us could speak for four and a half working days?'

'I was in Paris in December,' I said. 'I remember trying to call in for job details and you pretended to be an answerphone message.'

'Was it in February, darling,' said Daz, 'when you drank too much Diet Coke at once and had your funny turn? Perhaps you sped your way through the trip without realising it.'

She looked at her screen, exasperated. 'No. It's not on your chart anywhere. You have definitely, one hundred per cent never been to Bali.'

'What are you all doing over there?' said Diane in her no-nonsense manner.

There were now five of us gathered around the magazine of mystery and one of the phones on the men's desk was going unanswered. *Bleep bleep. Bleep bleep.* She strode over and peered between us to look at the pages.

'It's an unsolved puzzle, Diane,' said Lewis, 'the Great Bali Body Snatch. Someone has taken Ruth's head and used it on a different body.'

Diane straightened up and began to stride over to the men's desk.

'I have no idea what you could be puzzled about,' she

said, picking up the persistently bleeping phone, 'you're staring at pictures of Jessica Hart. Diane speaking, how can I help?'

Jessica Hart. So that was who she was. Not my face on a better body *at all,* but just an all-round better me. I felt deflated as Daz began to search for her name. A few images popped up – same tooth gap, similar boobs and in some pictures her face was identical to mine. But then, depressingly, in most pictures it wasn't. She was like a version of me that had been surgically morphed with a living Barbie – narrower in the body, longer in the legs and with a slightly more symmetrical, classically pretty kind of face.

'Since when has this girl been around?' said Lewis.

'Not that long,' said Daz, clicking through her search results, 'and she's based in Australia, thank God. But she's already doing big things by the looks of it. And she's very sexy.' She turned to me. 'You've got yourself a face double darling,' she said, closing the magazine and shoving it into the wastepaper basket. 'You'd better hope this girl doesn't make her way up to the northern hemisphere.'

'Or if she does,' said Lewis, 'pray that she has a really shit personality.'

Oh, this was *trés mal.* Was this what it was going to come down to? A battle of the personalities? I was relatively confident in mine – people always said how easy I was to work with and I was always up for a laugh – but what if this girl was some wisecracking, classic car-collecting brainbox who played sax in a progressive jazz band and liked to train police dogs in her spare time? What if she was just altogether more interesting?

Even worse, what if (and this idea really disturbed me for at least eight or nine minutes) we had *exactly the same personality*? If not only did we look the same but acted the same? Imagine if she came up from Australia and we bumped into each other at a casting! Imagine if we got booked on the same job! (We didn't. She did brilliantly well but we never crossed paths and the universe was saved from almost certain implosion.)

Anyway, I knew the score. There'd always be someone who looked better than you. And if you let yourself slip into a negative state of mind then you could easily believe that *everyone* looked better than you. After all, quite a proportion of the average model's time is spent being rejected in some way or another. If you got fat you were out, age was a ticking timebomb and there were numerous ways in which your own body could let you down – legs too spindly, teeth too big, shoulders too manly, nose like a pig. Few pursuits could make you feel more worthless, if you allowed yourself to fall into the pessimistic pit of self-doubt.

Which was why you had to get your kicks where you could. If there was anything to grab hold of that made you feel good about yourself, whether it was a sample size dress zipping easily closed or someone complimenting the clarity and tone of your skin, as though you were a breeder's prize-winning specimen, then you had to just grab it. Sweep up the scraps of self-confidence and try to stick them back on.

'She's going to be mega-famous, apparently,' said the editor from the magazine. 'Not only is she exceptionally beautiful, she's an incredibly talented singer.'

I nodded and kicked the wheel on the luggage trolley. It wasn't that I was jealous of this model that the editor would not shut up about, I was just very tired. I had returned from a shoot in Hamburg late the night before and had barely had time to get home, empty my suitcase and repack a larger one before having to get the tube back to the airport.

'I don't know where she's got to,' said the editor. 'We booked her car to be with her at seven, she should have been here by now.'

'I know that she was in the studio yesterday,' said the assistant editor. 'It's possible that they were recording until late.'

We were on our way to the Caribbean to shoot six different fashion and beauty stories for a popular women's magazine. Two models, one magazine editor, an assistant editor, a stylist, the stylist's assistant, the photographer with his assistant, hair, makeup and a production guy.

'We'd better go through,' said the production guy, checking his watch. 'We're boarding in twenty minutes and we still need to get to the gate.'

'God where is she?' said the editor. 'I hope she's not being harassed by fans.'

I rolled my eyes. I'd looked up this girl, Chambray, on the internet and there had been nothing to be found apart from a MySpace page. The only source of information was this editor, who'd not stopped banging on about her since I'd first been booked for the job.

Bloody Chambray. I'd heard all about how Chambray had been optioned for a Chanel beauty campaign, how Chambray had the voice of an angel, how Chambray had such gorgeous blonde hair and how Chambray's husband was a millionaire and so she didn't even need the money but she still worked because she was Chambray. I knew one thing for certain about Chambray and that was that her publicist was working overtime.

'We'll do the beauty shots with Chambray,' the editor said, leaning into the photographer and reading through his printed list of stories and shots. 'Her skin is an absolute dream, just flawless and with a real luminescence. This is a sponsored story, too, so the advertisers will love it.'

'Oh and the hand close-ups – definitely Chambray,' she continued. 'Did I show you her hands on her mocked-up album cover? There's something so . . . unusual about them.'

The photographer turned the sheet of paper over and ran his eyes down the list.

'What about the hair stories, the "seven sins of styling" feature?' he said.

'Chambray,' said the editor, without pause. 'Apparently her hair is like spun gold, falling about her shoulders like an emperor's cape, rippling in the—'

'*Apparently*?' the photographer said. 'Have you not met her?'

'Of course not,' the editor replied, 'Chambray doesn't have time for meetings!'

And now it was 8.02, with the mad rush to the gate still to go and no sign of a megastar – no paparazzi chasing a baseball-capped deity through the departures hall, no screaming of fans. In fact, the airport was eerily quiet, with just a cleaner emptying a bin, an Addison Lee driver blundering about in the wrong building and a sullen teenage boy in a hoodie stomping towards the check-in desk.

'We're going to have to go without her,' said the production guy. 'I'll get us on our flight and then call the travel company to organise the next possible one out for Chambray.'

'I'm Chambray,' said the sullen teenage boy.

The editor gasped.

Within the depths of the hoodie, Chambray scowled, her bloodshot eyes making her look like some sort of demon. I was interested to see that Chambray was quite short, at least three or four inches shorter than me, and that her fingers were quite weird, long and knobbly, with sticking out knuckles and quick-bitten nails. Interested and – I was apparently going to hell – silently quite pleased.

'You're . . . Chambray?' said the editor, her face suddenly pale.

Chambray handed her passport to the check-in attendant and gave a curt nod.

'Was-was your journey OK?' stammered the editor, who was deeply flustered. 'Did you get stuck in much traffic?' She looked as though she'd just walked in on her boss fornicating with a cow; shock and disbelief were etched upon her face and she seemed to be struggling to compute what she was seeing. Chambray, megastar-to-be, wearing Adidas bottoms and a ketchup-stained hoodie. Short Chambray. Rude Chambray. About to make us miss our flight Chambray.

'I wouldn't normally do a magazine like this,' said

Chambray, as we cruised at 37,000 feet. She had pulled her hood back to reveal skin that was sickly in tone and hair that had been cut short, shaved up the sides and dyed a dark, unforgiving shade of grey.

GREY!

It was ungenerous of me to be revelling in this real-life Chambray, so far from the editor's fantasy version. I knew that. But she had been a total pain in the arse as we'd sprinted to the departures gate, had kicked up a fuss that we were flying economy and now, seated with her chair in the fully reclined position with no thought for the passenger behind her, she was busy telling me in no uncertain terms what an absolute loser I was.

'My manager only let me do this because they said I'd get the cover,' she said, scratching at a large pustule in the crease beneath her nose. 'Why would I do such a nobody shoot otherwise? The issue with the cover should publish at exactly the same time as my album gets released. All publicity is good publicity, apparently, even if it's a magazine for sad, boring women.'

Across the aisle, I could see the photographer casting furtive glances our way and then writing things on his printed-out shot list. The editor was beside him, silently staring straight ahead. She looked traumatised. Chambray was absolutely nothing like the image on her mocked-up album cover, the image that the editor had printed out specially and passed around as we'd waited at the check-in desk. On the album cover, Chambray had wavy golden hair, porcelain skin that looked as though it had been lit by a candle and cherry-red lips, perfect and plump. Her lithe, pale-limbed body was sheathed in a long, grass-green dress and she'd been curled sensuously around the neck of a cello. She'd looked like a medieval princess, playing sweet music for her lord.

Here, on the Boeing 777, she had wiry grey hair, a face that looked as though she'd spent the past week sniffing glue from a paper bag, and dry, cracked lips. She looked like a roadie who'd fallen on hard times. There was a small tattoo beneath her ear, three cursive font letters that spelled out CNT.

Could Chambray even be the same person as the one on the cover? What had happened to this girl in between shooting that photo and now?

'I don't know why you'd do this job,' said Chambray. 'I started off in modelling but only did a month; singing was always going to be my thing. I mean, why be a model if you have a talent?'

I drank my mini bottle of Chardonnay and attempted to sleep.

The hotel we were staying at was idyllic. A true paradise edged with a perfect white beach, the bluest of seas and tiny, winding pathways that led between buildings. In the rooms, huge four-poster beds sat swathed in curtains of the lightest voile, the fabric billowing in the breeze from the creaking fans that turned on the ceilings.

'I've stayed in better,' said Chambray, as we walked down to dinner on that first night. 'There's not even TV.'

'Now Ruth,' said the editor the next morning, 'we're going to be doing your hair shots first.'

'Is this the "seven sins of styling" story?' said Lee, the production man. 'Beneath the palms on the east end of the beach?'

'Yes,' said the editor. 'Eight shots altogether.'

'Sorry,' said Lee, 'I have this down as Chambray shooting, not Ruth.'

There was an awkward pause. I looked at Chambray, who was still in her hoodie, despite the thirty-three degree heat.

Chambray shrugged. 'I don't do hair jobs,' she said. 'I'm not a model, I'm a singer.'

'Oh!' said the editor, far too brightly. 'Well, don't worry then Chambray, Ruth will have to step up and do this one. Lee, can I have a word?'

I was delighted, of course. The sponsored hair shoot meant three and a half thousand pounds added to my fee. I was also delighted because, secretly, it was always quite nice to be considered the better option. It was terribly Cutthroat-Nadia to even think it, but someone else's loss in this case was absolutely my gain. It felt good. My hair was better! My face was better! For God's sake, even my height was better! This boost of self-confidence made for a brilliant day; my poses were all spot-on, I angled my head perfectly to show off the hair, I even decided to go above and beyond and suggest improvements to some of the styles, which were, in my opinion, sort of samey.

'What's this one called then?' I asked the hairdresser, as he spritzed the lengths with sea salt spray for the thirtieth time.

'Undone root-lift beachy waves,' said the hairdresser,

whose name was Cal. He scrunched my damp hair violently in his fists and instructed me to sit out in the now-thirty-eight degree heat to dry it out quicker.

'Wasn't the last one beachy waves?' I said. I didn't have access to a mirror but was fairly sure that spraying in sea salt and scrunching, without any other tweaking involving heated tools or hair grips or even a brush, would result in a similar look each time it was done.

'That was undone tousled beachy locks,' said Cal.

I fried myself out in the sun for a few minutes, gladly, because frying myself in the sun was one of my favourite hobbies and getting paid to do it was almost too good to be true, then returned to base camp, under the palms.

'Erm,' said the editor, 'it's quite similar to the tousled beach locks, Cal?'

'The last one was undone tousled beachy locks,' I butted in. 'The one before that was redone wavy tousled roots. They're all totally different.'

'Go fuck yourself,' said Cal, jabbing me in the arm with the point of his comb.

'Listen,' said the editor at the end of the hair shoot. 'We need to have a chat about the rest of the week.'

We gathered round. All of the crew save for Chambray, who had returned to her room after breakfast and not ventured out since.

'Ruth,' said the editor. 'You're going to have to do the second beauty shoot as well as the first.'

'As well?' I said. I mean, it was a compliment and all but at this rate I'd be shooting every single day of the trip.

The deal had been three days shooting and three days off – lovely, languorous days to lie in the sun whilst Chambray flaunted her flawless skin and frolicked in the surf.

'I need you to,' said the editor. I wondered how it would feel to make her beg. 'We're in a bit of a bind. We'll shoot the cover story on Wednesday, both of you in, and then your beauty story will be the following day.'

'But we have to use Chambray for more than just that,' said the photographer. 'You've paid all this money, blown the whole budget, it seems mad not to make sure she's used?'

Paid all this money? Blown the budget? How much was this girl getting paid?

'You're right,' said the editor. 'OK, let's swap Ruth out from the sandals shoot tomorrow and use Chambray instead.'

'Has she had a pedicure?' said the makeup artist. 'You know that it's tricky with close-ups of feet.'

'Oh,' said the editor, 'really Monique. I'm sure it'll be fine. How bad could they be?'

'Sweet Jesus,' said the photographer before leaving the room.

We were sitting on Monique's bed, doing a quick hair try for the cover shoot the next day. Chambray was wrapped in a towelling dressing gown looking like a totally different person, ready for her sandals shoot with her blue-grey hair artfully styled and skin looking dewy, glowing and fresh. Cal had twisted my hair up and back, into a severe bun, giving me the masculine edge the editor wanted. The editor had asked Chambray to slip off her trainers so that they could take a look at her feet.

They were the feet of someone who had spent a year trampling shoeless through the Arctic tundra: slightly bluish, swollen in places and with thick yellow toenails that looked brittle and cracked. Monique's optimistic little pedicure set-up suddenly looked absurd; she needed an angle-grinder and chisel, not foot scrub and a pale pink nail polish.

'Right . . .' said the editor. 'OK!' She left the room.

I'd started to feel slightly sorry for Chambray, even though she could act like a bit of a dick. From our brief chats at dinner, I'd gleaned that her album wasn't a done deal, her manager had made her dye her hair grey for a poncey editorial and that the body with the cello on her mock-up album cover wasn't even hers.

The editor came back in to Monique's room, wringing her hands.

'Chambray!' she said, energetically and with a manic smile on her face. 'You lucky thing, you get another day off today. Ruth? You're in sandals.'

For God's sake! I'd already planned exactly my position on the beach and had packed a small tote bag with fags, my notebook and a copy of *The Da Vinci Code*, the new book the entire world was talking about. And now I'd have to spend the day wearing sandals and having yet more sea salt spray spritzed in my hair?

'Probably best not to use me,' I said, forcing my feet deeper into my hotel slippers. 'I chipped my nail polish yesterday and there's a mosquito bite on my ankle.'

'You'll be alright,' said Chambray, getting up to leave. 'Nobody looks at those pictures anyway. You're just there to fill space.'

Was it nice to have been considered the better option? Yes. Was it an easy win because Chambray had the feet of a thousand-year-old troll and the hair of one too? Of course. A bit shallow, this contest of physical attributes, but then her behaviour had left a lot to be desired. She'd spoken to the assistants like shit, refused to get up at 5am so that we could catch the sunrise and had stropped about moodily when her eye makeup wasn't just as she liked it. She'd blatantly learned nothing in her month as a model and that was a shame because most of the skills would have helped her out in her singing career, which would end up fizzling out, mere months later, before it had even begun.

Skills like knowing when to be humble and knowing when to shine; treating the least important person in the room in the same way as you'd treat the most important (easy when you were often the least important person in the room, but let's move on); being able to endure sub-zero temperatures wearing a bathing costume when everyone else was standing in the snow wearing UGG boots, ear muffs and Himalayan mountaineering parkas effective to minus fifty-five degrees. All of these skills were a necessity, as well as the genetic jackpots – the nice face, the good body, the Teflon hair that could withstand multiple tonging sessions in one day without turning to ash – they were all necessary and I was proud to have them.

Perhaps one of my best skills though, one that I had

honed over the past couple of years and was inordinately proud of, was my ability to stay still for very long periods of time. And by long periods of time, I mean that sometimes people would forget I was there and scream with shock if I spoke. I could hold still when my limbs began to ache and my neck began to tremble, push past the screaming muscles stage, brush off the short period of numbness that would follow, silently suffer the pins and needles epoch and then settle in for limitless minutes of absolute stillness. It was not just a skill, it was a gift. I could be a living, breathing mannequin, the very essence of a clothes horse; should it be required of me, I could go inside myself and completely detach from my physical being. Like a yogi. Or a monk.

Chapter 16

Her Face, it is Wrong

G oing within myself was a useful coping mechanism for the odd occasion I had to withstand near-inhumane levels of tedium. It didn't happen all that often – the fashion industry wasn't renowned for its dull, unremarkable characters and repetitive, uncreative tasks – but if it did, I could very easily slip away from reality, retreat into my own thoughts and leave my body behind to be a kind of empty, soulless shell. There was one particular job that I did on a regular basis and it was so dull, so absolutely mind-numbingly boring that sometimes I used to pray for a catastrophe. A crumbling studio wall, a falling ceiling beam, an overground train smashing through the side of the building. A rat infestation.

It was a trousers-wearing job. I put on trousers, they photographed the trousers – the front, the back, the sides – and I took them off again. The only issue was that every single pair of trousers was a UK size twelve and I was an eight. And so every pair of pinstriped slacks, every pair of bootcut stonewashed jeans or comfort-stretch jogger had to be very precisely, very carefully pinned to fit.

You may wonder why they'd hire a size eight model to wear size twelve trousers and then spend a quarter of an hour per pair – we would shoot thirty or so pairs a day – pinning them to size. It's because size twelve was considered the average size of a British woman at the time and so this is how the samples came. If they'd tried to hire a size twelve model, which was a niche concept at any rate, then the model would almost definitely have had legs four inches too long. And God forbid they consider using a woman with the size of body and length of legs for which the trousers were actually made. For this was 2004 and we were far, far off the idea of celebrating – indeed tolerating – any body size or shape that wasn't tall-tall-tall and thin-thin-thin.

The job was repetitive and torturous to the point that you wanted to set fire to your own hands just to feel something. The most exciting thing that ever happened on that job, and I must have done it two or three dozen times, was that one time, on a particularly rushed and stressful day, the stylist kimble-gunned me through the arse. The kimble gun was a special gadget that she used to reattach the labels to the trousers, once we'd shot them. Usually – for good reason – she'd wait until I'd taken the trousers off before she aimed her gun at the back pocket to shoot it with her little dart-headed piece of plastic. I have no idea what was going through her mind when she kimbled my arse, but it definitely jolted me from my bored stupor.

For almost two minutes, until we worked out how to extract the plastic without giving me a blood infection, I was a legitimate piece of merchandise. I had an SKU, a barcode and a retail price of £24.50.

It was far more likely, in the world of modelling, that you would be afflicted with a sense of acute frustration rather than boredom, usually because someone else on the team was marching to the beat of an entirely different drum, working in actual slow motion whilst everyone else tapped their fingers on their teeth and you stood there losing all feeling in your feet and wishing for an early, sudden death. Photographers who would artfully ponder how to best frame their photo whilst you balanced, in a totally sheer Alexander Wang sheath dress, on the edge of the fountain at Trafalgar Square. Stylists who couldn't make their mind up between the Dior with the thigh boot or the Celine with the shoe when it was shot number thirteen and nine o'clock at night. Art directors who wanted eight options for every picture because they didn't have the conviction to go with just one idea.

In these times of acute frustration, which often developed into episodes of silent, furious rage, I would amuse myself by imagining wicked things and hatching intricate revenge plans on the person or people who were holding things up and dithering about. In my tortured mind, the mind that had withstood about ten thousand hours of 'waiting for the Polaroid to develop whilst standing absolutely, perfectly still', I would wreak terrible havoc upon the fashion industry. These revenge dreams were strictly for my inner viewing pleasure only – none of them could have even remotely come true. They were purposefully abstract with absolutely no danger of them ever being executed. Until one day, a cold day in 2005, when I discovered that I possessed the powers of telekinesis.

It was 10th March 2005, I was twenty-four years old and it was the first time that I had made something happen by sheer force of will alone. I say first time, it was the only time – I'm not Matilda for crying out loud – nevertheless, the whole thing was pretty impressive.

We were shooting in a huge, derelict factory in Germany that hadn't been in use for a very long time. I'd been to a fair few abandoned places in Germany – it seemed to have the world's largest collection of creepy buildings, including Olympic training camps with long-forgotten swimming pools, airfields with rusted fighter jet hangars, TB sanitoriums with long, dark corridors and bare bed frames pushed up against mould-covered walls – but this place was spectacular. It was the industrial equivalent of shooting at the Grand Canyon or Yosemite park. Awesome in scale, with water cooling towers as tall as high-rise buildings and huge machinery cogs and wheels the size of small houses. Some of the machine halls were cathedral like in their proportions, bigger than cathedrals, with glass rooftops allowing light to flood down to the factory floors below. Everything had just been left as it was, so many decades ago, in this gigantic manufacturing plant that was the size of a small town. Vines hung down from the ceilings, turning corridors into indoor jungles, and every now and then, unexpected beams of light shot through the holes that had been made by collapsed roofs or through window frames that had been glassless for longer than they'd ever had glass in them. It was a photographer's dream. Unless you were the particular photographer on the shoot that day, who apparently had no dreams, no nightmares, no thoughts at all, and was physically incapable of being happy, or pleasant, or satisfied.

'OK Root,' he said, because that's what almost everyone called me if English wasn't their first language, 'I am not liking you for this shoot, but it was not me who picked you.' Well, that was a brilliant start to the day.

'She is perfect for this shoot, Fritz,' said the stylist, in a vaguely weary way. 'Please wait until we have hair and makeup done and you will see.'

She shrugged at me. I appreciated the fact that she'd said this in English so that I'd understand it and know she had my back – it was a small kindness.

'Her face, it is wrong,' said Fritz. 'There is too much softness. The face needs to show suffering. But we will proceed.'

I'd only been there a few minutes and already a number of my modelling pet hates had come together: the photographer was a knob – tick! it was going to be freezing cold – tick! the health and safety standards looked dubious – tick! and there were no proper toilet facilities. At least, there were no proper toilet facilities unless you wanted to have a wee in an unplumbed bowl in a totally dark, windowless bathroom stall that was one of eight in a room that no doubt contained the ghosts of a hundred Second World War steel workers.

There were five of us there – just five tiny people in

this immense world of unmoving cogs and endless hard concrete. I found derelict places spooky at the best of times but this felt like we were the last five people on earth. It was so big and so empty that there wasn't even an echo – in the smaller control rooms and staff quarters that branched off the main halls, there was just a deafening silence. No pigeons, no rats, no nothing. It was filled with a sinister sort of stillness that just didn't feel right. There was no sign of any previous human occupation – not one work overall or apron left slung over a rail or hung upon the cloakroom hooks.

I hoped to God that it was going to be a quick photoshoot. Death felt close. You could easily imagine falling down into a cooling tower or dropping through the walkways around the top of the turbine hall. The best thing that could happen in this situation would be that the photographer was a quick worker and that the four shots they'd said we needed to do would be easy, uncomplicated.

'Right, Root,' said the photographer. 'We are first going to examine all locations to find out which ones are best for shooting you. Then we are going to begin your hair and makeup to see if we can make you look acceptable for the shooting,' he continued. 'And then finally we will start the shooting in our eleven different locations.'

ELEVEN?

'We must make sure that we are finishing here before it is dark,' he said, 'as we do not have power and it is becoming unsafe to be around the machinery. It would be easy to be falling down a cooling tower or dropping through a walkway.'

HER FACE, IT IS WRONG

Seven hours later, dressed as a Cold War refugee (the magazine's actual reference) and leaning against a large metal wheel, I began my attempts at telekinesis in earnest. I had already devised a number of imaginary ways in which I could dispose of this deeply unpleasant photographer – tying him to a cog to be gradually eaten by the rats and pigeons who would surely emerge after dark; pressing him flat beneath one of the big iron sheets that hung suspended on chains; knocking him out and locking him in the toilets to be terrorised to death by ghosts – but nothing was calming my inner rage. Everything this photographer did was just jaw-clenchingly irritating.

Not only did he criticise every tiny thing in every shot, he was overly meticulous. He had a camera case containing six extra lenses, for example. He tried each and every lens before deciding on which one he'd go with and then often changed his mind again mid-way through the shot. He sighed if the light changed, if the sun suddenly shone beautifully through the rafters, or a cloud darkened the outside sky; he said that the floor was too grey, the vines were too green, the dress was too dressy.

I had never felt so uncomfortable – not least because my bladder was reaching 'distention' stage – and I had never, in my life, wanted to get out of a place more. I'd tried praying for a structural calamity – which to be fair was likely, considering where we were – but no walls had crumbled down, no tower had suddenly creaked dramatically and come folding over on us. I'd also willed the photographer to get horrible, unstoppable diarrhoea but so far he was just fine, finding fault with everything apart from himself and taking forty minutes per shot just to pick his camera lens.

It was late afternoon and it had started to grow dark inside the turbine hall. Fritz had taken pause to tell me where I was going wrong with my posing and had left his camera on the metal stairs behind him. I should say, at this point, that the camera was in no way perilously placed – it wasn't 'perched right on the edge' or 'worryingly close' or any other one of those descriptors that I'm sure people would come up with to diminish my story and deny my powers – the camera had the bulk of its body on the step with just a small portion of it hanging over the side.

As Fritz leaned in, giving me lengthy instructions as to how I should try to bend my arms in a more beautiful way and not part my lips because it revealed my undesirable tooth gap, and try harder to pose for the shape of the dress because I was not doing it justice, I focused my entire mind on the brainwave I'd just had. What better escape from this hellish place with this hellish man than to somehow bring about an equipment malfunction? There was his camera, unattended – imagine if it fell off the steps? And, readers, I thought and I thought and I willed it to happen and right then, to my absolute disbelief, the camera threw itself down from the step. Bounce, bounce, bounce it went, down the last few stairs and then shattered on the concrete floor.

Christ alive! I thought. *What is this newfound strength?* Watching Fritz step towards his broken camera, his smashed lens, I began to list all of the things I could do with this brilliant gift. Could I rob banks? Could I fly planes? Could I explode the headphones from the heads of people who played their music too loudly on the bus? Surely the applications were endless. But for now, I would be satisfied with having sabotaged the shoot. I could go for a wee, we could leave this godforsaken place before dark and I'd never have to work with Fritz again.

'Otto,' said Fritz to his assistant, 'please fetch camera case number two from the boot of my car.'

It never repeated itself. My telekinesis that day had obviously been an anomaly, a blip, born from sheer desperation and intense inner rage. (Another explanation would be that a spirit had moved the camera, perhaps the disgruntled ghost of a Second World War caretaker who simply couldn't abide people leaving obstacles on stairways, especially if those stairways formed part of the emergency evacuation route in case of fire, flood or turbine malfunction.) That's not to say I stopped feeling sheer desperation and intense inner rage on shoots, I just never managed again to laser-focus those feelings into anything productive. Probably because I was usually too cold.

Being cold was, for me, the biggest downside of the job. I also hated getting up very early, pre-7am, but this was more of an inconvenience. Being cold, to the extent that I moved beyond the shivering phase and stopped talking in order to conserve heat for my vital organs, made me feel physically ill. I hated it. Nothing made me happier than seeing a studio name on the call sheet; a warm, safe studio with a working toilet, and water to drink whenever you wanted because you didn't have to worry about needing a wee because *there was a working toilet,* and food you could eat without worrying about the eventual consequences because – you guessed it! – *there was a working toilet*. You could have thrown anything at me, workwise, and I would have endured it so long as it was going to happen in a warm studio. With a working toilet.

'Hey babe, so . . . tomorrow for this *Elle* shoot, they want to do a *Teenwolf* story and stick hair all over your face with eyelash glue.'

'Go on.'

'They want you to eat cow entrails from the mouth of a live leopard.'

'Right . . .'

'And then pose in a coffin wearing the pelt of a recently killed sheepdog.'

'Tell me, Texana,' I would say. 'Are we shooting in a studio?'

'Yes babe, Spring Studios.'

'I'm in.'

Chapter 17

It's the Bloody Teletubbies

Y ou never knew quite what you were going to get, when it came to your photographer; most I worked with were talented, respectful and a joy to spend time with, but every now and then you'd get a right sort. The angry man who made me hold a rowing boat still whilst he took a sunset portrait of the male model, for example – he was a treat.

'Hold the fucking boat *still!*' screamed the demented little man, puce-faced and hopping mad, as I lay beneath the waterline and tried to steady the craft. We were in the Seychelles, it should have been paradise.

'Er hello, it's *on water?*' said the hair stylist, who was holding a foil light reflector underneath his chin, trying to top up his tan with the last of the day's rays. His eyes were closed, he was in his happy place, only vaguely aware that I was being keelhauled every time a wave came in. Still, at

247

least he had my back. 'You can't keep a fucking boat still when it's on water, can you?' he said.

'Shut up! Shut up!' shouted the photographer, stamping his feet into the sand.

'You,' he said to the hair stylist, 'put that reflector down and get in the fucking sea. Hold the boat steady, go the opposite end to *her*.'

'Fuck's sake,' said the hair stylist, throwing the reflector down on the beach. He waded out to the other end of the rowing boat and grabbed hold of the bow. 'Fucking cun—' he said as he ducked down into the sea.

The boat didn't stay still, obviously, because it was being pulled back and forth by some of the most fundamental and powerful forces on earth, and we were but mere humans and not Olympian gods.

'It's still moving!' screeched the photographer. His chest was sunburned, his lips were flecked with spittle, his head was surrounded by dozens of small flies that he beat at wildly with the back of his hand.

'The fucking boat, it's still moving!'

The male model, who was looking more and more uncomfortable, went to step off the boat.

'No, you stay where you are, Jackson,' the photographer said to the model, temporarily calm. 'When these two morons manage to do their job properly I want you to be in the right position to shoot.'

We hadn't endeared ourselves to this photographer, the hair stylist and I. Firstly, we'd almost missed the flight out because we'd taken muscle relaxants with our vodkas in the airport lounge and lost track of time, and then we'd proceeded to get very drunk at every single opportunity from the moment we'd arrived on the island. We *were* irritating, undoubtedly. But when it came to getting down to work? The picture of absolute professionalism.

Anyway, the muscle relaxant thing had been an innocent mistake. The hair stylist had thought they were sleeping tablets and it wasn't until we'd had our names called twice over the tannoy system and attempted to stand up that he realised the error.

'Oh shit!' he said, as we both wobbled like newborn fauns and sat back down at the bar. 'Can you walk? I can't walk.'

'We're going to have to crawl there,' I said, which is basically what we did, boarding the plane mere seconds before they would have unloaded our baggage.

A photographer could make or break the day, essentially; they could be moody and pedantic and still testing out their 'new lighting idea' at 7pm or they could be fun and fast and finished by lunch. Or any sort of combination of the above, with the addition of all of the other traits that can be found amongst the human race, including kind/ egotistical/hilarious/unpredictable/clever/arrogant/down-right odd. Delete as applicable. But the thing that almost everyone wanted to know about photographers, as soon as you said you were a model, was this: were they pervy?

'Do they try it on with you though?' asked one girl, when I was still at my weekend insurance job. 'Do they try to take advantage?'

'Just be careful,' an older women warned. 'You can't

trust any man, especially not one who uses a camera lens as a penis extension!'

'Surely some of them are a bit *dirty*?' people would say. 'All those girls around, it must attract some wrong-uns.'

But the answer, for the most part, was no. Perhaps I was simply lucky or maybe because I started slightly later I wasn't quite so vulnerable, but apart from one guy who became very grumpy when I didn't return his text messages and a couple here and there who *really really* thought that a shot would look better if I whipped my top off, my twelve-year-long career was mostly pretty uneventful. In that respect, at least.

Yes, I'd had the almost mandatory rite of passage that was casting for Terry Richardson (I'd bailed when his assistant asked me to wear stupid glasses and hold an inflatable banana – he'd also asked me to take my top off, which I'd done, but I drew the line at the banana), and yes, there was one particular old-school photographer who held slightly outrageous castings and still seemed to live in the swinging sixties. But did I ever feel unsafe or traumatised? Thankfully not.

I mean, had I ever felt traumatised I would almost definitely have written it down in my diary to whip out at a much later date. Oh wait:

October 21st 2005

Today, I had to sit in a paddling pool with just my knickers on and have shower gel poured all over my face. I couldn't open my eyes and it felt horrible just sitting there in my pants and not knowing who was coming in or watching. I could <u>hear</u> the catering people bringing in lunch and setting it out but I couldn't <u>see</u> them.

Even with my eyes closed tightly the soap still ran in and it really stung; then when the last shot was finished the photographer just packed up and left! When I was still in the paddling pool! I couldn't get dressed or even find a towel to cover myself or wipe my eyes because I couldn't see to get out.

I felt like the brother in *Legends of the Fall* in the world war bit when he gets blinded by tear gas and stuck on the barbed wire fence. Except I didn't then get shot to pieces by the Germans, I *just had to wash soap out of my eyes* . . . the makeup artist stayed behind, she was really nice. Lucky, because washing my face turned out to be a right mission – the more I splashed at the soap the more it multiplied until it had filled my nose and my mouth with foam and soaked through every paper towel in the toilets.

Rich was really angry when he met me outside the studio and he wanted to go in and have a word, but the photographer had left ages ago, probably the same time I was blindly crawling my way over the soapy floor with nothing on. Anyway, I was too sticky to hang around, I just wanted to wash it all away.

The photographer was a woman.

So I had come across the odd perv, a sulky admirer and a woman who had left me for dead in a paddling pool, but apart from them, there were no particularly sinister people to report.

It was usually a photographer's other oddities and eccentricities that worried me more, anyway. Mainly because those might impact how quickly the shoot progressed and what time I would get to finish. A photographer obsessed with cleaning his camera lens, for example (I only worked with him once, thankfully), might double the length of time it took to finish a shoot.

On the opposite end of the scale, you had photographers like Barry, who almost always had an unlit cigarette clamped between his teeth and just couldn't wait to get things over with, to *get it done*.

'Let's get it done then,' he'd say, wearily, as though he wasn't being paid good money to be there.

He always had some sort of sardonic comment ready for the moment you arrived on set, whether it was an observation about the outfit or a remark about the amount of time it had taken everyone to get you ready.

'Come on then, Simon Cowell,' he once said when I walked out in high-waisted black trousers. 'Let's get it done.'

'Come on, Alice Cooper,' he deadpanned, on the beauty shoot with the 'distressed smoky eye'. 'Let's get it done.'

There was one time I had to wear a bright yellow bodysuit, the only skin visible being the skin on my face, which poked through a round hole at the front. It would have been hideously humiliating, really, had there not been another three girls also wearing the same suits in different colours.

'Oh Jesus Christ,' muttered Barry, as we descended the steps of the location van one after the other, 'it's the bloody Teletubbies.'

He lit his cigarette, possibly to hide his mirth.

'Come on, then,' he said. 'Let's get it done.'

In a chapter about photographers, it would be remiss of me not to mention the one I lived with, Filthy Rich; after all, he'd taken my very first pictures, booked me for my very first shoots and then used me as a live-in muse for the first few months of our relationship, testing out lighting techniques and trying out new ideas, and generally using this as an excuse to get me naked. But the thing was that – after those first few months – we worked *terribly* together.

For once I had moved past the initial politeness phase, that bit in the relationship where you'll do anything to please one another and just sit there staring lovingly into one another's eyes, once that had passed, I found it simply impossible to take instruction from him. It was like a mental blockade that I couldn't circumnavigate. I heard him asking me if I could kindly move my left leg, or make my right hand less claw-like, or point my toe or tilt my chin, but, due to some sort of subconscious control issue, I physically could not carry out his requests. It was a problem.

'Can you just turn your head to me slightly?' he'd say.

'Well, does it look good like that?' I'd reply. 'Isn't it better this way, the way I have it?'

'Are you looking through the lens,' he'd say, 'or am I?'

'I don't need to be looking through the lens,' I'd argue, 'I know what my face looks like.'

And so it would continue. And as chance would have it, we were booked on quite a few jobs together, sometimes when our relationship was completely unknown to the clients or other people on the shoot. Which you'd think would be exciting and would add a little sexy frisson to proceedings, but no: it simply meant that I couldn't chat back.

One of my favourite photographers was a minor aristocrat who lived on a farm and who gave a running commentary on absolutely everything and anything, incessantly and with a wide-eyed sort of fascination. As though he had been kept in a cellar since birth, just reading about life, and only recently let out.

'Ah, a wind chime is chiming!' he would say. 'And this – a cat flap – look at the way it's like an exact replica of the bigger door it sits within!'

He was long limbed, his legs and arms like pipe cleaners, and I suspect he was double-jointed because his walk was bandy and the way he held his camera meant that he could take it off the tripod and twist it this way and that in his hands without ever changing his grip.

He touched everything – 'feel this traffic cone, very smooth to the touch' – and noticed every tiny event, reporting on it with barely disguised glee.

'A lorry, reversing *very* close to a parked car over there. Beep beep beep.'

'Fifteen starters on the menu!'

'Eight different fruits in the fruit salad, including kumquat.'

If you can imagine how excited he was about life in general then there's no need to tell you quite how enthusiastically he did his job.

'Woohoo, here she comes!' he would say, as I emerged from hair and makeup.

'Frog green!' he said about one of the swimming costumes when we were away on location. 'High leg, low-rise bikini bottoms, pink vest top – not matching – let's shoot!'

His favourite words were 'smashing' and 'fantastic'. And 'corking'.

'Corking!' he said as the sun started to drop behind the horizon and the light changed. 'The sun is dropping behind the horizon and the light has changed, let's get another Polaroid there please, Davros.'

'There she is,' he said, looking at me through the camera, 'face in profile, angry frown, wishing I'd stop talking and just get the bloody photo taken! What?'

You didn't need to be observant to notice that, it was plain for all to see.

Chapter 18

Living, Breathing Jackson Pollock

You never really knew what you might be doing on a shoot, or who you might meet, but it was (apart from the trousers-wearing job) almost never dull. You could be modelling pop socks in a west London studio one day and pretending to be a lion tamer in an East Berlin circus tent the next. One week, you'd be doing an ad for cat food, smiling as you padded around softly in a warm, plushly carpeted penthouse, the next, you were being tied up in string like a Christmas ham and shot at with paint from a Super Soaker.

'Good God, darling,' said Daz, as I staggered into the agency afterwards. 'Are you alright? You look as though you've just done three rounds in a bear-baiting pit.'

'I've been stripped down to my underwear,' I replied, 'and blasted with cold paint through a gigantic water pistol. Three rounds in a bear-baiting pit might have been easier.'

'Oh, that sounds terrible darling,' said Daz. 'How did the shoot go?'

I looked at her incredulously.

'That *was* the shoot,' I said.

'Goodness,' Daz replied, 'what fun.'

That particular job had been sold in as one of Daz's 'golden opportunities' – a job characterised by its long working hours, dubious long-term benefits and total lack of fee. In this case, one of the most prolific and highly regarded photographers in the world was working on a personal project with one of the most renowned makeup artists in the world, but the most they'd given, information-wise, was that it would be filmed in a studio and used for a website.

'It'll only take a few hours,' Daz had said. 'What have you got to lose?'

Oh, I don't know. My dignity? My will to live? My brand new La Perla skin-toned knickers, worn because I considered it a 'special occasion' and didn't realise I was going to be turned into a living, breathing Jackson Pollock?

I'd thought – stupidly, because it was always a mistake to set great expectations – that this might finally (again) be the pivotal shoot in my career. It was becoming something of a stuck record but in the back of my mind, I did believe that this one could be *the one*. Again. That's not to say I was some disillusioned, naïve twit still hankering after her five minutes of fame; I was working a lot and earning good money. A quick trot down the high street and you'd see me in five or six fashion store windows at once and maybe up on some billboard for something or other, and if you nipped into a newsagent then you might be able to scoop up two or three magazines with my face on their inside pages.

I wasn't hankering after supermodeldom, after super-anything, really, but the idea that I might strike it lucky and suddenly be elevated to the financial heights of proper star status wasn't an unappealing one. And before this shoot I had allowed myself a small daydream: I imagined a plain white studio, beautiful in its bareness, with an antique wooden stool placed in its centre, lit by one simple softbox.

'Wow,' the famous photographer would say, folding onto his stool in a louche kind of manner, crossing his legs and resting his elbows on his knees, 'you look incredible. I can't believe I've not shot you yet. How long have you been modelling for now?'

'Just a few years,' I'd say.

'Just a few years.' He'd ponder this for a moment, touching his chin and staring at the white studio floor, and then he'd pick up his camera and the special, soul-stirring, one-on-one photographic alchemy would begin. The cover of *Vogue* would be mine.

But obviously this is not what happened. You know the drill by now.

There were already seven girls at the studio when I arrived at ten o'clock and there were still another four to come. And when an assistant rushed up to me and asked in a panicked voice, 'OK, who are you? Model or paint-thrower?' I knew that my daydream had just been a silly little fantasy.

I sat in the makeup chair, listening to the famous makeup artist outline her concept: she was the painter and we, the twelve girls, were to become the living canvas on which she would work. Standing only in our underwear, flesh bound in string and distorted into unfamiliar lumps and bulges, we would become abstract, a mere texture. Faces obscured with masks, thick eyebrows, false noses.

Oh well, I thought, *maybe they'll do something good with my hair*. I imagined it coming out of rollers and bouncing itself into a Linda Evangelista-esque masterpiece.

At that point, the makeup artist came over and placed her hands on my shoulders. 'Carlos,' she said, looking over to the hair stylist. 'Put this one in a bald cap. I want her to be particularly featureless.'

Once prepped, we girls stood there like beasts at an abattoir, shifting from leg to leg, waiting to be shot with the paint guns. And we laughed – how we laughed. What a weird old job we had, hohoho.

'In real life, this wouldn't even be called a job,' said one girl, through her rubber mask, 'seeing as though we're not being paid.'

There seemed to be a correlation in the modelling world between 'not being paid' and 'having a really shit time'. The world of modelling very vaguely mimicked the real world in that usually, the worse the job, the less you got paid and the less likelihood there was of having a good lunch spread put in front of you. Conversely, it seemed that the more you got paid for a job, the better you were treated and the more likely it was that you would have to do something so piss-easy and quick that you would barely believe your luck. You'd get no pounds and zero pence to risk life and limb riding a penny farthing around a notoriously rough East End estate wearing a sequinned leotard and a feathered cape, or you'd get £10,000 to sit in a reconstructed diner booth for twenty minutes, pretending to bite into a burger. Fees for modelling jobs bore no relation to amount of effort or degree of inconvenience. A twelve-hour shoot in a town square in Siberia, where you had to pose for three hours at a time holding a concrete sphere weighing forty-eight kilos? £105 plus agency fee, no transport provided. Oil of Ulay-sponsored magazine feature? Half an hour in makeup, a lunch spread from Carluccio's and one close-up shot of your right eye? £6,500 and a car back home. None of it made sense. The more you made, the easier the job and the better you got looked after.

TV and advertising were the best. You'd be given a dressing room, sometimes, or if you were on location then maybe even your own trailer. And people would bring you whatever you needed, whenever you needed it, and if you ever had to leave the confines of your assigned temporary living quarters there would be someone with you, probably in case you got lost or stolen and ended up costing production a ton of money in wasted time.

Once, I got paid an outrageous sum to fly to Cape Town in British Airways first class and appear for four seconds in a shampoo commercial. I had a large suite at an expensive hotel and had a driver, my own trailer on set and something called *per diem*, which was basically pocket money for you to spend on anything that wasn't covered by production.

Which was . . . nothing. Because everything was covered by production.

I didn't realise it at the time, but this job really was to be the very best of my career, both financially and in terms of auxiliary perks. Never again would I be given actual pyjamas to change into on a flight, never again would I return from the toilet with my complimentary Anya Hindmarch washbag to find that my seat had been transformed into a small bedroom, complete with duvet, pillows and a hot toddy nightcap resting on the side table. I'd go business class, again, yes, but this first class journey was the closest I'd ever get to being the president of the USA. Lobster thermidor. *Oysters*!

And the money. It was outrageously good. So good that then, in 2006, the initial fee alone was enough to put down as a decent flat deposit. On top of that, it was a TV commercial, which meant that you got paid again and again, every time the company wanted to use it. More money for usage in Europe, another big payment for North America, same all over when they wanted to play it after Christmas. It was a blinder of a job, so much so that when I had done the casting for it, I had been very specifically told not to fuck things up.

'Darling,' said Daz. 'You absolutely cannot fuck this up. And I mean that both rhetorically and as an order. They saw your first audition and they all loved you, so just do what you did before and I think it's in the bag.'

'What did I do before?' I asked.

'It's the head-swinging one,' said my agent. 'You're playing fine and fat.'

'Fine and fat?'

'Sorry darling, misread that, force of habit. I meant fine and flat! Fine and flat hair.'

'Oh yeah,' I said. 'The one where I have to throw my head down behind a pillar to get bigger roots? Piece of piss.'

'Well, get an early night, darling, and look fresh-faced. Oh wait – it's Declan DeLorean's party tonight at the Shadow Lounge, so come to that and then go home and get an early night. So long as you're in bed by three . . .'

I arrived at the casting studios grossly hungover at 8.55 on the dot, sweating an unknown spirit from my pores and holding onto the reception desk whilst the casting assistant retrieved my form. I felt like a drowning sailor grasping onto the beam of a sinking ship. The room swayed, my mouth tasted salty, the floor appeared to swell and retreat beneath my feet.

'Ruth!' said the casting director. Her voice was loud on a normal day but that morning it was as though she'd bellowed at me down an ear trumpet. My vision broke into wavering lines, as though my signal-receiving aerial was experiencing interference.

'You're first up, you'll be pleased to know!'

She led me into the studio that surely would be the scene of my final demise, for a human body can only experience so much pain, and she shut the door behind us.

'Thanks for coming in at such short notice. This is Wade from the agency in New York, his associate Danny, and this is Tonya from Silvestre Haircare.'

Oh God. Four people to witness my undoing? I could feel vomit churning at the very top of my stomach, my vision was swinging in and out of focus. I could smell, acutely, an egg sandwich lying on one of the tables in front of the clients. The casting studio was so white. Too white! It hurt the backs of my eyes. I didn't know the clients would be here! Why were the clients here? At least there were only three of them.

'Behind them,' said the casting director, 'we have Peter, Laurence, Mandy and Keisha, all from the UK agency looking after Silvestre, and then over on that side of the studio,' she waved her arm across the room, 'another Peter – sorry, Pete – Vim, Rachael, Jamal, Leisha . . . Petra? Ah, I was right! Petra, Simon and Candice.'

I glanced about. It was like one of my worst recurring nightmares, where I find myself on a stage in a theatre with an audience waiting for me to start speaking, but I have no clue which play I'm playing in or any idea as to what my lines might be.

'Hi everyone,' I said, as brightly as I could. All of the clients, ad execs and people from the ad agency (who were basically just having a day out of the office) glanced up momentarily from their clipboards.

God, I felt so ill. The air outside looked so fresh, so cool. I just wanted to open a window and hang my head out of it like a dog. Or just hang my head, full stop, it didn't even have to be out of a window. But I had to pull myself together. I'd be fine. So long as I could keep my head relatively still on my shoulders and not jig about too much, I would be absolutely fine.

'Now, what you're going to do is this.' The casting director handed me a piece of paper with some cartoon drawings on it. 'You've done this before, I know, but I'll recap. Imagine you're a confident, happy woman about town. Everything about you is bright and bold . . . except for your hair.'

Vom, vom, vom.

'You have fine, flat hair and can never get any volume whatever you try. Don't worry: as you know, there's no speaking in this part. All of this – or most of it – is given to the audience by voiceover. What we need you to do is give a really visual, extra-physical kind of representation of what you would do to try and get volume into your roots.'

The room was silent, expectant.

'So . . . you remember this pillar?' The casting director pointed to a large, square pillar holding up the ceiling in the middle of the studio. 'You're going to duck behind it, played comically at first, just like we did before, but then we'll probably take it down a bit, get a bit more *real,* and you're going to flip your head over, shake it about in a really exaggerated way, like a dog with a dog toy, then flip it back up again as you come out from behind the pillar.'

I considered the dilemma. I would almost certainly pass out if I had to perform such acrobatics. I felt as though the top of my spine had somehow fused itself onto my skull; my brain felt as though it was sitting inside a stewpot of acid. What the hell had I done the night before? I had woken up still holding a section of kebab in my fist with an un-drunk pint of Alka-Seltzer balanced precariously on the shelf next to my bed.

'We'll do it a few times just to warm up,' said the casting director, placing a comforting hand on my shoulder, 'and then we'll start rolling.'

'Rolling?' I said, weakly. I wanted to hold her hand and keep it on my shoulder forever. The weight of it was so . . . reassuring. Rolling? I couldn't manage rolling. Hair-flipping was one thing, rolling would finish me off.

'We'll start recording you on tape,' said the casting director. 'Rolling.'

'OK, thanks Ruth,' she said as I performed my eighth 'hide behind the pillar and flip hair dramatically' move. I detected a note of disappointment. 'We're all going to take ten. If you can stick around for a bit, we might need to see you again.'

I exited the studio as cheerily but speedily as possible and sprinted to the loos. Oh, the safe haven of white porcelain and closable doors. Had I just completely ruined my chances at a life-changing job? It was difficult to care, such was the ferocity of my hangover. I needed to sleep. It was even possible that I needed actual medical attention – a drip. A cool flannel wash. Clean sheets and one of those beds that went up and down with a remote control so that I could adjust my position to suit. Slightly upright for when the room was spinning. Totally upright for throwing up. Back down flat for the resting and recovery phase.

'You look like shit!' It was Laura/Elsa/Laurelsa. Laura/Elsa had two names: her real name and her given name. Except that she had been given her given name by Daz, rather than her parents. I had witnessed the entire ceremony at the agency, which had taken place between the gurgling water cooler and the mammoth printer that printed out our cards and our portfolio pictures. We had only been two days' old, Laura/Elsa and I, but I had been allowed to retain my name because I – quote unquote – 'looked interesting', whereas Laura was 'slightly on the dull side'. Bear in mind that Laura looked as though she had been designed by a computer programme – her proportions were as near to perfect as was feasible and her facial features were almost symmetrical.

'Your name should be something interesting, darling,' Daz had said to her. 'To make up for the lack of interest elsewhere.' She sucked on her cigarette thoughtfully. 'Scandi is big right now, if you can't be Russian.'

'Sveta?' said Laura.

'Sveta?' said Daz. 'Sounds like Sweater. Total no-no.'

'Bianca?' said Laura.

'I'm not sure that's very Scandinavian,' said Daz. She continued to thumb through her copy of Swedish *Vogue*.

'Bianca Plunkett,' said Laura. 'If you say it quickly in a Swedish voice it sounds quite convincing.'

'Christ!' said the booker, almost dropping her fag. 'You didn't think you were keeping your surname, did you? It's an absolute car crash of a name! It's like the word equivalent of the Fat Controller riding a space hopper. No, darling, you will be . . .' Daz paused dramatically. 'Elsa Sondgarten.'

And thus, to the whoosh of the printer and with a sprinkling of holy Marlboro ash, Laura Plunkett was laid to rest and Elsa Sondgarten was born.

'What time did you leave last night?' said Laura/Elsa, who was now widely known as Laurelsa through a sense of solidarity and pity.

'I don't know.' I really didn't.

'Oh my God. Why have you got a twenty-pound note sticking out of your bra?'

'Have I?' I looked down. Sure enough, for all to see, a folded banknote was poking out – in reality, an emergency taxi fund, but looking for all the world like a stripper tip. 'I think it must have become dislodged with all of my hair swinging and head flipping.'

'Oh, are you fine and flat? I'm here for blonde hair with brassy tones.' Laurelsa swished her hair. 'It doesn't have any orange in it so – get this – they have to dye it ginge and then dye it out again afterwards.'

'That sounds,' I said, 'as though it could go horribly, horribly wrong.' I rested my head against the toilet door.

'Do you want a Pro Plus?' said Laurelsa. 'I have six.'

'Why on earth have you got those?' I said. 'Are you doing your GCSEs?'

I held out a hand to receive. Caffeine did odd things to me, energetic sorts of things. It was potentially not a great idea to imbibe during the casting for what could be the most important job of my life, but I could barely move my head. My eyes were on fire. I had to possibly go and do a second round of head-flipping, hair-swishing madness and nothing, absolutely nothing, could make me feel any worse.

'Laurelsa,' I stage-whispered across the waiting room. Fourteen minutes had elapsed. 'Elsa! Laura!'

My heart was beating out of my chest, my eyes were now popping rather than on fire. My hands were shaking, my jaw had locked, my elbows had taken on a mind of their own, sawing back and forth over the pleather armrests as though I'd recently escaped my straightjacket.

'Laura!' It was difficult to shout through gritted teeth.

What? She mouthed. She was busy. Peter from the UK ad agency was with her, touching the roots of her hair and saying something about dying it strawberry blonde.

'Help . . . me . . . Laura!'

'Elsa Sondgarten?' The casting director stuck her head out of the studio door into the waiting room. 'Ah, there. Come back in Elsa, let's chat about your hair colour . . .'

Laurelsa and Peter walked into the brightly lit studio, leaving the door open. I could hear the scraping of chairs as people inside the room stood up and I could see a few of the agency people gathering around Laurelsa's head, examining her colour and holding strands up to a board that was covered in silky loops of dyed hair. My senses, since taking the Pro Plus tablets, were heightened to the point that any noise above a whisper was painful. It was like being Superman – I could suddenly see ants crawling along next to the bin and the droplets running down the inside of the watercooler were vividly three dimensional.

Perhaps I would die like this, hearing every sniffle of snot that the receptionist kept snorting back up her nose instead of blowing it, seeing every mote of dust suspended in the close air, smelling the Glade plug-in with its vanilla-scented insert. I felt a pain in my left arm – a sure sign of impending heart attack. My dad had always warned me it started that way, that it would kill you stone dead. I clutched it with my right hand and rocked back and forth, clenching and unclenching my teeth. I realised I was gurning and tried not to gurn.

'Right then,' said the casting director. 'Where's our fine and flat?'

That was me. Fine and flat. My heart was pounding. It was me! Fine and flat! All of a sudden, I had a huge surge of energy. I unclasped my arms from around myself, stopped rocking, stood up forcefully and *confidently*, held my head high, swished my hair from side to side. I was back in the room.

'Then one time,' I rabbited on, 'at National Children's Woodwind Orchestra, I thought that natural tights meant black tights, because naturally I'd wear black tights because that's the normal colour of tights, right? But they meant natural to match your skin tone, so I should have been wearing some of those light beige-coloured tights that grannies wear, but instead I was the only person wearing these thick, woolly, black tights with bobbles on. I think they might even have been those ribbed ones, you know, with knitted lines of knitting down them—'

'Just your name and agency, Ruth,' said the casting director, 'that would be great.'

The entire room was gawping at me. I could see why. My sheer energy, my wit, my comic timing, my ability to retrieve anecdotal material at the drop of a hat – I knew that, if they weren't exactly won over with my first performance of the morning, they would be now.

'And just give us your profiles to camera again – I know we've done this but this tape is being sent straight to New York so that we can confirm as soon as possible. Did we mention that flights out to Cape Town are in three days' time?'

'No, Barbara, you hadn't, but I am *ready to rumble*!'

God, I was on form. Superhuman, you could have said. I couldn't stop smiling! I couldn't stop moving! I jauntily jigged from side to side as they set up for the pillar-hide-head-swing-reveal shot.

'The money shot,' I said, punching the air in front of me and skipping on my toes like a boxer. 'Just tell me when.'

I remember thinking, *I should do this Pro Plus stuff more often.* And then I remember flinging my head towards the pillar. And then not much else. 2006: the year I got high on drugs, knocked myself out on a pillar and *still* got the job. Maybe I could be a supermodel after all.

Chapter 19

Our Experienced Yogi

Hair-flinging wasn't the only skill I could turn my hand (or head) to at a casting. I was happy to give almost anything a go in the name of a hefty paycheque – anything but dancing, that is.

This was mostly because I was terrible at dancing and hated the idea that someone else would witness my inadequacy. If I knew that my frenetic, uncoordinated limb-flinging was being actively observed then I became frozen with mortification, overcome by the sort of intense humiliation most people reserve for being caught receiving oral sex from their hoover. Call me uptight, but I had never really understood how anyone could dance in front of a watching audience without dying of embarrassment. The moves were all so base, so sexual – the gyrating and the thrusting and the slinking of hands over the body that suggested manual self-manipulation of the erogenous zones. That's not to say I *never* danced. Drunk with friends? Fine.

Careering about the dancefloor at a wedding reception with no shoes on and ABBA blasting out from DJ Derek's mediocre speakers? Also fine. But *performing* to an attentive crowd? Or, even worse, singular person? No siree.

So dancing was a total no-no for me. And a surprising number of castings required you to do it – even, I had noticed, when the end job itself had no identifiable need for dance skills. I developed a hunch, after a while, that some casting directors used dance as a weapon, a hook-ended stick to poke around with and root out those who lacked confidence or who might be less pliable than other contenders.

'Dance like a dying hedgehog,' said one director, who was casting a television advert for a company who made stainless steel pans.

'Jig like a German barmaid,' said another.

'OK, Ruth,' said one man, at a request casting for a bikini shoot, 'if you could just give us a few seconds of your best dancing when we play the music, that would be brilliant. Dance like nobody's watching!'

But that was my problem. Somebody was watching. And often, when the advert came out that I had cast for but inevitably failed to get, there would be absolutely no dancing involved.

'Just a quick dance, now,' said one woman who was casting the part of a mortgage advisor at a high street bank, 'if you don't mind.'

I did mind.

'Sorry,' I said, because this was in 2007 and I was a weary veteran model by this point, 'I've looked over the script but I can't see anywhere that the mortgage advisor starts dancing . . .'

'It's just to see how you move,' said the woman, who wore a cravat and had a cropped thatch of hair the colour of sand. 'The client has asked for ten or fifteen seconds of dancing on film after you deliver your lines.'

The lines were schmaltzy and twee, to be spoken with feeling by the mortgage advisor to a made-up couple who were in the process of buying their first house. Except that the couple weren't there, so I had to say the lines to a coat thrown over a tripod.

You buy your home, I had to say, *but we hold your hand.*

And then: *That's why first-time buyers love us. And second-time buyers. You move, we move with you.*

'So just say the lines . . . then dance for ten seconds?' I said.

'Ten or fifteen,' said the woman in the cravat.

I was nothing if not brilliant at remembering instructions.

'You move, we move with you,' I said and then, without pause and without waiting for any sort of musical cue, I immediately burst into violent limb throwing that propelled me out of my chair and onto my feet. Ten seconds of pure dance carnage ensued, the woman in the cravat watching slack-jawed whilst the soles of my shoes squeaked horribly on the studio floor in the awkward silence. No mortgage advisor job for me; twelve grand down the pan.

Fortunately, not every casting required a talent for dance. There were plenty of other skills in high demand, usually ones I didn't possess. Not that it mattered, apparently.

'Babe,' Texana would say, 'can you ski? It's for Breitling watches and you need to be able to slalom down into shot.'

'I've never skied,' I said, 'no.'

'Never?'

'No.'

'Babe, anyone can ski. Just tell them you used to ski as a kid, you'll be fine.'

'OK but when I get the job, surely I'll then have to actually ski?'

'We'll deal with that if it comes to it.'

Or,

'Hi darling,' Daz would say, 'can you drive a scooter? . . . OK, but if push came to shove?'

The worst 'sporting pretender' casting was one for a newly launched women's sportswear brand and their range of yoga garments. And the fault, this time, was entirely with me.

'Babe, do you do yoga?' Texana asked when I phoned to check in.

'Nope, but my mum teaches it.'

There was a pause.

'OK babe, but . . . do *you* do yoga? It's just that this casting, you'll have to go through a series of poses so you kind of need to know the lingo.'

'Yeah, I can do the positions,' I said, 'the stretching up and the crossed legs. I can probably still do a headstand.'

'Right . . .' said Texana. 'I just . . . I'm wary of having a repeat of the beer commercial situation.'

'Where I did the Karate Kid moves?'

'Oh my God, babe, what the hell. They said it was

like watching someone drop acid and then try to fight themselves in a hall of mirrors.'

'Huh,' I said. 'I'll make sure I practise some yoga positions then.'

'Poses, my babe,' said Texana. 'They're called poses.'

'Fear not,' I said. 'I'm limbering up as we speak. Going in for the warrior dog and the downward spiral.'

The yoga casting took place in a dance studio, beautifully bright with sunshine streaming in through two full-length windows, reflected from a wall of mirrors onto the wooden floor. The clients, three friendly women in their thirties or perhaps forties were seated behind a table that was piled with model portfolios. They looked very serene, hair loosely pulled into ballerina buns or flowing onto shoulders, all of them clothed in the sort of soft fabrics and gentle colours that make your own clothes look as though they've been stolen from an eighteenth-century vampire.

'Lovely to meet you, Ruth,' the first client said. 'We've been desperate to book you for a campaign so it's brilliant that this yoga range could be a good fit. You've got exactly the look that we want.'

'We'll start with the warrior pose,' said client number two, putting on some spa music.

Warrior pose? What an earth was this? Couldn't they just see me in the leggings and crop top and be satisfied with that? Surely on the shoot day someone could just arrange my legs and arms?

'It's important for us,' said client number three, 'that whoever we use genuinely practises yoga.'

Oh.

'We really want the campaign to feel authentic and for the images to call out to our customers – we're not just a brand using models who look good in our clothes, we're a brand using models who will wear our clothing in real life. Actual sportswomen, athletes, mountaineers, and you, hopefully, as our experienced yogi.'

Wait. What?

'Yogi?'

'Let's get started and see how the samples look,' said client two. 'I can't wait to try the taupe harem pants on you.'

For warrior, I pretended to hold a spear in one hand and put the other on my hip. In fairness, it wasn't a million miles away from the correct pose: I'd put my legs in a strong, wide-apart stance that looked relatively convincing, actually. Bending forward pose was pretty self-explanatory and, miraculously, I actually knew the bridge. It was when the other poses, the more abstract names, came along that the shit really hit the proverbial fan. Who would ever have thought that 'mountain pose' would be 'standing up straight'? What mountain is tall and thin and not large and round, like a boulder? Which would obviously make more sense, explaining completely why a person would think that they should turn themselves into a big ball, hugging their knees and tucking their head between their legs . . .

'OK,' said client two, with just the slightest tremor of confusion in her voice, 'let's move on to the downward-facing dog.'

I mean, how would a dog face downwards? Isn't it

already mostly down-facing, due to the fact that it walks on four legs?

'That's more the cow pose,' said client one, 'but with four straight legs. I'm not sure I've ever seen it like that but OK. Let's now move into the child's pose.'

Well. Even under such intense pressure my mind was spraying out ideas left right and centre, God bless it. It had sensed extreme career danger and had risen to the occasion, providing pose solutions to each and every prompt with only ever a second or two's hesitation. It was as though I was on a weird version of Charades *Mastermind*, in which the presenter called out a random word and I had to work out which action might possibly – as in, a one in a thousand chance – be the correct match.

Never had my mind and body had to work so hard as one. And now, after the cow and the downward dog and a mountain pose and a boat pose (which I had been pretty pleased with, seeing as though I'd managed to use my arms as oars *and* one leg as a mast) I had one last challenge. The child's pose.

'Do . . . you need any help?' asked client three, as I stood quietly upon the mat, eyes closed, breathing in through my nose and out through my mouth. Buying time.

'No,' I said, eyes still closed, hands over my ears, because it just felt right, 'I'm fine thanks, I'm doing some breathwork before I do the next position.'

What poses did children do? There was the foetal sleeping position, which didn't seem stretchy enough to be a yoga pose and so was my least favoured option, and then I had thought about skipping. But you couldn't hold a skipping pose, or skip in slow motion, unless you wanted to look like a complete fruitcake, so that one wasn't likely either. Children liked to climb trees, but I'd done the tree pose with my branches stretched out and my toes wriggling into the floor like roots (nice touch!) and so what were the chances they'd get me to repeat myself? No, it would have to be my fourth choice and I was pretty confident about it because so far, they hadn't asked me for either of my solid, tried-and-tested yoga moves. And I wasn't mad keen on doing a headstand in front of them, and so I dropped down into the most childish pose of all, the position that all under-tens must adopt for hours in the schooling week, in a hall stinking of boiled vegetables: sitting cross-legged.

'Er,' said client one.

'Uhm,' said number two.

'I'm not sure that's quite the one we're after,' said client three, as I clumsily rose to standing position, or 'normal pose'.

'It's alright,' I said, 'I know that my type of yoga's not for everyone.'

Chapter 20

Never Sit Down in Lingerie, Darling

It was funny, I hated dancing at castings because it felt demeaning and humiliating, yet later on that year I was more than happy to snog an eighty-three-year-old man whilst straddling him on a park bench. At a casting.

In all fairness, I went along to the snog-a-pensioner casting happy in the knowledge that a) nobody needed to actually snog anyone for the casting itself, you only had to do it if you got the job, and b) there was no hope in hell that I was going to get the job anyway. Mainly because Perfect Candice was also auditioning and had cracked out the Hervé Léger bodycon bandage dress that she liked to sheath herself in if ever a casting called for something particularly erection-inducing. In case you're not familiar with the concept of bandage dresses, it wasn't made of actual bandages. Candice didn't arrive looking like a leper, or a mummy from *Scooby Doo*; the bandage aspect was merely that the dress looked like it had been formed from hundreds of individual tight strips. Neon pink strips. It was a showstopper.

And so in I went to the casting, whistling a jolly tune and having an inward chuckle to myself about how weird my job was, fully assuming I wouldn't get the part. I strode in, joyfully said my vital statistics to the camera, straddled the old man, leaned in to pretend-kiss him, did some hair-flicking, acted out some gum-chewing and then left.

I have to say that I was pretty pleased with my performance, for once. I had pulled out all the stops in terms of meeting the brief and had managed to faux-snog an ancient man who looked like Touché Turtle, all without grimacing. In fact, I'd done better than that: I'd made my attraction for him seem believable. To the point where perhaps I should have been thinking about an acting career.

The ad was for a nicotine replacement gum, so tasty as to be absolutely irresistible, to the point where a young, sexy woman would tongue-wrestle a pensioner to get at some. And I totally aced it. Whether it was the professional way in which I straddled or the friendly banter I had with the old man as we waited for the camera to roll, I don't know. Perhaps it was the fact that I was so relaxed, knowing that I would never actually get the job because Candice was there, and even if Candice *hadn't* been there, my odds of getting the role were forty to one.

'Darling, great news,' said Delia, who was my commercials agent.

Being Delia must have been a bit like being one of the

people who phone up the monthly winner of the Premium Bonds million pounds prize: nobody would ever be displeased to hear from you. She was the bearer of good news, the harbinger of financial optimism, the literal keeper of the pot of gold. If Delia was calling it meant that you a) had a casting for something potentially very lucrative, b) were in the running for something potentially very lucrative and needed to not book a holiday over certain dates, or c) had been booked for something that was almost certainly very lucrative. In this case it was option c.

'Darling, great news,' she said. 'You got the nicotine gum commercial. It's shooting tomorrow in Spain, £8,000 plus commission, flying out tonight.'

There was a pregnant pause before I answered, and it didn't escape Delia's notice.

'Great,' I said, in a slightly trembly voice, 'I'll go home and grab my stuff.'

'You don't sound too happy, darling,' said Delia.

'No, no,' I lied. Who wouldn't be happy about having to tongue a man almost four times their age? 'I'm just trying to remember where my passport is.'

'Well, you've just got back from Paris, darling, so it must be close to hand. Are you sure you're OK? You're not worried about the kissing part of this, are you? It's so bonkers, darling, the things you end up doing!'

'Well,' I said, feeling a sense of relief at being able to share my anxieties. 'I did sort of put it out of my head because I knew I'd never get the job.'

'Oh darling, they *loved* you,' said Delia. 'Of course you were going to get the job. Apparently nobody has ever looked so convincing kissing someone they didn't want to kiss. It was as though you enjoyed it, they said.'

'Well, that's because I was pretending.' I heard the petulance in my own voice and felt instantly ungrateful. 'It's a bit different having to actually make mouth-to-mouth contact.'

My stomach did a little flip just thinking about it. I mean, Bert had been a lovely man, and all that – if I had been doing some kind of harvest festival provisions delivery or a Help the Aged social call, he'd have been top of my list.

'Oh darling, you'll be fine,' said Delia. 'Just think, one day Rich will be that age and you'll kiss him for free.'

I walked up to Oxford Circus tube questioning my entire existence and feeling sick with worry, not for the first time, that I was somehow selling a vital part of myself just for money.

But isn't that what a lot of people do? my devil's advocate said. *If you'd been a lawyer, you'd have been representing disgusting people and trying to get them reduced sentences. If you'd been a journalist, you'd have been forced to find stories that might have ruined people's lives . . .*

This was true. If I had been a hotshot lawyer, then I probably would have faced daily moral dilemmas. Defending child molesters or psychopathic billionaires. Surely kissing an old man, once, for money, was somehow less character-wrecking?

Think about estate agents, said the devil's advocate, as I fed my zone 1–6 travelcard through the ticket barrier. *They sell houses that they know have damp issues, or a roof that's about to fall in, or with neighbours that throw wild parties every other Friday until 3am – do you think they stay up at night questioning their life choices?*

Perhaps every career required some kind of moral compromise. Apart from the essential and wholesome ones, like nursing and teaching and driving buses and planes.

Even a doctor has to make distressing decisions, continued devil's advocate, as I stepped into the tube carriage. *Who to save first in a mass crisis, whether to operate on someone when they've only had three hours of sleep and just toasted their phone instead of the bread . . .*

Devil's advocate was right. Kissing an OAP for thousands of pounds wasn't a big deal. It wasn't as though the OAP would find it sexual. It wasn't as though I was being paid to sexually gratify another person. It wasn't *prostitution*, for God's sake; it didn't even come close to the definition of *engaging in sexual practice with someone in exchange for payment*. Not one little bit.

By the time I arrived home, I was at peace with the situation. It was fine. It would be a few takes, hopefully no more than a dozen, and I could pretend the man was dying and I was performing life-saving resuscitation on him. Not all heroes wore capes.

All I had to do now was explain to Rich that I was going to fly to Spain to repeatedly snog an elderly gentleman. In a minidress.

'Hahaha,' said Rich, whose jealousy trigger remained permanently off. 'This could only happen to you.'

'Aren't you even a bit cross that I'll be kissing another man?'

'You'll make his day,' said Rich. 'It's almost an act of charity.'

'Well, I'm going to hate every second of it,' I said. 'I can't think of anything worse.'

'At least they're not making you dance,' he replied.

As it happened, and to my utmost relief, the kissing job cancelled at the very last minute. As I was walking to the tube to get to Heathrow, in fact, travel bag slung over shoulder.

'Hello darling,' said Delia. 'Bad news I'm afraid.'

But it was never bad news with Delia.

'The job in Spain is off,' she said. 'Most annoying, darling, I'm so sorry, but you still get paid.'

See? Always the bringer of good fortune.

It had been a lucky escape, but I wasn't so lucky with the next couple of jobs. When it came to embarrassing things that I didn't especially want to do, the next jobs took the proverbial biscuit, and the worst thing was that I didn't even have any choice in the matter. At least with the old man casting I'd known exactly what I was letting myself in for – I'd made a fully informed decision when I'd dropped onto his lap and pretend-kissed him. The two jobs that followed gave absolutely no indication whatsoever that they'd involve anything unusual or – I'm just going to come out and say it – humiliating.

When the job for the Italian makeup company confirmed, nobody casually mentioned that I'd have to have a rubber penguin hat pulled over my head and that I'd be swinging from a rope over shark-infested waters.

In lingerie. And when a German high street brand wanted me for a womenswear shoot, I was never forewarned that at the end of the shoot, someone would snip clippings from the ends of my hair, glue them to my face as a moustache, put me in a mad wig and then photograph me in (again) lingerie as a 'Sexy Einstein'. It was just never put out there as a possibility. Would I have refused to go? Would I have drawn the line at such degradation? Probably not, but it would have been nice to have had the choice.

'He's going to get you!' screamed the photographer, as I swung back and forth across the studio in my rubber penguin hat. I had been suspended above the floor on a rope and the floor had been painted blue, to suggest sea.

'Argh, argh, the shark!' she screamed again. 'Look scared!' She placed her camera down on the floor and mimed looking scared, her knees pressed together and her arms hugging her body. Which was a pointless mime because I could not press my knees together and nor could I hug my arms to my body, seeing as I was gripping onto a rope for dear life. It was the sort of physically demanding activity you'd give to a new marine if you wanted to put them through their paces – a marine on some sort of special task force where you needed to be able to stay strong amidst extreme mental stress and degradation.

'Look scared, even more scared!' said the photographer. 'You're really being scared now, little penguin, and please, remember to breathe in.'

There was no rope at the Einstein job but there was a freezing lake, which was put to good use. The indignity of having my own hair glued to my top lip was lessened, ever so slightly, by the fact that I was in Germany with two other girls and they were also being made facially hirsute. We turned to one another and laughed uproariously about it and then, later, shared our collective sense of fury when we were herded into the lake to be shot.

But these minor humiliations, these little degradations, you just had to shrug them off. Because if there was one talent that you needed as a model then it was to be able to grow a thick skin. You had to be able to survive hearing not-so-nice things about yourself and not let those things enter your psyche. You had to stand there and take it if a Parisian casting director huffed that you were too fat, or someone in Milan whipped out a measuring tape in front of an audience, or someone in Tokyo said that you had a Pinocchio nose.

It was cruel, in a way, that as a model, you had to carry around a whole book of pictures that looked barely like you did in real life. You went to a casting, you passed them this portfolio, filled cover-to-cover with the most glamourised, perfected images of yourself, and then you had to sit there whilst the client looked from book to person, person to book, and tried not to look shocked.

Can this really be the same girl? they would undoubtedly have been thinking, a lot of the time. *The person before me looks like she's from* The Nightmare Before Christmas, *yet in her photos, well, she's a total babe.*

One of the things about fashion models, the models who did shows and billboards and pages of high fashion for good magazines, was that the majority of them looked very normal in real life. Sometimes just plain odd. In fact, quite often, the better and edgier the model, the weirder they'd look in the street. And even if you weren't the best or the edgiest, you'd still be met with looks of disbelief if you told normal people what you did for a living.

'You?' they'd say, these people who had no inkling of just how brilliantly barmy the industry was. 'You're a model? You don't look like a model.'

The majority of people associated modelling with the traditionally pretty sort of girls that you might have seen at a beauty pageant or Miss World, whereas the fashion industry – especially the higher up you got – craved uniqueness, alternative beauty, types of beauty that were largely unattainable because their characteristics were so rare.

'I can't believe it,' they'd say, the non-industry people. 'A model! You!'

Thank God for the hair and makeup professionals and their unbridled talent for polishing up tired, pallid girls who looked as though they'd been dug from a shallow grave. At 9am, at 7am, sometimes even at 5am, they were masters of transformation, magicians with hair wands, lip brushes and lash glue. I could forgive them the little scalp burns, which were par for the course when someone had been given eight minutes to curl your entire head of hair; I could even forgive the time that a makeup artist almost set fire to my face because the hair stylist was spraying hairspray and she chose that exact moment to light up her cigarette. (This was in Paris, obviously, and she kept it clamped between her teeth the entire time she applied my mascara, puffing out smoke straight onto my eyeballs.) These were just hazards of the job and they were many and varied. At one shoot a woman glued beetle wings to my eyes and at another, a stylist merrily re-pierced my ears with the prongs of some cheap-metalled H&M earrings, giving me balloon lobes and an antibiotic-requiring infection.

The opening of my ear-piercing holes was actually a running theme over the course of my twelve-year-long modelling career. There could only have been a handful of shoots where someone *didn't* claim to be the person who would finally get an earring through my closed-up lobes once and for all. It almost became a challenge because nobody could quite accept the fact that I had earring holes yet nothing could pass through them. The closed-over holes were a tease. An invitation. And there was always someone on the team who would see that as their area of expertise. Either they'd had more piercings than a pin cushion or they knew someone who knew someone else who was a professional piercer, and it was simply not possible, in their view, to have holes yet not be able to pass something through them.

'Listen, babes,' said the makeup artist, 'my boyfriend works at Tits and Tats. There's nothing he can't pierce. Clits, bumholes—'

'Why would you pierce your bumhole?' I said. 'It's already a hole. How can you pierce a hole? It's like a double negative.'

'The sphincter,' said the makeup artist, waving her eyelash curlers (a torturous device, another health hazard), 'not the hole itself.'

'Your ears have holes,' said the hairstylist, who had

changed his name from Pete to Bethlehem, 'and you can pierce those.'

The makeup artist looked at him and snapped the lash curlers like crab claws.

'Yes, whatever, *Bethlehem*. That doesn't even begin to make sense. All I'm saying is that he can pierce anything and I've seen him do it a million times – I could re-pierce her ears, piece of piss.'

'Oh,' I said, it dawning on me suddenly that the conversation was taking the turn that seemed to be customary whenever my lobes were discussed, 'I'd rather you didn't. Many have tried, all have failed.'

Lash-crabber's face darkened. 'I never fail, babes,' she said. 'Bethlehem, fetch me some ice.'

Lobe-piercing, scalp-burning, arse-kimbling . . . you had to be – quite literally – thick skinned. But at least I could rely on Daz to soothe my fears and offer up her usual confidence-boosting mantras.

It was 2006. I was twenty-five and she was taking Polaroids of me in my underwear next to her new antique stool.

'How can it be a new antique?' I said.

'It's old,' said Daz, 'so it's an antique, but new because I've only just bought it. I don't know why that's so hard to understand. Anyway, it makes the perfect prop. You can lean on it, stand next to it, interact with it . . .'

'Sit on it,' I added.

'Good God, no!' said Daz. 'Never sit down in lingerie, darling. You may as well go home and eat a hundred cheesecakes. It's instantly fattening.'

I sucked in my stomach and stood beside the stool, touching a hand to the cracked wooden seat. The whole thing felt ridiculous. Who stood next to a stool rather than sitting on it?

'Come on, darling,' said Daz, 'get with the programme. Why are you patting the stool on the head like it's a favourite nephew?'

'I'm just having an off day,' I said. 'I feel chunky and gross.'

'Chunky and gross?' said Daz, putting her Polaroid camera down on the table. 'Darling, don't be ridiculous, you could never be chunky and gross.'

I very nearly fell over sideways. Had Daz just paid me a compliment?

'Really?' I said.

'Well, I wouldn't be bothering to do lingerie Polaroids if you were chunky and gross,' said Daz. 'It would be a total waste of my time. Why would you ever think you were chunky and gross?'

Er, I thought, wanting to list at least a dozen reasons.

'Well,' I said, carefully, 'my arse is on the cusp, for a start.'

'The cusp of what, darling?' said Daz. 'What on earth are you rambling on about?'

'My arse,' I said. 'The first time I met you, you said that my arse was on the cusp. Unlike Milla Jovovich's.'

'Oh, Milla's arse,' said Daz. 'She works hard on that arse. Goodness darling, that was years ago, why are you still thinking about that?'

'It stuck in my head,' I said.

'Well,' said Daz, 'there was nothing wrong with saying that your arse was on the cusp. It was a friendly warning.'

'It meant I had to constantly worry about it falling to the wrong side of the cusp,' I said. 'You were basically saying that it was nearly too big but not quite.'

'Well, darling,' said Daz, 'it's still on the cusp, so well done, you're fine. No cusp-falling-off for you.'

I rolled my eyes.

'And you said I was too short and that my boobs were on the big side.'

Daz sighed.

'Look,' she said. 'I didn't say you were too short, darling, I said that you were *quite* short. For a model.'

'OK,' I said, 'well, it didn't fill me with confidence, that's all.'

'Oh darling,' said Daz, 'think yourself lucky. At least you were relatively young, then. Now you have your age to worry about, too.'

Chapter 21

This is Not My First Rodeo

It was the tail end of 2006, I had just turned twenty-six decrepit years of age and I thought it was time to get serious about finally giving myself that honed, chiselled Victoria's Secret body that I'd set out to get almost half a decade earlier. The gym I joined was – handily – three minutes away from the flat, door to door, and allowed just enough time for a leisurely cigarette as I ambled there through the graveyard. The main floor of the gym looked over this same graveyard, incidentally, which I thought was quite good motivation – *don't end up lying in there! Pump those legs! Strengthen that heart!* – but I rarely went into the posing pen; I preferred to go to classes. In particular, one that was carried out in a dark room with flashing lights. A class called spinning.

'Like turning around and around really quickly, darling?' asked Daz when I told her about my new regime.

'No,' I said. 'It's cycling to loud music, in the dark, but on a bike that's stuck to the floor. It's all the rage in America.'

'Goodness,' said Daz, 'I can't see that catching on.'

I'd exercised before, of course I had, but this time I took it to a new level. I was dedicated. Spinning three times a week, weightlifting twice a week, chain-smoking (excellent for arm and wrist mobility) seven days a week, and the usual six or so miles of walking I did per day to get to all of my castings. I began to develop quite impressive calf muscles, like Mrs Trunchbull, and the thighs of a Tour de France competitor. But still, I did not lose weight. My gym routine did not yield a stick-insect level of thinness and my six pack never appeared. Why? You might well ask. It was because of the gym cafeteria, which specialised, apparently, in trying to give its diners an immediate coronary.

The lunches in this cafeteria had undoubtedly been designed by an eight-foot-tall giant with thighs as thick as pirate ship masts. The baked potatoes were gargantuan, like partially deflated rugby balls, and a typical sandwich could have served as an emergency mattress in a baby's travel cot. The chicken salad, which was my default lunch choice, contained the following: three whole hard-boiled eggs (sliced), approximately fifteen cherry tomatoes, shaved parmesan pieces that would amount to perhaps a matchbox-sized chunk if you rewound time and stuck them all back together, about nine (giant's) handfuls of salad leaves and – I do not exaggerate – at least two chicken breasts, cooked and shredded. All of this was doused with the tastiest salad dressing I'd ever been treated to, a French-style vinaigrette that was mildly mustardy, nicely sharp, slightly eggy and probably contained six or seven tablespoons of olive oil.

The calorific content must have been the same as the average man's daily allowance. No athlete needed that much energy. It was too much of a meal for an NFL quarterback.

Yet I, Ruth Crilly, five feet eight and eight stone four, tucked into one of these 'extra healthy' chicken salads two or three times a week, rarely leaving a scrap behind because I didn't like waste. This huge plate of food, which was served in a pasta dish that was almost the same diameter as the table, cost a whopping £5.50 – none of that was going in the bin. Gym-going was a pricey affair, especially if you had a six-banana, three-avocado smoothie to wash the salad down with.

I wasn't a natural exerciser because why would anyone be? Exercise was punishment, all the eighties' kids knew that. Every daytime TV programme we'd watched as children had its shiny Lycra-clad women doing aerobics in the studio, burning off all the extra calories they'd naughtily eaten. In PE, there'd be the kids who'd had to do a few extra laps of the field because they were on the tubby side – *run, fatty, run* – and the magazines we'd steal from our parents were filled with tips on how to firm up, lose pounds and get back into shape. Usually after having a baby, a.k.a. 'letting yourself go'. Nobody could afford to let themselves go, not least a model.

A model had to be ahead of the game. Nobody wanted to be on the cusp of being too big. Because once you were the wrong side of the cusp, well. That was just asking for trouble. But it was difficult to know when you were on the wrong side of the cusp, or even just heading for the cusp, because lots of people had a different opinion on what that cusp was – the important thing was that you had to have your cusp radar turned on, you had to keep an eye on the cusp-ometer. Listen to what others said about what was an acceptable body shape and size – listen to the media, listen to other models, listen to friends. And how lucky we were, as models, that the very people who wrote the stuff in the media and who created the trends – the magazine editors and the designers and the art directors and the stylists and so many more – how fortunate we were that we had direct access to their opinions on our weight and fat distribution. Straight from the horse's mouth.

For what was the point in *thinking* you were thin, or gorgeously curvaceous, or androgenous, or whatever it was you needed to be, if the editors were saying that you were slightly hefty, or not quite curvy enough, or rather too womanly to be truly androgenous? (Delete as applicable.) You needed this validation or else. It was no good looking in the mirror and liking what you saw – what was important was, *what did everyone else see*?

'I see a fat girl wanting to get out,' the stylist had said, a week before the exercise regime began.

'She eats too much, that's for sure,' said the editor, whom I'd thought was quite nice. She'd shared some personal snippets over dinner – I'd almost have popped her down as a friend, if I'd had a written list.

We were in Paris shooting a high-fashion story for a high-fashion magazine in a lovely old hotel. It had one of those old-fashioned lifts, with a metal gate to noisily pull across and an open shaft. You could hear everything through this shaft, all the way up the hotel, regardless of which floor you were on. The stylist and editor were on the ground floor; I was getting in on the third.

'Everything looks awful on her,' said the stylist, stepping into the lift. 'Frumpy. I'm tearing out my hair.'

'She should smoke more,' said the editor, pulling the rattly gate across. 'Or give up the wine.'

'Or take up running,' said the stylist. 'Like me. She said over dinner she doesn't work out.'

I waited for the lift to rise up to my floor. My hands trembled. How had this happened? I'd been fine two days before, when I'd stood in the fashion cupboard and the editor had tried on outfit after outfit, cinching in here and nipping in there. Surely they should have bailed on me then, rather than bringing me out to Paris. Had I ballooned in two days? Was it the wine? We'd all laughed at dinner, the night before, and drunk red after red, but nobody had put a quiet hand out to stop me. Nobody had raised a brow. Had they? The lift stopped, dinged. The editor opened the gate.

'Oh hi, Ruth,' said the stylist as they stepped from the lift. 'Have you had breakfast yet?'

'No,' I said. 'I was just going to go and have a cigarette.'

'You should have the croissants,' said the editor, 'they're utterly divine.'

This was why it was important to listen to criticism when

it came to your size. It might have been degrading, it may have reduced you to what was essentially just a soulless flesh bulk (hopefully not too bulky!), but you needed to know. For professional reasons. If someone else, who you might never work with or even see ever again in your life, thought that you were too fat then you had to take that on board. Being the right size was surely just a requirement of the job, after all, in the same way that a pilot needed to know what the big middle stick did and a healer needed to have magic hands. A good model apparently needed to be thin, possess unique beauty and to be able to pose – you couldn't very well expect to do the job with only two thirds of the attributes. Could you?

The models I knew were a broad church when it came to their attitude towards exercise: some were diligent, dedicated to sculpting their bodies into near-masterpieces of physical beauty, and many of them were well ahead of the curve – concerned with wellness and 'maintaining a healthy vessel' years and years before it became a trend and then a multi-billion-dollar industry. They did yoga and Pilates, and strange classes in obscure little studios using machines and weighted balls and stretchy bits of elastic band. Others, like me, worked out just enough to keep the wolf from the door, and lots did no exercise at all because they seemingly had more in common genetically with a giraffe than they did a human. Some – some, though – took things to the extreme. And now and then you'd share a flat with them.

Astrid and Loes were my flatmates in Milan. I hadn't

wanted to go to Milan but Texana had said that Milan was small, basically a village. I'd love it. I could get it done, see all the people I needed to see, in less than a week.

'Babe it's *tiny*,' she said. 'Milan is cute and compact, you'll love it. And you could literally get round all the go-sees you need to do in a day. Definitely a week. Or two.'

Texana was from the states and said *Mill-onnn* instead of Milan, like Patrick Bateman from *American Pyscho*. She also had a completely warped idea of size when it came to geographical areas, mainly because the ranch she'd grown up on was larger than the whole of Berkshire. From her description of Milan as 'cute, basically a village' and also 'ancient', I built a picture up in my head of some sort of medieval walled citadel with all of the magazine offices and photographic studios and designer showrooms quaintly packed inside. *Vogue Italia* was at the top of a turret; the Missoni offices would be down a narrow, cobbled street, sandwiched between a blacksmith's workshop and a stall selling whittled wooden spinning tops.

'It's *so* cute Crilly,' said Texana as she finalised my flights. 'You'll love it. Love. It.'

Reader, I didn't love it. As the plane began its descent over the grey, sprawling city, I knew that I had been duped once again. For where were the old city walls? Where were the turrets?

Bloody hell, I moaned inwardly as I stood outside of the apartment block that was to be my home for the next fortnight. Even to the uninitiated, the newcomer, the city of Milan virgin, the apartment block looked unpromising. For a start, there were a number of women loitering around the frontage who were definitely not dressed for the office. One, wearing a neon yellow Lycra tube dress, eyed me coldly and folded her arms across her ample chest. Two others huddled to the side of the doorway, lighting their cigarettes from a single lighter flame.

'*Buon giorno*,' I did not say, as I perused the row of buzzers and singled out the 47. I needn't have buzzed, as chance would have it, because when I went to push it, I realised that the front door was propped open with half a brick, but at least it had given my roommates prior warning of my arrival.

'Hey,' said roommate number one as I walked up to the apartment door. It was open just a crack and I could see her large eyes and a long, blonde ponytail. 'Come in,' she said, opening the door just wide enough for me to pass through and then quickly shutting it behind me, 'we're just getting started.'

Getting started with what? you may wonder.

It turned out to be their exercise routine. As I wheeled my suitcase over the lino, I saw that they had pushed the one small sofa to the edge of the living room, placed the wooden-legged coffee table upside down on top of the sofa and laid two yoga mats out on the floor. Roommate two, who had black hair cut into a severe bob, was already in situ on the yoga mat, wearing cycling shorts and a vest top, and doing very expert-looking abdominal crunches. Both girls were lightly sheened with sweat and very slightly breathless. I got the impression I'd interrupted proceedings.

'I am Astrid,' said roommate number one, 'and this is Loes.'

Loes gave a quick wave and a grimace of a smile in between crunches.

'We are just getting started with our fitness routine and you are welcome to join us,' said Astrid.

'You look as though you've already got started to me!' I said.

'No, we have just completed the one-hour warm-up,' panted Loes. 'Two hundred and thirty five,' she said, under her breath, crunching upwards and touching her elbows to her knees.

'If you like, you could do a short period of stretching and then join us for the main fitness?' said Astrid. She was wearing a kind of shiny Lycra catsuit, black and long-sleeved; she looked a bit like a liquorice lace. 'Are you wanting to join us, yes?' she said, stepping onto her mat.

'That's OK,' I said. 'I'm wiped out from the journey. I might just have a cigarette out of the window and then go to bed. Unless you have wine.'

Loes stopped her crunches abruptly and pulled herself up, a look of horror upon her face.

'We do not smoke,' said Loes.

'Or drink wine,' said Astrid.

'There is no smoking in the apartment,' said Loes.

'There is no wine here,' said Astrid.

I looked from one to the other.

'Fair enough,' I said. 'At least I'll go home detoxed!'

I wheeled my case into the bedroom and identified the spare bed. The occupied beds had outfits neatly laid out on top of the blankets. Low-slung jeans, spaghetti-strapped vest tops, high-heeled sandals, studded belts. There were other items meticulously hung up on coat hangers on a metal clothes rail and on the small desk in the corner were two oblong makeup bags, a hairdryer and a set of straighteners.

OK, I thought, *so they're that type of model*. I had realised quite early on that there were two sorts of girl who did what I did: the organised ones, who took things very seriously and treated their career like a proper job that needed some level of commitment and dedication, and then the ones who were more like me. Who were rather more haphazard and reactionary, who refused to let the job completely dictate their lifestyle and who moaned endlessly if the requirements of actually being a model – travel for example, or having to be thin – encroached on normal life. I didn't tend to get on too well with the first type, mainly because I was British and any sort of naked ambition made me feel uncomfortable, but also because their sense of determination made me feel as though I was merely coasting along and not trying hard enough.

I lay on the bed with my feet resting on my unpacked case, eating a packet of salted nuts from the plane. 'Do you think you're better off alone?' sang Alice Deejay from the living area. I felt twitchy. There was no way I was going to be able to read or snooze through the Europop they were playing through their portable speaker, but by my estimations they still had over an hour and a half of their routine left to go. I got up and stuck my head out of the bedroom door.

'Is it OK if I smoke out of the window, if I close the window behind me?'

'No smoking in the apartment,' said Astrid, not breaking her stride as she changed from one leg lunge to the other.

Loes shook her head. 'It is very bad for you and for us, yes?'

'And how would you close the window behind you?' panted Astrid.

They began doing a sort of hideous movement like mountain climbing but faster and on the floor. You'd think that horizontal climbing would be both pointless and non-tiring but they were dripping with perspiration, their ropy muscles standing out from their arms.

'I've done it before,' I said, sounding strangely proud. 'I'm an expert at it.' And I was. I would lean out of the window as far as possible and then reach behind me to close the window down on top of my lower back, like I was being guillotined in half.

'There is no smoking in the apartment but it is not raining if you would like to smoke outside of the lobby, yes?'

Astrid looked at Loes and raised an eyebrow.

'I probably won't,' I said, thinking about the Lycra-clad women who had been fiercely eyeing the passing traffic.

'Probably this is for the best,' said Astrid.

After another hour of Euro dance hits and panting, I stuck my head through the bedroom door again.

'How long left to go with the dance marathon?' I asked.

'Eighteen minutes,' said Astrid. 'You should join us. It's the final crunches, the best bit.'

'You're all right,' I said. 'I went to the gym yesterday and did sit-ups.' I pulled my t-shirt up a bit and tensed my stomach muscles.

305

Loes stopped crunching and peered at my proffered flesh. 'The final abdominal exercises are very beneficial,' she said, 'they target the fleshy part of the belly that sits at your waistband and around the sides.'

'Oh my God,' I said, looking from one girl to the other. 'There's not an ounce of flesh on either of you, what are you on about, "fleshy belly"?' I rolled my eyes comically.

'I said *your* waistband,' said Loes, before dropping down to the carpet.

Which was how I found myself lying on a mat with my knees bent and both girls instructing me on how to do sit-ups 'the proper way' – Astrid directing from the head end and Loes holding down my feet, as though they were attending a royal birth.

'You have terrible form,' said Astrid as I strained my head towards my kneecaps. 'You should have your head relaxed into your hands, not pulling you up.'

'Don't you worry,' I said, between heavy breaths, 'this is not my first rodeo.'

'But Ruth,' said Loes, the warmth of her hands spreading through my socks, 'you must have your head supported, yes? Otherwise, you will damage your neck and your head will stay in only one position.'

She rolled onto the mat beside me to demonstrate, contracting up and unravelling down, up and down, her body rolling smoothly and fluidly, her pretty head dropped back into the cradle of her hands.

'Don't you worry about my neck,' I said to her as I launched myself into another juddering, desperate sit-up. 'It's as strong as an ox.'

Chapter 22

She Has a Bleeding Anus

'Ruth,' said the Milan agent, 'why are you walking like a chicken?'

It was the next morning and my neck had frozen so completely that my entire upper body could only move as one piece: face rigidly pointing forwards, eyes wide and frantic as anyone's eyes would be if they had woken up to find they couldn't turn their head.

'I did some sit-ups last night,' I said, 'at the apartment.'

'You are like a chicken,' said the Milan agent, whose name was Giuseppe, 'peck peck peck.'

He pulled a tape measure from his back pocket.

'Ah, now I remember, you are sharing an apartment with the crazy crazy keep fit twins!' said Giuseppe, slapping his thighs with the flats of his hands. 'I am going to measure you, so please, Mrs Chicken, take off your clothes and stand in your underwear.'

We were at his desk, right in the middle of the open-plan office.

'No, you're alright,' I said. 'You can measure me over the top of them.'

It was 2007, I was twenty-six-years old and I owned a house. I was an adult now and I wasn't taking any shit. Giuseppe narrowed his eyes and then, as though he'd decided I was a battle not worth fighting, he shrugged.

'OK,' he said, 'but the clothing will only add to your size.'

My size, my size. A size that, a decade or so in the future would have been a UK eight and probably a tiny one at that, but in 2007 was edging into definite top-end-of-UK-ten territory. (A Topshop eight, in 2008, had a thirty-four-inch hip and a twenty-five-inch waist – by 2023, the same UK size would accommodate a thirty-six-inch hip and a twenty-six-inch waist.)

When I returned to the brothel, after a painful day of castings, the 'crazy crazy exercise twins' were just heading out for food.

I was fascinated by what Astrid and Loes ate. Or, more to the point, didn't eat. I had such a low tolerance for hunger that I ceased to function properly if I didn't eat at least every four hours – anything significantly past that crucial window spelled rapid mental and physical deterioration. True, the Marlboro Lights curtailed my appetite to a certain extent, but nevertheless, if I went too long without food then my body would soon begin to shut down.

But Astrid and Loes could survive on what would

probably be classed as emergency rations. If emergency rations consisted entirely of avocado, kale, cheese and meat.

Had it been a decade or so later, I'm sure that someone would have gently and tactfully pulled them up on their behaviour, identified a problem and found them help, but it was the 2000s and the world was still too busy munching away on its tabloid media diet and being happily force-fed grossly misogynistic worldviews to care about women struggling with things that were ultimately their own silly fault. Society was busy gossiping about Paris Hilton's drink driving and laughing at Nikki Grahame's high-pitched, emotional cries for help on *Big Brother*.

At any rate, Astrid and Loes were faring better than the girl I'd met a few years before, in Paris, who had spent spare moments off-set eating her way through the small, foil-wrapped pats of butter that you get at a hotel buffet. She had eaten at least seven of them that I had seen, quietly unparcelling the neatly folded packages and nibbling the oblong pats of fat whilst she waited her turn for hair and makeup in a terry towelling dressing gown. By the time it had reached late afternoon (the girl had not eaten any of the lunch provided by the studio), the butter had softened in the wrappings and she'd had to scoop it out with her little finger to get it to her mouth, delicately licking her fingernail after each scoop to clean all evidence from her skin. Everyone in the studio had noticed but nobody had said a word, because – as always – it wasn't even the strangest or most notable thing about the day. There the butter girl sat, as quiet as a churchmouse, little nibbling teeth and a fine down of fur upon her arms.

And so I was weirdly fascinated by Astrid and Loes' special diet and their non-standard foodstuffs, which weren't readily available at the corner shop. The supermarket they needed, which also sold protein powder, multi-packs of cheap steak and a strange, jellified, calorie-free dessert in little plastic pots, was three quarters of a mile on foot down a busy dual carriageway. There was no pavement and so we squeezed ourselves as close to the edge of the road as we could, risking life and limb in pursuit of the girls' next high-protein, low-carb meal.

And it wasn't just Astrid and Loes who were in pursuit of the next high-protein, low-carb meal; the Atkins diet was something of a worldwide cultural event.

Everywhere, previously normal people were eating steaks for breakfast and bacon and eggs at teatime, with a side of cheese, and at lunchtime they were becoming a bit unstuck, if they were honest, because a sandwich from the sandwich shop wasn't *quite* the same without the bread and, unsurprisingly, a lot of them weren't losing any weight at all. They were probably just fattening up their hearts and their livers to the point where the rest of their bodies had just become a kind of fleshy perambulator for their organs.

But for Astrid and Loes, it was working, mainly because they were probably consuming the same amount of food as a squirrel at a rest stop.

'This is what we like the most,' said Astrid, as we moved down the cooked meats aisle. She picked up a packet of individually wrapped salamis, finger-sized.

'Oh, they're like Peperamis,' I said. 'We have those at home.'

'We call them taste sensations,' said Astrid, lovingly placing the salamis into the trolley, and I suddenly felt very sad.

I wasn't just there in a voyeuristic capacity though: I needed to buy a ball of my most favourite dairy product of all time: *mozzarella di bufala*.

Mozzarella di bufala was not even remotely the same thing as mozzarella-the-normal-stuff. It had a different taste – creamy, almost liquid inside – and an entirely different texture, like a slackened out stress ball. I went to the cheese counter and surveyed the wares, leaving Astrid and Loes slavering over the cured meats section. To my horror but also, I'll admit, mild delight, the only *mozzarella di bufala* they had left was the approximate size and shape of a newborn baby's head. Or a medieval wet-nurse's bosom. Neither being things that you'd want to eat, but I'm trying to convey some of the grotesqueness of this thing's size. It was submerged in its own cloudy water, as buffalo mozzarella should rightly be, but rather than being in the usual little plastic container you'd expect, about the same size as a coleslaw tub, it was languishing like a great white alien foetus in a clear plastic bag, the sort you'd win goldfish in at the fair, and the clear plastic bag was in turn in a small bucket. A bucket! It was ludicrous, this cheese, and so I used up all of the cash in my back pocket and bought it.

'You can have cheese on the Atkins,' I said to the girls, when we got back to the apartment. 'It's allowed.'

'But I do not want to eat this cheese,' said Astrid. 'It looks like it is living.'

It was true. The cushiony sphere of mozzarella seemed to pulsate as I placed it onto the chopping board, and when I pierced the skin with a knife, a whole cupful of liquidy inners poured out and trickled down the side of the kitchen unit.

'It is enough cheese for one month,' said Loes, who was standing the other side of the chopping board. Both girls were staring at the *mozzarella di bufala* as though I'd brought a brain home and had decided to dissect it in the kitchenette. They were at once fascinated and disgusted.

'It's delicious,' I said. 'You have to try it. With some sharp tomatoes, a little balsamic vinegar, a drizzle of olive oil, a sprinkle of sea salt . . . I honestly think it's one of the greatest foods in the world.'

'We have some taste sensations,' said Loes, wiggling a handful of wrapped salamis like fingers.

I placed my mozzarella into a fruit bowl, as gently as a midwife weighing a newborn, and then set about eating it with a soup spoon.

I did not eat the whole thing. That last bit wasn't a big preamble into an admission of a tendency to undereat or to overeat; disordered eating was thankfully (amazingly) not my Achilles heel. No, my one Achilles heel, health-wise, was actually my bladder. I was plagued with cystitis, every time I let my back get cold or my immune system became run down, or I made the radical decision to actually have sex and a glass or two of wine ON THE SAME NIGHT. It happened infrequently enough that I would forget it was even a thing and then, shazam! There it would be, so painful and so utterly debilitating that I'd wonder whether

I'd ever feel normal again. And it was one thing getting it in the UK, where I had access to antibiotics and a sympathetic ear; abroad, it was a living nightmare. And it happened just two days later, while I was on a magazine shoot in some far-flung village, three or so hours from Milan.

I was there, in this village in the middle of nowhere, to shoot three pictures dressed as a stone statue – this was as much information as I had been given – and, luckily for me, if you could call anything lucky on that day of acute bladder pain, I was going to be shooting in the second half of the day.

But I had woken up that morning and felt the familiar ache deep down in the very base of my body – the intense urge to empty my bladder alongside the knowledge that there was nothing within it save for a trickle of pure fire that would burn almost unbearably on the way out and leave me with an even worse feeling of needing to empty my bladder. Anyone who's ever suffered with cystitis will know that there are few things so completely incapacitating, because you're not just dealing with pain – pain can be temporarily medicated to allow you to function – you are dealing with a feeling that quickly becomes part of your psyche for the day or the week (or year, or following entire decades) and makes you terrified to drink too little water, or too much water, or anything but water, or to venture too far from a toilet.

I needed antibiotics. I needed heavy-duty painkillers. I needed to nip this cystitis in the bud. I reached for the telephone and dialled the hotel's reception.

'*Buonigiorno!*' said the man on reception.

'Hello,' I said, 'I need a pharmacy.'

'*Si, si,*' he replied. 'There is one in Montebiale, the next village.'

'OK,' I said. 'How far is it to Montebiale? Can I walk there?'

There was a short pause.

'*Si,*' the man said, but he didn't sound massively sure of himself. 'Yes, I think you can walk there. It opens at nine. You take a left out of the front of the hotel and follow that road all the way to Montebiale.'

It was four minutes past seven. I pulled on my jeans, doubled over in pain, and set off for the village.

It was four miles to Montebiale, along a fast road with only the narrowest of pathways beside it. Lorries charged past and pulled me into their wake; wing mirrors skimmed inches from my body. Cars honked, vans honked, a busload of people looked down upon my hobbling form and I cried quiet tears as I slowly made my way to Montebiale, on the quest for whatever miracle cure they might have at the *farmacia*.

It was two minutes past nine when I reached it and the little shop was full. And when I say full, there was barely space for me to stand next to the counter let alone have any modicum of privacy. Not that I cared by that point. I was desperate – at crisis point, in fact – to relieve myself of the mineral water that I had drunk before leaving on my pilgrimage. Every ounce of my being wanted it expelled from my person – the foul, bacteria-infested, sulphur-scented-liquid that was simmering away inside me and multiplying its germs.

'*Buongiorno*,' I said to the lady. 'Do you speak English?'

'*Si*!' said the lady. She looked absolutely ecstatic to have been asked and immediately ducked beneath the counter to retrieve a big navy blue book that she plonked down next to the till. The display of reading glasses rattled.

'*Parlo bene l'inglese*!' she said, opening the leatherbound book. A little cloud of dust puffed into the air. She ran her finger down an index and flicked some of the pages over, pages as thin as tissue with faint, faint typing upon them. Her eyes landed upon something that obviously satisfied her.

'How can I be of help to you?' she said.

I felt the tears swell behind my eyes. 'I have a urine infection,' I said, pointing to between my legs.

'*Pregnante*?' she mimed, running her hands over an invisible bump. The ancient audience muttered in excitement, the old man nearest the door slowly clapped.

'No,' I said, 'I have—'

'*Momento*,' said the lady at the counter. She reached behind her where a paper packet was being passed through a hatch by a disembodied hand. 'Signor Colombo!' she said. Signor Colombo, the man nearest to the door, ambled forward to the counter to collect his package.

'OK,' she said, turning back to me. 'No pregnante?'

'No,' I said. I mimed squatting down to wee and pulled my most pained expression. 'Ow ow ow, pssss!' I said. The woman peered at her book.

'Leaking?' she said.

'Yes! Leaking!' The relief. I would soon be out of there, medicated, on my way to recovery.

'Leaking from the vagina,' said the woman.

'No,' I said. I placed my head in my hands.

'Headache.'

'No! Please wait.'

I stood back up and pointed at what I hoped was my urethra and mimed a gushing of liquids, which wasn't really accurate but I was desperate.

'Ah,' said the counter lady, returning to her book and carefully examining the pages. '*Si*! *Si*! Now I know it!'

The OAP contingent babbled with anticipation.

'She is bleeding from the anus! *Sta sanguinando dall'ano*!'

A cheer went up from the audience, the counter lady slammed her book shut and the disembodied hand appeared through the hatch to give a thumbs up.

In the end, I arrived back at the little hotel with both heavy-duty painkillers and antibiotics, and there was barely an hour to spare before I had to don my flesh-coloured underwear and go downstairs to meet the fun bus.

'Ruth!' said the stylist, who was jolly and permanently smiling and never had a bad word to say about anything. 'We have missed you. It has been so much fun. Did you have a wonderful lazy morning?'

I didn't want to do anything to dampen her brilliant optimism and so just nodded, feebly.

'I took a lovely long walk,' I said, 'to Montebiale.'

'Montebiale?' The stylist looked alarmed. 'Along the notorious four-mile-long road of many pedestrian deaths?'

When we got to the shoot location, they dressed me as a stone statue. I was to be the centrepiece in the middle of an old, beautiful fountain – my hair was swept up and pinned in a romantic chignon, my body was draped in a gorgeous silken robe and fine silver bracelets were stacked upon my wrists. It was actually a very good, very inventive idea for a story: a crumbling old *castello* with its overgrown grounds and this woman, this statue, alone in the fountain. Very good.

Or it would have been very good had I not been having a code red medical breakdown. As I looked at the plinth I'd be balancing on, which was in the middle of a large, completely stagnant pond, I realised that frequent trips to empty my bladder of its satanic contents would be impossible. It wasn't an easy trip to the plinth, either; I had to be carried by the photographer's assistant, who was wearing rubber waders covered in brown sludge and smelled as though he had been living inside a rotten buffalo carcass.

Once there, I had to stand perfectly still, waiting for everyone to be happy with the shot. If any tweaks had to be made then the assistant had to wade out, through the thick green sludge, and do hair or makeup or styling adjustments by proxy.

'*Scusa,*' he said, as he brushed a hair from where it had fallen across my eye. '*Scusa,*' as he arranged some fabric folds on my shoulder, the stylist laughing gleefully at the sight of a man in stinking waders doing such an intricate job. '*Scusa,*' as he dabbed some lip gloss with the utmost concentration, like a painter putting finishing touches to the ceiling of the Sistine Chapel.

Bloody hell, I thought, *never mind* scusa, *let's just get this show on the road before I develop a full-blown kidney infection*. And we did. Yes, at one point, the assistant had to wade over with some more heavy-duty painkillers that the stylist had retrieved from my bag and yes, at another time, I did have to let out a small trickle of wee, which ran down my leg unnoticed and dropped into the pond. But after two hours and three (pointlessly similar) gowns we were done.

'That was amazing,' said the stylist. 'We've really loved to work with you, Ruth, I am so glad we could do this shoot.'

I smiled.

'But you should have said you were in pain,' she continued, 'and we could have moved your shoot to tomorrow!'

I was momentarily confused and then remembered she'd been in my bag to get the painkillers.

'Oh,' I said, 'don't worry. It's nothing.' I thought about the Monty Python sketch where the knight has his arms cut off and still carries on. *Tis but a flesh wound.*

The photographer looked up from where he was kneeling on the ground, closing up his camera case.

'What is the matter, Ruth?' he said. 'We were noticing how you were quiet today.'

'She is bleeding from the anus!' said the stylist, who had read the label on the box.

Chapter 23

Too-Small Shorts

'Darling,' said Diane, 'how do you fancy going back to Tokyo?'

I couldn't lie, the idea of making quick money was a tempting one. And I was a Main Board girl now, a woman, a million years away from the naïve little thing I'd been the first time I'd gone to Japan.

'The agency would love to have you,' said Diane. 'Your portfolio is strong, you look great and your measurements are fine. They'll take you after the summer, in September. Just remember they like you pale, darling, so stay out of the sun.'

I rocked up to Tokyo in September with a 'softening of the curves' and a mega-tan. I had spent the summer of 2007 burnishing myself to a crisp on various beaches and drinking rosé through a straw. Of course I was tanned. The skin on my feet, as I shoehorned them into the high heels provided for the purpose of 'initial Polaroids' (straight off the plane) was so tanned that it had gone crepey and soft.

In terms of the curve-softening, there was no real difference on the tape measure, if you pulled it taut enough; I just looked slightly more fulsome. Sexier. Yeah, maybe there was some increased diameter, but with my long, gloriously highlighted hair and sun-kissed face, I looked more similar to the Brazilian bombshells I'd envied in the earlier years of my career than I ever had before. Bingo.

Had I walked into my Paris agency looking like a Brazilian supermodel, they would have been absolutely cock-a-hoop. I usually turned up looking like a medieval peasant woman who survived on raw celeriac. This agency, though – they were a bit startled about my tan, startled to say the least.

'Ruth-*san*,' said the agency boss, 'you are a different colour!'

I looked down at myself. Looked down at my honeyed, caramel-cream skin. I had never felt so good. Even though I knew I wasn't supposed to have tanned, I just couldn't understand their horror because I just looked *so much better*! I looked like a model crossed with a volleyball champion, crossed with one of those Californian girls who drank health juices and wore cropped jumpers with white jeans. I looked strong, I looked lithe . . . I looked happy.

The Tokyo model market was at the same time very particular and completely nonsensical. I had established this the first time around. What worked for one girl might not necessarily work for the next – one very popular Slovakian girl when I was there in 2002 had long, straight black hair and yellowish eyes that were so round and big and popping-out that it looked as though she was perpetually in the middle of being strangled by an invisible pair of hands. She'd looked like a lemur with a wig on. And yet she worked constantly, mostly for lingerie, even though she had absolutely no boobs. But the same long, straight black hair on Darnel from Ohio had been disastrous. They'd made up some excuse or another to get rid of her. Rebecca from Surrey worked constantly, with her wavy blonde hair and deep blue eyes, but Genevieve from St Tropez barely managed to scrape three jobs together.

Was there any rhyme or reason as to which physical attributes were desirable? If there was then I couldn't work it out. It was a complicated algorithm kept secret. The only sure things were that you needed to be thin but not painfully so, tall-ish but not tall (yay!) and that you couldn't have a tan. The tan thing was very important. The fairer you were, the more English peaches-and-cream your complexion, the better. One makeup artist had explained it thus: 'We do not want to see . . . Asian complexion. We do not want to see . . . Asian hair. Western skin and Western hair, this we like to see. We aspire to Western beauty.'

Ugh. It was completely my fault. I should have avoided the sun for the summer – worn a big hat, stayed in the shade, not had so much fun. I'd only had two rules to follow and now here I was, back in Tokyo, looking like Ursula Andress in *Dr No*.

'It's OK,' I said, smiling as the agency boss threw the loop of her tape measure over my head like a lasso, pulled it tight around my waist, 'don't worry. Give me a week and I'll be back to looking as though I've been raised underground.'

'There is no week,' said the boss. 'You have immediate job tomorrow, 8.30am.'

'Oh amazing,' I said. See? A tiny thing like a tan wouldn't stop me. 'What's it for?'

'Beauty advertising,' said the boss. 'Skin lightening cream.'

And so that was me, back in Tokyo, with feet as wrinkly as a ballsack and a suitcase filled with forty-seven tins of tuna. Because I wasn't starving this time around, no siree. It wouldn't matter if strawberries were eight quid or I didn't understand any menus; if ever in a bind, I had a John West Tuna Light Lunch to fall back on.

The other thing I had changed for my return visit was that I asked to have my own apartment. Which was punchy, considering that the first time I'd gone I'd made no money and here I was basically pre-spending all my money on the apartment, but I didn't want to be sharing with some girl I'd have to look after. Especially not the infamous Sicilian who screamed in her sleep or the sixteen-year-old girl from Leeds who said she saw dead people. That wouldn't do, not with my overactive imagination. OK, so I was mature, sensible and had wisdom to impart, but did I want that responsibility on my plate? No, I did not.

This plan massively backfired almost immediately. I realised, within forty-eight hours, that no matter how much people annoyed me when I shared a space with them, this inconvenience paled into insignificance compared to how utterly terrified, how completely and utterly fear-stricken

I was, living in Tokyo alone. It wasn't that the apartment was in a dodgy area, not at all. In fact, in comparison to the first one I'd stayed in with its miniature death bath and view of the cemetery it was decidedly uncreepy. The problem was the lift. It was near-identical to the elevator in the Japanese-inspired film *The Grudge*. There's a part in this film where the lift, which has a window in it so you can see out into each floor, goes up and then all of a sudden there's this absolutely terrifying *thing* in shot with jerky movements and messy hair. As the real-life lift rose through the floors one, two, three, I was just waiting for the dark scuttling in the corridor and the face at the porthole window and then my certain, horrendous death.

I was reasonably OK in daylight hours but once darkness fell, I went into what I called 'zombie apocolypse mode'. Twilight hours were a time of utter terror and total panic. It would take me twenty minutes each evening just to prepare my barricades – at both the front door and my bedroom door – and even then I would try to stay awake until the sky began to lighten, which was around 4am.

So I was genuinely ecstatic when Danish Dani turned up and had to share my apartment because the others were all full.

'Why is the dining table next to the front door?' she asked as she walked in. 'This is really fucking weird. Why are the chairs stacked on top of one another and tied together with . . . what are these? Elastic bands?'

I explained about *The Grudge* and my fear of the Hollywood-imagined Japanese demon.

'OK,' said Dani, 'so . . . you're not afraid that on the

next street there is a man showing pictures of vaginas and you're not afraid that you have been leaning out of your window to smoke when there is a fifty-metre drop below you, but you *have* been blocking the doorway at night so that a film character doesn't murder you?'

Even with Danish Dani in situ, life in Tokyo did not improve. Other than the initial first job, I hadn't really worked; none of my castings had been even remotely successful and part of me thought that it might not just be the tan that was holding me back. I had come out to Tokyo with such high hopes, such confidence and total conviction that I'd do OK. If this was me feeling at my very best, my most sexy, my fittest, my most desirable, then what was I supposed to do if this just wasn't good enough? How would I ever have the right body, the right hair, the right face – and what would I have to give up to get them? Would I always have to be chasing the market, seeing if I was right for Paris, or a fit for New York, or precisely the right kind of edgy to work in Milan?

The days went by and the castings continued, and not one client called to confirm.

'Ruth-*san*,' said the boss on the ninth day. She called me at 6pm, as the agency was closing. 'You have a casting for a sports clothing company, for a possible sports clothing job, but they need pictures now in a special outfit. Kind of lingerie.'

It was 6.30pm by the time I walked into the agency. I had already eaten my evening meal (chicken teriyaki burger from McDonald's, no fries, bottle of water) and the idea that I now had to do lingerie photos wasn't ideal. There was a little changing cupboard in the agency and the outfit had already been hung up. I felt confused. Had I developed some sort of condition that changed my perception of the sizes of things? Because the cycling shorts and crop top on the hanger were tiny. Not usual model tiny: child sized. Smaller even than Tokyo Teena – Teeny Tokyo Teena. I checked the labels. The cycling shorts were C&A and said 146cm on the sizing label. This all just seemed very wrong.

'I think the shorts are for kids,' I called out of the cupboard, sticking my head around the door.

The agency boss looked up, the lenses of her glasses glinting in the office lights and obscuring her eyes. Sinister.

'No, not for children Ruth-*san*. Please put on the outfit and come for pictures.'

The shorts did just about pull on but, blimey, they were tight. Every remotely moveable bit of flesh from around my bottom and tummy squeezed up and out of the waistband and then sat there, like a little doughy ring, strangely weightless and disconnected. With the tiny crop top in situ, it was as though any flesh that was not directly anchored to a specific limb had been cajoled into meeting up in the middle.

'OK Ruth-*san*,' said the boss as she pointed her camera. 'I will take these pictures and send them straight to the sports clothing company. It is for a sports clothing company job.'

I wondered why she was saying sports clothing company so much. I also wondered why they needed the photographs now, last thing in the evening.

'Is the sports clothing company' – for Christ's sake, I was at it now! – 'is the sports clothing company job tomorrow?'

I wanted to know, because the next day was a Saturday and I had planned to go back to Shibuya to buy a new camcorder – priorities.

'No job tomorrow,' said the boss.

Maybe her glasses are purposefully reflective, I thought to myself. *To retain power over others*. It was unnerving not being able to see her eyes. Maybe she didn't have any eyes, just empty robot sockets. Cable ports.

'Tomorrow is Saturday,' she said. 'Job with sports clothing company is . . . next week. Maybe.'

Strange. I was sure she'd said that the job was tomorrow.

I didn't have to wait long to find out what the hell was going on.

'Darling, it's Diane.'

Diane didn't have to introduce herself by name, I could tell when it was Diane calling from the very first syllable. Possibly from the very short, split-second pause or intake of breath before the 'D'. Diane, my saviour, the pillar of strength and of security and sensibility in a world of complete madness.

'Explain to me,' said Diane, 'why the agency boss has just emailed me three pictures of you looking very odd in some miniscule cycling shorts?'

'She's emailed them to you?' The cogs began to turn.

'She's emailed them with a message about your weight and how your measurements have increased.'

'Oh my God!' I said, incensed. 'She said the pictures

were for a sports clothing company. And I told her that the shorts were for kids but she still made me put them on.'

'This doesn't look good darling,' said Diane. 'She's saying your measurements are bigger than the ones on your contract.'

'So she's trying to get out of the contract? But she didn't even do my measurements, she just put the shorts on and took the photos.'

I wanted to fight. I wanted to rage. I wanted to go back to the agency and confront the boss, but by now the office would be closed and there was a whole weekend stretching out ahead of me, in which I'd have to stew and be miserable, and question my entire worth and wonder why I wasn't thin enough to properly fit into some age eleven C&A shorts without giving myself a muffin top. Is this why the boss had chosen a Friday night, just before she left for home? It was cowardly and I hated her. I wanted to march in there, nothing to lose, and show her the label on the inside of the C&A shorts. But then I pictured her poker face, her calm demeanour, the way she had disposed of Marie-Cecile the French model, who was never seen again (in Tokyo; again, I'm not saying she killed her) and the sudden severance of Olga who had fainted one too many times on shoots. And I knew it was over. That I couldn't win.

'Darling,' said Diane. 'Just come home.'

Betrayal in Tokyo: the too-small shorts.

© Taken by modelling agency's assistant

Chapter 24

Lucky Rat

I couldn't help feeling as though I'd failed, as I sat in the restaurant window watching the flood waters recede. I would be leaving Tokyo in the morning with my twenty-nine unopened tins of Tuna Light Lunch and I had virtually nothing to show for my stay.

In the few weeks I'd been in Tokyo, I had made 314,000 yen, which was around £1,600. My flight had been £817.80, my apartment had cost £753.92 and therefore, I had made a total of – drumroll please – £28.28. Which was a weird sum of money to land on because twenty-eight was supposedly my lucky number. There'd been nothing lucky about this trip. I'd turned up as tanned as David Dickinson after a week in the Bahamas, failed spectacularly at living alone because I was afraid of a ghost from a film and, in the ultimate act of model degradation, I had been tricked into wearing too-small shorts.

Even the weather had been against me – I'd taken one

final walk into Roppongi and the heavens had torn the dark sky open, pelting down rain so hard it was like standing beneath a power shower. Immediately, the roads had turned into rivers, carrying anything that wasn't attached rapidly downstream. Plastic chairs, bins, every type of litter and detritus. I'd ducked into the nearest restaurant to take shelter, grabbed a seat at the big window and was now waiting for the storm to pass.

Tokyo. It should have been an amazing cultural experience, especially the second time around, now I was older and wiser. Once again, I'd been a rubbish traveller and failed to take full advantage of my amazing model side-privileges. So what if I'd only had two jobs the whole time I was there? The rest of the time I should have been learning Japanese, or exploring the shrines, or tasting new foods and drinks. But what had I done? Smoked, barricaded myself into my apartment at night and spent at least two hours every daytime mooching around in the department stores. Instead of diving into little sushi bars at lunchtime, I'd eaten my tuna from a tin, or I'd gone to Subway to have the same nuked chicken teriyaki baguette I'd eaten every single day the first time I'd stayed in Tokyo.

What the hell was wrong with me? I'd been travelling around the world since the age of twenty, trotting into metro stations here and boarding long-haul flights there, not a soul with me and sometimes without knowing where exactly I was, but had I really travelled? Had I really stopped to experience anything? Where was my sense of adventure? Even now, in this restaurant, watching the last of the flood waters swirl on the road, why was I not appreciating the novelty of the situation? Why hadn't I ordered the sea urchin from the menu, or the chicken cartilage 'crunchy snacks', or the fried beef tongue or the plate of intestines?

'Miso soup,' said the waiter, placing a bowl in front of me that looked and smelled like dishwater. It was the plainest thing I could find on the menu and I wasn't even keen on that.

So I was a bad traveller, I was bad at living alone and I was beginning to think that maybe I was a bad model. Certainly, the agency boss thought so, with her age eleven fat-trapping shorts and her 'regretfully, I cannot pay out your contract'. I had to wonder whether any of this was making me truly happy. This rollercoaster of rejection with its amazing, life-affirming highs and dreadful lows. It felt so good when you were at the top, when the great jobs came in and you were wanted and valued. But at the same time, when you were at the top, you always knew that you wouldn't be there for long, that a fall was imminent. You spent the majority of your time waiting for the high or falling from it; rarely did you get to stay at the top and admire the view.

Oh for Christ's sake, pull yourself together, I thought, as I sipped bland, calorie-less soup from a pottery spoon. *You have one of the best jobs in the world*, I thought. *You get to travel, to meet amazing people and you get paid to look beautiful. To stand there, knowing that you're there because other people think that you look good. Pull yourself together and count your lucky stars.*

The rain was lighter now and the water on the road was

receding just as quickly as it had risen, leaving rubbish scattered across the wet ground like the landed flakes in a snow globe. It was as though the world had been turned upside down, given a shake and then left to resettle. I noticed a rat at the edge of the road, pulling itself up onto the pavement. Weren't rats supposed to be lucky in Japan?

See? It was an auspicious moment. At my lowest ebb, the universe had sent me a sign. The rat nosed at a sodden food carton lying crumpled on the pavement and then scuttled beneath it, pushing the white cardboard upwards then flipping it over. *Look at it*, I thought. *If a rat can escape the churning waters and get back to work, then so can I.* It was all about positive mental attitude. Where was my thick skin? Where was my self-belief? I needed to be more like the rat.

Go, lucky rat, go, I thought, as the rat tired of the carton and looked around for new delights. And then the rat did go, scuttling full pelt into the road with its greasy fur slick and shiny. The rat hit the wheel of a moving taxi, was flung violently up into the air and then landed with a thonk on the bonnet of the car before bouncing onto the tarmac. Killed. Killed stone dead.

Chapter 25

Squared-Off Brows

It was 2008. I was twenty-seven years old. My measurements were 32D–25–35 and my hair was pale blonde.

In July, Rich and I married and then went on a sixteen-day trip down Route 66 for our honeymoon. It was finally the sort of travel I could get on board with – not alone, not for work and with unlimited food and drink. We had a brilliant time, staying in quirky motels and driving through creepy abandoned places (which was quickly becoming my *Mastermind* specialist subject) and I filmed the whole thing on the camcorder I'd bought in Tokyo. Then I spent weeks editing the film, adding effects to it, putting on a soundtrack and properly throwing myself into a project that didn't involve worrying about my appearance. It was the happiest I'd been in a long time.

At the end of August, a few weeks after returning from honeymoon, I declared very boldly and with great certainty that I did not want to have children for 'at least a couple of years,' and then the following month, in September, I set about trying for a baby.

This must have been a pretty confusing time for Rich because I didn't admit that I had changed my mind and wanted to try for a baby after all. Instead, I simply made some small but very crucial changes to our (dubious, Catholic-style) contraceptive routine, that were obviously quite alarming to him when they suddenly happened during our most intimate moments.

'Wait . . . WAIT! Are you . . . wait! What are you doing? No, you can't – WAIT!'

And so on. You get the gist.

But after three months, nothing happened. I had assumed, because I hadn't done any research, that it would happen straight away. Why would it not? I had spent the past ten or so years utterly fixated on *avoiding* pregnancy, fearful that it could happen so easily – *even if he doesn't put it in properly! Even if you just roll in it afterwards!* – and now I was expecting instant results. Surely any couple who were even remotely trying, in a half-arsed sort of way, would be pregnant within three months? Six at the very worst?

Nothing.

I started to feel pretty annoyed that my body was failing me in this particular mission. Getting pregnant was the one physical thing I felt I had control over; I could be too curvy for some jobs, too tanned for others and my tooth gap might be too edgy for many, but my pregnancy? It would be perfect. And all mine.

Except that it just didn't happen. And with every period I felt more and more detached from my body and more and more angry that it wasn't doing what it was supposed to be doing and then, just when I thought that I couldn't feel more annoyed with how things were going, three things happened in relatively quick succession that made me feel as though I had absolutely no bodily autonomy whatsoever.

The first was that my face nearly exploded on an aeroplane. This was probably caused by a combination of my horrendous hangover, the size of the aircraft (miniscule, it looked like a baked beans tin with the label taken off) and the fact that I had a lingering sinus infection. I was hungover because I'd spent the previous day drinking champagne over and over again from a specially made flute, shaped to look like a designer stiletto (what a job!) and had then celebrated a successful shoot by passing five hours on Hamburg's infamous Reeperbahn, drinking shots in strip clubs and showing everyone my magic tricks. (Not a euphemism.)

The air hostess on the flight to Milan Linate had taken one look at me and asked whether I'd like a blanket and a pillow. That was how hungover/still drunk I looked.

My state worsened as the plane climbed into the air and the noise of the engines grew louder and louder. The pressure in my ears just intensified the sound, it was almost unbearable, as though I was inside a gigantic blender. I managed to sleep for a while, feeling for all the world like one of those drug-addled revellers who pass out inside a speaker at a rave, but the flight was bumpy and more than once I knocked my head hard on the plastic ridge that ran around the window and woke myself up.

So I couldn't help feeling a huge sense of relief when

the pilot announced that we were preparing for landing. Finally, I could go and sit for a while in the cold toilets at the airport, perhaps rest my head against the partition, which wouldn't move or vibrate, perhaps hold my face under the tap, or maybe even a foot, both feet – God what I'd give to immerse my entire body in cool water!

But it was at that moment, when the pilot announced our descent, that I began to realise that I had quite a serious problem with my face. Throughout the flight, it had started to ache and I had put it down to the hangover coupled with my sinus infection, but now there was a strange stretching sensation in my skin, as though a different – bigger – face was trying to burst out from my own. And as the plane dropped further towards the ground, the pain became unbearable. My ears were under so much pressure that the insides felt as though they were bulging out into the ear canals, and not only could I not hear, my eyes had started to blur around the edges. Then, suddenly, there was an indescribable feeling behind them, as though my head was being pumped quickly full of air. (With one of those powerful car-tyre inflators at the garage, not the phee-phoo, phee-phoo, phee-phoo type of pump that you have to do with your foot.)

There was the pain behind my eyes and inside my face, but then there was a surface pain. My skin was as taut as a balloon. It was ready to split open, like an overripe plum.

I was aghast. I needed to tell someone. Surely when the air hostesses looked at me they would notice – surely my face would be puce, or covered in raised veins, or it would look like a big round balloon?

I pressed the call button.

The air hostess who had given me a pillow and a blanket waggled her finger at me. 'No, no,' she mouthed. 'Landing.'

I know we're bloody landing! I thought. *My face is about to explode from it!* How would I convey to her just how serious my facial predicament was? I had already complained about a small shard of metal on my seat belt clasp, returned a mineral water with a broken seal and had also apparently overreacted to a 'small knee bump' when one of them had wheeled the trolley into my leg – why would they believe me if I told them that my face was about to explode?

I needed to calm myself. When had anyone ever heard of someone's face exploding? If it had happened on a plane then the world would have known about it. There would be precautionary exercises, like with deep vein thrombosis. It would have been on the news. People wouldn't travel on them if they had sinus problems or bad colds. It would be a *thing*.

But God, I could easily be the first, I thought, as the throbbing and stretching became more and more unbearable. There's always a first! Maybe nobody has had this precise combination of blocked sinus, blood alcohol level and absurdly small plane size.

Had there been someone sitting next to me I would have grabbed their hand at this point. My vision had almost entirely disappeared. My lips had begun to distend, no doubt pushed away from the main muscle mesh by the pressure. It was now or never; I needed to make the crew aware of the situation at the very least so that there wouldn't be mass hysteria when my face finally exploded.

I went to press the call button again but couldn't locate it, for I was almost blind by now, but then, at that moment, we hit the runway with an enormous, bone-shattering bang and my face felt instantly better. I felt instantly better. I had regained control of my face.

The second thing happened only an hour later: my eyebrows disappeared. The worst thing about it was that I'd said no to their removal but the makeup artist had continued to do it anyway. Other than staging a walkout, which in hindsight I should have done, I felt I really had no choice other than to let her get on with it.

'Do you mind if I remove your eyebrows?' she said.

Beg your pardon? She said it so casually that I hardly registered it as an odd request; it was as though she'd asked me if I needed any water, or whether I was allergic to any products.

'I'm just going to bleach them out,' she said, seeing the reluctance – nay, horror – develop on my face, 'and then before you go, I'll dye them back in.'

If there was one thing people couldn't touch it was my eyebrows. I'd had them professionally shaped early on in my career by a brilliant makeup artist – Alex Box – and she'd given me a piece of advice I'd always held on to. Not to let anyone, anyone at all, fuck with my eyebrows. I could let people pluck the strays, I could allow the plucking of the middle hairs, so that I didn't develop a monobrow, but nobody could touch the shape.

'I'd rather you didn't,' I said. 'I don't let anyone change my brows.'

They're the things that frame your face, I remembered Alex saying. *If you let people mess with them, you'll never get them back.*

'I'm not changing them,' said the makeup artist. 'I'm bleaching them out and dying them back.'

I pondered this for a few seconds. She was making it really hard for me to say no, because I am British and we don't like to disappoint but also because I needed a confrontation with this woman like I needed a hole in the head. She was wearing a stiff black shirt that looked as though it was made from cardboard and her leather trousers were spray-on tight. If she could endure such extreme levels of discomfort then who knew how long she could continue an argument? She kept her tools in a leather toolbelt that she wore across her chest, like Rambo's ammunition belt, all of the little brushes lined up like bullets, and her foundation bottles were set out so evenly on the makeup desk that I was sure she'd used a ruler to space them.

'I mean, I'd still rather you didn't,' I said. 'My agency wouldn't like it. In fact, let me give them a ring and maybe they can speak to you about it.'

Ah, the agency helpline. The equivalent of Greenflag, or the RAC, but for models who needed rescuing from potentially terrible work situations. Somebody wanted to give your hair a 'quick chop'? Check with the agency. A photographer wanted to show 'just a bit of boob'? Agency. Shoot might overrun by six hours? Stylist wanted you to wear fur? Nobody told the client that your hair was temporarily red? Agency, agency, agency. Phoning the agency was the saving grace, the lifeline, the thing that would spare you the awkward conversations and the potential confrontations, and, ultimately, tell people who wouldn't listen to you a *big fat NO*.

'Your agency is not open yet,' said the makeup artist. 'We are an hour ahead. And I must hurry with my makeup.'

Which was how I found myself in the makeup chair, masking tape strips across my forehead, having my eyebrows bleached. I was livid. As I wiped away the bleach, alone in the studio bathroom, I wondered why I couldn't just stick up for myself. For Pete's sake. I looked like an alien; where before I'd had brows, I now had strange ridges of bone beneath the skin that were entirely unfamiliar. My whole face was now entirely unfamiliar. The makeup artist drew in the thin black lines for eyebrows she'd wanted from the start and I sulked for the entire shoot.

'They will look exactly like they did before,' the makeup artist said as she applied the dye at the end of the day. In fairness to her craft, she had spent twenty minutes colour matching the dye to my hair colour so that my returned brows would look natural, but anyone with half an ounce of common sense would have known that they would not look exactly the same as they did before.

But I was late for my flight, my taxi was waiting outside the studio entrance and by the time I reached the airport, even if I left at that moment, I'd have only forty minutes before the plane took off. I just wanted to get home. Eyebrows be screwed. I didn't even look as she wiped off the dye, cleansed my face and hurried me out of the door. I didn't get a chance to look at the brows until I was in duty free, doing my customary airport thing of taking massive dollops of La Prairie moisturiser from the sample pots and slathering it all over my face, neck and hands. As I bent towards the mirrored counter to check whether I'd massaged it in enough, I saw a different face. A face with two very large, grey, slug-shaped hair patches instead of eyebrows. Three times as thick as they'd been before and oblong, rather than shaped into any sort of arch or curve, because the dye had simply coloured every hair on my skin within the squared-off masking-taped areas.

The squared-off brows took a while to reshape but it was the hairdo from hell, a few weeks later, that really tipped me over the edge. It was January in New York City, blowing a bitterly cold gale, and I was staying in a very cool hotel on the Hudson that had leaky window frames, noisy room heaters and what felt like a twenty-four-hour club night going on in the downstairs bar. I was cold in my room most of the time, but when the heaters fired up – on the hour, every hour, with a cacophony of clangs and groaning sounds – it was suddenly like a furnace. Unbearably hot. This intense burst of searing heat lasted for precisely eight minutes and then the heaters went off, the warmth escaped straight out through the gaps in the window frame and I was left to return my entire being to beneath the duvet, wearing a hat, my coat and a pair of woolly bedsocks I'd taken from the flight.

I was in New York for a haircare advertising job and it had been agreed, as part of my fee, that my hair could be cut and coloured. They didn't want to do anything drastic, they said; it was for a blonde hair range, so I needed to be blonde, and they wanted long hair, so my hair needed to be long. I had, already, long blonde hair and so nobody felt as though I might be in imminent danger of being radically transformed – there was little threat of me coming away with the mullet of a seventies German pornstar, for example, which is what had happened a few years previously on a different haircare advertising job in Amsterdam.

New York was different. When it came to advertising they took things seriously. It was all about the money. My hair was being coloured at one of the most expensive salons in the city and my trim, just a bit off the length to neaten the ends up, was going to happen at the shoot. Casual, easy, nothing to worry about.

'So they've said a warm blonde,' said the New York colourist, fanning my hair over his forearm and examining the existing dye job. It was a beautiful, expensive-looking, cool-toned blonde with shots of honey running through it – it was the best it had ever looked.

'We don't wanna go too far from these tones,' he said, speaking to his assistant rather than to me. I was irrelevant. I was being paid to be in the hair ad, I was being paid to have my hair coloured – for the next two days, my hair was not mine.

And so when my hair ended up being gingery at the roots and a strange, straw yellow through the lengths I tried to disassociate from it. When I glimpsed my terrible orange roots in the mirror at Bergdorf's and involuntarily grimaced, I told myself it was just renting my hair out temporarily, that I had to stay calm. And then, on the shoot, when the hair stylist began hacking away at the ends, I tried to imagine that it wasn't even my hair she was cutting.

Think of the money, I thought. *That's all it is: you're selling your hair for money.*

Did I want to sell my hair for money? I wasn't sure. I'd had all sorts of haircuts and colours for money and I'd had all sorts of haircuts for free, but this felt different. Out of control. I couldn't get pregnant, I couldn't stay thin, I'd recently lost my eyebrows as I knew them and now my hair, the hair I was feeling pretty pleased with, was starting to look like the hair of a person who'd tried to 'get a Britney Spears' using Sun-In and a pair of pinking shears.

'I'm going to have to go shorter,' said the hair stylist, tutting as though her having to cut my hair was all my fault, 'it's so dry that it's just snapping.'

She had already cut two inches from the length and the ends were hovering worryingly close to my shoulder blades.

'They put a lot of bleach on it,' I said, 'and then dyed it darker again – well, yellow – so that's probably why it's dry.'

'It's not yellow,' said the hair stylist. 'I instructed the colourist myself. It's exactly as I said I wanted it. It's dry because it needs conditioning.'

I imagined the hair stylist being singed with a dozen of her own heated-up curling irons and bit my tongue.

'This is ridiculous,' said the hair stylist. 'It's like straw. I just don't know where I can cut to that'll make it look good.'

I stared in the mirror. My hair was just below shoulder length whereas ten minutes before it had been long. Tousled. Two days ago, it had been long and also honeyed. Delicious. In fact, the clients had booked me *because* of my hair – 'Your hair,' they'd said, 'is the exact hair we want in the campaign.'

Now it was sticking out, dry, yellow – I looked like Worzel Gummidge. She hacked more off and before I could exclaim, or shout, or do anything at all, it was suddenly short, the hair ends skimming just above my shoulders.

'It's short!' I said. 'It was supposed to be just a trim!'

The clients arrived at the studio and hmmed at my hair.

'It's not *great*,' they said to the hair stylist. 'It's not what we imagined.'

'She has totally the wrong shade,' said the hair stylist, as though I'd been and dyed it in the toilets, 'and her hair is so dry. I just can't do a lot with it.'

She pulled a wig from a suitcase – luscious, long, blonde – and that's what I wore for my haircare campaign. A wig, almost identical to the hair they had ruined.

'Marco will absolutely know what to do with your hair,' said Daz, the following week. 'He's an absolute genius, darling, when it comes to the era-defining cut.'

I was back in the agency in London, massacred hair in hands, and Daz had started up on one of her favourite topics of conversation: the era-defining haircut. The era-defining cut was kind of the same as the drastic cut I'd identified as a New Face model. It was the hair makeover that would, if you were lucky, win you the best editorial shoots, grab the attention of the big designers and send your career stratospheric. The cut was bold, unapologetic, *different*, and was usually the sort of style that only a model with the most exquisite bone structure and long, elegant neck could carry off. A mere mortal with an era-defining haircut would just look like Wee Jimmy Krankie.

'Yes,' said Daz. 'That's who we'll call, we'll call Marco, darling. He did Natalia's cut, he did Sarah McDermish's—'

'Who's Sarah McDermish?'

'Sorry, Svetlana's.'

'Svetlana is really called *Sarah*?'

'Yes,' said Daz.

'Is she even Bulgarian?'

'No, darling, she's from Aberdeen. Anyway, that elfin crop he gave her was to die for. She has no tits, of course, so it works. Androgynous elf sitting next to the garden pond, etcetera, etcetera. You'd look like Cheryl from the twenty-four-hour garage on the Euston road.'

'Don't know her.'

'For the best, darling. Anyway, Marco will sort you out. Just don't go shorter than jaw length, darling, I'm not sure your neck can take it.'

Marco worked from a corner chair in a friend's salon. He had a completely shaved head, which I instantly thought suspect. It was like meeting a dentist with bad teeth – or no teeth! Or a manicurist with terrible nails. Or none!

I arrived at 4pm and, at six, when the neighbouring businesses were pulling down their security grills and putting out their bins, he was still there, snip-snipping away with precision at each and every strand, as though pruning the world's most precious bonsai tree. He had not stopped cutting and neither had he stopped talking, an entirely one-way conversation in which he detailed all of his accolades – very bizarrely in the third person – as though dictating his CV to some secretary or PA I hadn't realised was hiding behind the backwash area.

'He's cut Natalia's hair,' he droned, 'and he's done Svetlana's. He gave Beatrice Muldowney the crew cut she had when she walked for Prada last month.'

Wow, a crew cut, I thought. *How long did that take when you can only cut three millimetres off an hour? Did you start last year?*

'He assisted at the Versace show but didn't do Gucci,' he went on, in his strange monotone, 'he then flew to Paris to help prep hair for Jalouse.'

Another of Marco's quirks, in case the previous one wasn't enough, was that he didn't like to cut in a mirror, and so he had swivelled the chair around so that I faced the middle of the room. He regularly moved to the front, to check how it looked, and then to each side, to make sure the lengths matched up, and then he returned to the back to scissor his miniscule snippings and continue his autobiography.

'In ninety-nine he attended Central St Martin's,' he said, 'but soon realised that art history wasn't for him . . .'

At twenty past six, he swivelled the chair to face the mirror and I gasped. I had been promised a miraculous transformation, something directional and edgy, and I didn't know whether to be disappointed or relieved. My hair looked identical – 100 per cent exactly the same – as when I'd walked in.

'Thanks Marco,' I said, shaking off the cape and stretching my legs. 'It's really great.'

'Ruth Crilly,' said Marco, 'was another cool model he successfully coiffed.'

Chapter 26

Body Like a Turgid Penis

'Crikey, darling,' said Daz, as I strode into the agency in a pair of new boots. 'You're looking very . . . healthy.'

'It's stopping smoking,' I replied. 'It's over a year, now. My whole body feels different.'

My body did feel different. It felt great. It had still not acquiesced to my wishes when it came to producing a baby and my period still appeared, stubbornly, every single month, but apart from that saddening let-down, it felt pretty amazing. Not that I'd particularly given up for health reasons, I was ashamed to admit. In the end, after years of people banging on about lungs and arteries and the smell of stale smoke, it had been vanity that had made me quit. Vanity and a self-styled white witch called Davina.

Smoking had been so intrinsically linked with my time as a model that for a long time it had seemed almost inconceivable to separate the two. Cigarettes had been my friend, the only constant in a sea of change and unfamiliarity, and I'd used them as a crutch. New York one week and Paris the next? Who cared if nobody was in town and I had to sit on my own at my window ledge looking like someone who constructed haikus about the rain – if I was smoking then I was never truly alone. Arriving in Frankfurt at 2am on a Sunday and there's nothing to eat? The turn-down mint on your pillow will do for actual sustenance; leave it to the Marlboro Lights to satisfy the mental hunger.

You could buy Marlboro Lights everywhere and anywhere, and they were cheaper than food and didn't need cooking. In a way, they cooked themselves – the perfect lazy-person's meal. No cutlery required. A bit like a banana but less calorific. And, being completely calorie-free, they were the ideal reward for just about any minor achievement throughout the day or night. Made it through another one of your (nine) castings? Cigarette celebration! Finally home to your empty hotel room, looking forward to an evening of leftover sandwich for dinner and listening to the next door room's television through the wall? Commiserate with a Marlboro Light! Marlboros punctuated my schedule and provided a familiar 'open and close brackets' to each and every batshit crazy casting or go-see I doggedly fought my way to, through rainstorms in Paris and perverts in Soho.

But if there was one thing I loved more than smoking

it was my skin. I was proud of my skin. It was what every single makeup artist seemed to comment upon when they started working on me – in the absence of any sort of striking height, admirable musculature, noticeable thin-thinness or glorious hair, my perfectly clear, completely flawless skin was my *pièce de résistance*. My money-maker. I hadn't thought that my skin was anything particularly special until I'd started modelling, but for years it had been handled with something bordering on reverence, as though it was the finest silk or rarest animal pelt.

'It's just so . . . perfect,' one makeup artist had said, quite early on. 'I cannot see a single mark on it.'

'I've never seen skin so clear,' said another. 'It's almost like glass.'

And then the compliments had come thick and fast, to the point where I had wondered whether I should keep my face in a protective dome, like David Duchovny's hand in *Zoolander*. Never a shoot went by without somebody commenting on the quality of my skin – its smoothness, its evenness of tone – and after years of this hype, I still had not become complacent. If I sat in a makeup chair and *didn't* get some form of skin-admiration spiel then I'd have to wonder whether they were looking closely enough at their canvas.

And so, when Davina, a makeup artist who also read fortunes and liked to diagnose people's hidden diseases with the force of her mind, made a comment about my skin, I was instantly all ears.

'You have very fine skin,' Davina said.

'Thank you,' I said.

'No, what I mean is,' said Davina, swirling around in her warlock's cape to reach for a different foundation stick, 'it's very thin. Fine.' There was a rummaging as she tried to locate the product in her suitcase. 'Easily damaged.'

Very thin? Easily damaged? What was she rollocking on about, the crazy witch? I'd been with her on a week-long shoot in Spain and for five days she hadn't shut up about various people's undiagnosed ailments. The photographer had gout but didn't know yet, the stylist's cystic acne was down to the malfunctioning of her right ovary. It was both irritating and slightly unnerving.

'It's the smoking that'll do it,' Davina said.

Aha! So that was her game. This was just like Davina. She'd had a bee in her bonnet about my smoking since after the first dinner, when she'd seen me in the lobby having my bedtime Marlboro Light. She had then mentioned that smoking was no doubt the cause of my digestive issues (of which I had none, mainly because smoking kept me regular), my sleep problems (of which I had only one – the fact I had to be in her coven at 5.30am every morning), my hormone imbalances (moodiness, again due to the fact that I had to be in her room at 5.30am every morning) and wisdom tooth pain. I hadn't told her about my regular bouts of cystitis – I wasn't insane.

'If you keep on smoking,' she continued, 'I'll tell you what will become of your skin. One day, you'll wake up and it'll have just turned.'

'Turned?' I rolled my eyes, but there was something sinister about all of this. I didn't like the way that she was predicting the future of my skin, as though she was enjoying it. Was this a prediction or was it a curse? I felt uneasy.

'What do you mean "turned"?' I said. 'What will have turned?'

'Your skin,' said Davina. 'Yes, you will see. It is a fine skin but a weak skin, and once it crinkles it will be beyond repair. Heed my words.'

In the interests of full transparency, I'm not entirely sure she said 'heed my words', I can't remember exactly the phrase. But whatever it was gave me the creeps. None of Davina's other health-related prognoses had remotely bothered me – according to her, I only had half a functioning intestine and one working ear drum – but my skin? On my *face*? Back off, bitch.

'But there's not a single line on my face!' I said. 'I'm sure I'd get some sort of warning if it was suddenly going to go crinkly all over.'

'No,' said Davina, fanning me with a raven's feather to set my base, 'I told you. It is fine skin. It's not robust, it won't snap back. Once it transforms, it will transform for good.'

Transform? For good?

I didn't need telling twice. I gave up smoking straight away – OK, almost immediately, a few weeks later – so horrified was I by the idea that I might have wrinkles. And I hadn't smoked a single cigarette since.

'Well, it's all jolly good, darling,' said Daz. 'I have to say that you've inspired me to give up too. Not that I've quite managed it yet.' She fiddled with her packet of Marlboro Lights. 'Slow and sure wins the race, as they say,' she continued. 'I have a stab at quitting every few days, just to see. I tried last Friday *and* I attempted to quit yesterday as well.'

'How did it go?'

'I did four whole hours on Friday,' said Daz, 'but then there was that party at Big Sky Studios and so obviously I had to abort mission.'

'Obviously.'

'Yesterday was better, darling,' said Daz. 'I did a full fourteen hours fag-free.'

'Where did you fall down?'

'Just off the Kings Road. They'd dug up the pavement outside of Raffles and I didn't see the sign, darling. Absolutely tipsy as a trifle.'

I paused to process.

'I meant, when did you fall down with the smoking? What made you quit quitting?'

'Quit quitting?'

'Stop stopping,' I said.

'Quit quitting, stop stopping?' said Daz. 'Are you quite alright, darling?'

I took a deep breath.

'You stopped smoking for fourteen hours,' I said, speaking slowly and clearly, 'and then you started again. What made you start?'

'Oh,' said Daz. 'I woke up.'

Ah, how I loved my family at the agency. They had been there for my entire adult life, just about. I had seen them most days apart from on weekends – dropping in to get cards, or do a casting, or just to say hi. I had come so far from the early weeks, when I'd creep in to see Beryl in accounts and ask for an advance, or rush from the office to catch the train back to Birmingham or rescue my car from some nondescript multistorey off the M25.

And here I was now, striding confidently out of the agency door, going to a lingerie casting around the corner – a lingerie casting! at almost thirty! – feeling absolutely at the top of my game. Inspiring people to give up smoking, wearing my new, not-too-tall boots that gave me a bit of a sexy wiggle when I walked but wouldn't hobble me too terribly should I need to try to outrun a kidnapper. (Which had recently become my criteria for a good boot.) And I'd just shot a very nice editorial for a prestigious magazine, too – that was a bit of a self-esteem boost if ever there was one. Twelve pages of fashion – high fashion – with some beauty shots thrown in. *At almost thirty!*

Was this what people meant when they said that things only got better with age? If so, I couldn't wait to see what happened next in life; nothing felt as good, at that moment, as knowing that I couldn't be knocked down.

My phone rang just as I arrived at the door to the casting.

'A word in your shell-like, darling,' said Daz, 'and I don't want you to go flying off the handle, it's just so you're forewarned.'

My heart sank. How could I be feeling so buoyant one second and so utterly deflated the next, without even knowing what was about to burst my bubble? I lingered in the doorway.

'You know that big editorial you just did, darling?'

'Yes.'

'Well, the fashion editor you shot with just rang, and—'

'It was my hair, wasn't it?' I interrupted. 'They've complained about my hair because of the stupid greenish tint it had on it. I knew this would happen!'

'No . . .' said Daz. 'Nothing about your greenish hair. It's not even green, darling, I told you that. It's a hint of olive if it's anything and even then, you can only see it in certain lights. Anyway, darling, they were all very apologetic about that at *Half Cut Hair* magazine. They're never using that colourist again, that's for sure.'

There was a pause, the click of a lighter, the crackle of a cigarette beginning to burn.

'Anyway, darling,' said Daz. 'It wasn't about your hair, it was about the rest of you. They said you were . . . a bit turgid.'

'Turgid?' I said. 'Like a penis?'

'You're probably thinking of the word tumescent, darling, but yes. I suppose. Turgid like an almost-erect penis, when it's nearly there but not quite. Or immediately after, you know . . . it—'

'Sorry, I'm confused,' I said. 'They said I was like a semi-erect penis? Can I have some more context?'

'They said you were a bit bloated,' said Daz. 'Blobby. None of the clothes looked good on the shoot, apparently. It was something of a struggle.'

'Right,' I said.

'They're not sure they even got any pictures – the editor is in an absolute stew about the whole thing. The McQueen ruffles dress in particular was a key piece that they didn't even put on you because it would have been . . . what did they say?' I heard Daz flick through her notebook. 'Pointless and ultimately disappointing.'

'OK,' I said. I felt strangely bereaved. I wanted Daz to tell me that she had my back, that it was all fine. That the stupid fashion editor was obviously deluded because I looked great – so healthy! The best I'd ever looked! But she didn't.

'Anyway,' she said, 'I just wanted to give you a heads-up about it, darling.'

'Right.'

'Are you on your way to the lingerie request?'

'I'm at the door,' I said.

'Well,' said Daz. 'Remember, it's a big one, darling – nice money. Lots of confidence, knock 'em dead!'

I felt dreadful. I was back to the bottom of the modelling rollercoaster and something told me that I'd never again return to the top. How many more ups and downs could I take without driving myself mad or making myself ill? All enthusiasm drained away from me. I was the walking, talking example of how not to be a supermodel. How not to be any model.

I made a modelling pros and cons list while I waited my turn at the casting.

Pros of being a model, I wrote, in the inside cover of *Silence of the Lambs*:

flexible working hours,
good money (if you can get it),
getting to meet amazing people
travel

The next girl in line had a bruise on the side of her thigh, suitcase-handle height, a hazard of the job. How bizarre was it that all of our private goings-on were exposed in that room? That we were all just sitting around in lingerie whilst three fully dressed people assessed us?

Cons of being a model, I wrote:
never knowing whether you might work again
travel
having to stay thin

Had my name not been called at that moment, I'd have added *being cold, standing still* and *getting up early* to my list, but it was my turn to parade in my knickers, and so I clicked off my pen, closed my book and slipped both items back into my bag. At any rate, I was glad not to add the extra things to my cons list – they made me sound petty and spoiled. Whoever heard of a person who disliked their job because they had to stand still? Some would kill for that luxury.

I sucked in my stomach, put on a smile and passed my portfolio to the clients.

As I stood there, alternating between three of my strongest tried-and-tested standing-awkwardly-in-lingerie poses, I thought about what Daz had told me on the phone and I felt angry. Why had the editor of the magazine – let's call it *Bellendio* – booked me if I was so unsuitable for her shoot? She'd seen me four days before. I'd stood there in my knickers while her assistant had pinned things around me and pushed various shoes onto my feet. She had seen me, quite literally, laid bare.

It had been a female editor, again, who'd made the

comments about my size. Not the same one as in Paris, who'd stood at the bottom of the lift shaft and shared her thoughts with the stylist, a different one. But I'd thought we'd had the same sort of rapport. We'd laughed on the shoot and chatted about dogs, the tiny dogs that people had started to get and that seemed slightly pointless. I had her mobile number, she had mine, but she'd phoned the agency and called me turgid. Blobby. Bloated. A bit of a struggle. Pointless, she'd said, and ultimately disappointing.

What was it about these women letting me down? When I thought about all of the lowest moments of my career – the disappearing brows, the too-small shorts, the Einstein 'tache, the penguin head, the lift-shaft body-shape assassination – there had nearly always been a woman at the helm of my temporary mental destruction. Was I being too sensitive? Did I need a thicker skin? How many times could I bounce back from feeling utterly deflated? How many plunges on the rollercoaster ride could I take?

'Good news, darling,' said Daz, phoning just as I exited the casting. 'The editor from *Bellendio* just called back and apparently the photos look amazing, so . . . not to worry. They just got the contact sheets through and the pictures are incredible, they're really pleased. Just wanted to let you know, I knew you'd be happy to hear it.'

'Oh,' I said. My heart felt light, as though it had been attached to a helium balloon and was trying to lift itself out of my body. 'Well . . . that's great news,' I said.

Crank, crank, crank went the rollercoaster, pulling the car back up the track.

Epilogue

It was a job that stopped it all in the end. Of course it was. There was always going to be one shoot that combined all of my biggest peeves and hates and that would finally push me over the edge. Fate demanded it.

That job would forever be known as 'the job that almost killed me'. Without even the slightest hint of melodrama. It ticked almost every one of my most-hated boxes, with a pedantic photographer, a freezing outdoors location and a client who was never quite satisfied.

I was pleased for the job – of course I was – because for the past year or so paid work had been horribly thin on the ground. I'd barely earned enough to pay tax in 2008 and 2009 had been even worse. So a money job? At the start of the year? Surely it was a positive omen. It was just the cold thing that made me feel miserable; I really, really hated being cold. And I definitely had, I realised, as I slumped down into the makeup chair, the start of a throat or chest infection.

'Not a good day to be out in the cold,' the makeup artist – Sandra – said cheerfully.

'You're going to freeze your tits off!' said the hair stylist.

'And it's not going to be quick, he's got a new camera, apparently,' said Sandra, nodding at the photographer. 'And he wants to test out a new lens.'

I should have known that it wouldn't be a straightforward shoot. I should have known when the client said at the casting: 'We do love you for this job, sweetheart, but we only love you as a brunette.'

I had never been a brunette. I had no photos of myself as a brunette and the casting request had specifically said that they were looking for blondes. They wanted a blonde, they *had* a blonde, but the client had decided that what he saw just wasn't enough. He wanted me, but more. Me, but different.

The agency said no, of course. Brunette, for Ruth Crilly, was entirely out of the question. Which was why, as I sat in the makeup chair, the hair stylist unzipped a sports bag and extracted eight tiny cans of spray-in hair paint.

'Brown hair paint,' he said. 'Your agency said we couldn't dye your hair.'

'Isn't this . . . still dying it?' I said, weakly. My throat was on fire. My forehead was burning.

'It washes out,' said the hair stylist. 'Don't worry, it'll look *exactly* like it did before.'

'Ooh, what shade do they call that?' said Sandra, as the hair stylist sprayed the first strand.

'Mahogany,' replied the hair stylist, then got straight to work.

There was an additional stress to my day. Namely, the lateness of my period, which possibly meant – could it? Could it possibly, finally be? I had, after all, the tender breasts, the moodiness, the pounding headache, the bloating, some strange stretching pains in my lower abdomen – *the feeling of sickness!* Yes, most of these symptoms were the same as the ones for PMT, but I was sure that this month's were different.

Perhaps the sore throat was a sign? Maybe that's why I had a temperature? I suddenly felt strangely, violently protective over my body. Being heaved into the various skirts and blouses, feeling the zips close me in and the buttons pull the fabric around me, felt like a constant, low-level violation.

'Stop touching me!' I wanted to scream but didn't. I just wanted to crawl home, insert myself into a nest in the duvet and then sleep. Tiredness – another sign.

One of the only plus points on the shoot was that there was a working toilet and I took advantage of that benefit almost hourly, semi-delirious with my fever, checking on the tissue to make sure that there was still no blood. My period had been four days and six hours late when I'd arrived at the shoot; now it was four days and seven hours late. By elevenses, it was four days and nine hours late and my throat was so swollen I could barely swallow; by lunch (four days, eleven hours) I was nil by mouth.

My throat, my chest, my possibly inhabited womb, they all became one in my mind as I muddled through the day, trying to keep it together during shooting and then collapsing in between, nothing ever good enough for the client. Only the highest of heels would do, only the reddest of lipsticks – 'You must have a redder lipstick than that one, Sandra!' – and the sheerest of tights. Bearable on a normal day, had I not been suffering a thirty-nine-degree fever, but by three o'clock, I was ready to just lie on the floor and die.

Meanwhile, outside, the snow had been fluttering down, making Spitalfields look like Christmas in a Dickens' novel. Which was all very nice, through the window, until I had to go and sit in it.

'Right, sweetheart,' said the client, 'let's get those outside shots done, shall we?' He cracked opened the front door slightly and stuck out his hand. 'God, it's absolutely freezing,' he said. 'Does anyone have a spare blanket or scarf?'

'I do,' said the stylist, passing him a large woollen throw. He draped it around his shoulders, over the top of his thick coat, and stepped out, into the snow.

I sat upon the doorstep in my office-worker's attire, the cold from the stone seeping through to my very core. (Was the cold freezing the baby?) And, as the client very meticulously detailed every element he wanted represented in the photo ('You're an office worker, OK, sweetheart? But you also have some ambition. I want to see the ambition in your eyes; show me with your eyes, sweetheart'), the gentle, soft snowfall became a blizzard. Silent and beautiful, but oh so fast and so cold. It quickly began to settle on top of my stiff, painted hair so that the stylist had to bend in every few seconds and brush off the flakes; it started to pile on my shoulders.

EPILOGUE

This is it, I thought. *Death awaits me, finally.*

I began to shake, imperceptibly at first, but then a few minutes later violently and uncontrollably.

'She'll catch her death,' said a man as he hurried past the step, disappearing into the snowstorm.

'He's right,' said an old woman, appearing through the flakes. She was hurriedly wheeling a cart towards the market. 'She'll be wanting a coffin not a coat if you don't take care!'

The photographer ignored them as though they hadn't even spoken and continued snapping away, every now and then looking at the screen on the back of his camera and nodding his head. My throat pain was searing, my head felt as though it had some sort of large, round ballast within it, moving around of its own accord. Something twinged in my belly.

'She's bleeding!' screamed the stylist, taking her hand from the top of my head, where she had swept away the snowflakes. Her palm was a dark, metallic red.

I am not long for this earth, I thought, sadly. *This is surely the end.*

'It's just the hair paint,' said the hair stylist, 'the snow is making it run. Try not to touch it, Sandra.'

The snow continued to fall; the street was silent but for the sound of the camera shutter snapping again and again.

'We'll call it a day out here then, shall we?' said the photographer, suddenly, throwing his camera cable over his shoulder. I stood up shakily, barely able to feel my own body, and turned to go back inside.

'Pointless trying to shoot someone who looks almost dead,' said the photographer. He stepped around me and pushed open the door to let himself in. 'Oh by the way,' he said, 'there seems to be blood on the back of her skirt.'

I didn't think very deeply about life decisions whilst we ploughed through the last two shots, which were thankfully both indoors. I was too busy trying to stay upright, having successfully ticked off the other challenges of dealing with the cruel arrival of my period and managing to swallow without ingesting my own tonsils. It was only once I'd dragged myself home through the snow and collapsed into bed that two words rose slowly through the fog in my head and planted themselves firmly in front of my closed, aching eyes: SOD THIS.

I had a masterplan, of course. You don't think I'd have bailed from the modelling rollercoaster without something else to ride? There was this thing called *the internet*. And while I'd been gadding about as a model, posing in many pairs of trousers and swinging on a rope with a rubber penguin hat on, the internet had been gaining traction and had become really quite popular. People were using it for all sorts: shopping, watching funny videos, downloading books and even checking the news.

A few people, just a couple, had even become famous for – get this! – existing on the internet. Just existing, as normal people. They wrote things or they made videos and they published them – themselves – on the internet, to rapt audiences. It was mind-blowing and I wanted in. It was 2010 and this new internet idea wasn't even a viable career option yet, but still I wanted in. Even though the thing I wanted in on happened to have the worst name for itself – it sounded like the Klingon word for 'toilet' or the Viking word for 'deforestation' – I had an inkling that it might change my life. It was called blogging.

It had been my ambition to be a world-famous writer for quite a few years. I'd done my creative writing course with the Open University, I'd finished my literature degree (first class honours, thanks very much, work completed mostly whilst sitting alone in airports and sad little hotel rooms) and I'd decided – with my grasp, as ever, firmly on reality – that I wanted to be a world-famous bestselling novelist. If being a supermodel wasn't achievable then I'd go for something more within reach. A super*writer*.

'You can't just become a world-famous writer,' said one of my friends as we were propping up a bar.

'Why not?'

'It just doesn't work that way. Not everyone lives out their dream just because they want it to happen. Anyway, you'd have to be a writer before you became a world-famous one. I'd say that's probably the very first step.'

'I am.'

'You are what?'

'I am a writer.'

My friend snorted.

'I've been writing every day for the last few years,' I said. 'In my notebook.'

'Yes, well,' said my friend, 'you have to be a writer that somebody else *reads*. I'm a fucking world-class opera singer when I'm belting it out in the shower but it doesn't mean you'll see me performing at Covent Garden anytime soon.'

I had to be a writer that somebody else reads, she had said, and of course she was right. And this was why blogging was so perfect. You wrote it, you edited it and you published it onto Blogspot for other people to read. It was the most brilliant, genius first step to becoming a superwriter.

I realised that I had all of the material at my fingertips that I could possibly need for this thing called a blog. Because who had written online through the eyes of a model? Who had shared beauty tips and posing tricks from this unique – and ultimately massively qualified – perspective? Nobody that I could see, not yet. I would be the one to provide the world with this service, generously and without charge (and definitely without the long-term goal of creating a personal brand and monetising it) and I would put every single waking hour into making it happen.

So long, modelling. *Sayonara*, suckers! Yes, modelling had provided me with some of the best experiences of my life – what other job could have thrown me around the world so chaotically, could have introduced me to so many wild and fabulous people, could have made me so many life-long friends? How many jobs could give you a champagne lifestyle even when you were struggling to find enough loose change for a zones 1–2 travelcard? Yes, modelling had been this bizarre and brilliant time, but it was over. The clock had chimed midnight and Cinderella needed to leave the ball. I would write my book about modelling and blog my blog about modelling and it would be a whole new era. Completely different to the era before.

For one was a wild and wacky era of self-discovery, of

brutal criticism and of great financial instability, where nobody really considered my job to be a proper job. This, the world of social media, it would be a totally new and different era. One of self-discovery, of brutal criticism and of great finan—

Oh.

ACKNOWLEDGEMENTS

I think that this is where I'm supposed to do my Oscars speech. Winning an Oscar was always going to be my Plan C, if supermodelling and superwriting didn't work out and so I've practised this a lot – settle down because we're going to be here for a while. (My editor threatened to cut me off midway through these acknowledgements if I didn't get my word count down, but we all know she'd never do that!)

Firstly, I'd like to thank the many agents and managers I've had over the past twenty-four years: your varying levels of belief in me have made me the highly resilient person I am today.

Family, friends: your unwavering support from the sidelines does not go unnoticed. I love that you are, on the whole, such an undramatic bunch: not so much noisy, pom-pom waving cheerleaders as scarf-wrapped soccer moms, setting out your folding chairs and sipping from a Thermos of tea. Many of you have continued to sit there in your anoraks through drizzle, pelting rain and lightning storms and for this I cannot thank you enough.

My biggest thanks though – and I'm sorry to go all soppy on you – must go to th—